The
FLOWER CHAIN

SIPHONANTHUS FLORIBUNDUS Britten.

Now called *Clerodendrum floribunda*, this meticulously engraved plate was one of the hundreds Joseph Banks commissioned to illustrate his great Flora of the *Endeavour* voyage. (Illustration: Linnean Society collections.)

The FLOWER CHAIN

The Early Discovery of Australian Plants

Jill, Duchess of Hamilton
&
Julia Bruce

Kangaroo Press

THE FLOWER CHAIN

First published in Australia and New Zealand in 1998 by Kangaroo Press
an imprint of Simon & Schuster Australia
20 Barcoo Street, East Roseville NSW 2069

A Viacom Company
Sydney New York London Toronto Tokyo Singapore

© Jill, Duchess of Hamilton and Julia Bruce

All rights reserved. No part of this publication may be reproduced, stored in a retrieval system, or transmitted, in any form or by any means, electronic, mechanical, photocopying, recording or otherwise, without the prior permission of the publisher in writing.

National Library of Australia
Cataloguing-in-Publication data:

Hamilton, Jill, Duchess of.
The flower chain: the early discovery of australian plants
Bibliography.
Includes index.

ISBN 0 86417 922 7

1. Botany - Australia - History. I. Title.
580.994

Set in Goudy Old Style 10.5/13

Printed by Colour Symphony Pte Ltd, Singapore

10 9 8 7 6 5 4 3 2 1

Contents

*Chronological Table of the
European Discovery of Australia* 7

  1 The Flower Chain Begins *11*
  2 Terra Australis Incognita *20*
  3 The Plant Hunters *23*
  4 Fire and Flora – The Origins of Australia's Plants *31*
  5 The Scurvy Coast *38*
  6 The Dutch – Australia Seen but Forsaken *43*
  7 William Dampier – The Botanical Buccaneer *51*
  8 Joseph Banks and the *Endeavour* *59*
  9 Botanists in Botany Bay *65*
10 Disaster and Home *73*
11 Cook Returns to the South Seas *79*
12 A Forgotten Florilegium *87*
13 Sir Joseph and the Settlement of Australia *95*
14 Mutiny *101*
15 The British and the French in Botany Bay *109*
16 The Surgeon, the Convict and the Gentlemen *116*
17 The French Discovery of Australian Flora *124*
18 Spain and Britain in the Pacific *130*
19 Australia at Malmaison *137*
20 Australia Circumnavigated *143*
21 The Fate of the Flower Chain *152*

Acknowledgments 155
Suggested Reading 156
Index 157

To Gina Douglas in England and
Maureen Sheriff in Australia

Chronological Table of the European Discovery of Australia

1606
The first recorded European landfall was made by the *Duyfken* at the Gulf of Carpentaria. There are no known observations of the flora.

1616
Dirck Hartog discovered Eendracht Land (Western Australia).

1622
The *Leeuwin* coasted south-western Australia to latitude 35 degrees south.

1623
Jan Carstensz sailed around the Gulf of Carpentaria. Arnhem Land discovered and named after his ship.

1627
The *Gulden Zeepaert* coasted Nuyts' Land as far as Streaky Bay.

1628
The *Vyanen* ran aground on De Witt's Land.

1629
The *Batavia*, commanded by Nicholas Pelsaert, was wrecked on the Abrolhos Islands off the coast of Western Australia.

1642
Abel Tasman discovered Tasmania, naming it Van Diemen's Land. Tasman himself did not land but members of his crew did, the ship's carpenter swimming ashore and planting flags representing Holland and the Dutch East India Company. Tasman later sighted, but did not land at, New Zealand.

1644
Tasman's second Australian voyage. He sailed round the coast from Cape York to Eendracht Land. Although Tasman added more than 3000 kilometres to the map of the coast of New Holland, the illustrations that accompanied his account are crude with titles such as 'A view of the coast when you are six miles [9.6 km] from it'.

1652
William Dampier born in East Coker, Somerset, England.

1660
The first steps were taken in London to form the Royal Society, and shortly afterwards the Academie de Sciences was formed in Paris.

1688
In January, the *Cygnet*, a stolen pirate ship, under the command of Captain John Read, with William Dampier as an officer, visited north-western Australia. This impromptu visit by pirates was the first British landing in Australia.

1697
Willem de Vlamingh, sailing for the Vereenigde Oost-Indische Compagnie, discovered the Swan River. He collected some plant material for Nicolaas Witsen, a director of the VOC in Holland, but this has since been lost. It is likely that it was on this voyage that two specimens, *Synaphea spinulosa*, and *Acacia truncata*, wrongly described by Burmann in his Flora Indica as Javanese ferns, were collected. The *Synaphea* is now in the Herbarium of Geneva Botanic Gardens.

The Flower Chain

The illustration of Vlamingh's ships at anchor, which appeared in a history of the Dutch in the East Indies, is the first known attempt to portray the Australian landscape apart from Tasman's crude coastal profiles.

Dampier's book, *A New Voyage Round the World*, dedicated to Charles Montague, President of the Royal Society, was published in England. The book made Australia known to a wide public and also described South Sea islands, their people and the breadfruit. The book prompted the Admiralty to consider sending further exploratory voyages to New Holland.

1699
On 4 January, Dampier left England on HMS *Roebuck* for New Holland and made the first collection of Australian plants 'for the most part unlike any I had seen elsewhere'.

1701
Dampier returned to England after a hazardous journey and shipwreck, but with his plant collection intact. This he passed on to 'the ingenious Mr Woodward'. They were listed in both Ray's *Historia Plantarum* as an appendix in volume III, and Leonardi Plukenet's *Amaltheum Botanicum*.

1703
Dampier's account of his second expedition, *A Voyage to New Holland*, was published in London. It contained nine coastal profiles and three plates depicting nine land plants.

1715
Dampier died in England.

1726
Jonathan Swift's *Gulliver's Travels* was published. It was partly based on Dampier's voyages.

1728
James Cook was born in Yorkshire, England.

1736
Carolus Linnaeus published *Genera Plantarum*, introducing his method of plant classification and nomenclature to the world.

1743
Joseph Banks born in London, England.

1745
John Hawkesworth edited Swift's works, relating them to Dampier's voyages.

1760
George III came to the throne.

Joseph Banks went to Oxford to study botany.

1766
Joseph Banks went on a botanising expedition to Newfoundland and was elected to fellowship of the Royal Society in his absence.

1768
The *Endeavour* departed England bound for Tahiti to observe the Transit of Venus. She was commanded by James Cook and included in her complement Joseph Banks, Daniel Solander and Hermann Spöring (pupils of Linnaeus), two artists and four servants. This scientific team had been assembled and paid for by Banks to record and collect natural history specimens.

1770
The *Endeavour* landed on the east coast of Australia. Cook would later annex the land under the name of New South Wales. He named the first site of their landing, where Banks and Solander made extensive plant collections, Botany Bay.

1771
The *Endeavour* returned to Britain. Banks and Solander were lauded for their natural history observations and their huge haul of plants, particularly from Australia. Banks met George III, and under his auspices eventually became the unofficial director of the King's gardens at Kew.

1772

Cook returned to the Pacific with the *Resolution* and the *Adventure*. The *Adventure* stopped briefly in Tasmania where Captain Furneaux collected seeds of *Eucalyptus obliqua*, later grown at Kew.

1773

Stanfield Parkinson published his brother Sydney's journal of the *Endeavour* voyage.

1774

The official account of the *Endeavour* voyage was published. It was an amalgamation of Cook's and Banks's journals, with embellishments by John Hawkesworth. In it, Hawkesworth compares some of Banks and Solander's observations of the flora with those of Dampier.

1776

Cook's third and final voyage to the Pacific. David Nelson was sent as a plant collector and William Bligh was the sailing master. The expedition again visited Tasmania where Nelson collected specimens of *Eucalyptus obliqua*, which were to provide the type specimen for L'Héritier's description of the genus.

1778

Linnaeus died.

Banks became President of the Royal Society.

1779

Banks suggested to a House of Commons committee that Botany Bay was a suitable site for a penal colony.
Cook killed in Hawaii.

1787

The First Fleet departed with 1486 convicts and their keepers, bound for Botany Bay. No European had visited the place since the *Endeavour* voyage. No gardeners, botanists or farmers were sent to help establish the colony.

William Bligh, commanding the *Bounty*, left on a mission to collect and transfer breadfruit plants from Tahiti to the Caribbean to provide food for the slaves. David Nelson and William Brown embarked as gardeners.

1788

The First Fleet arrived and the new colony was established at Port Jackson. Within days of the First Fleet's arrival the French explorer La Pérouse with his two ships, *Boussole* and *Astrolabe*, anchored in Botany Bay, staying and observing for six weeks.

The Linnean Society of London founded by James Edward Smith.

1789

Mutiny on the *Bounty*. Bligh survived an open boat journey to Timor. David Nelson died in Timor. Fletcher Christian and the mutineers, including William Brown, established a colony on Pitcairn Island. Mutineers introduced the orange to the Cook Islands.

1790

The journal of the first months of settlement by John White, surgeon to the New South Wales colony, was published in England with illustrations and descriptions of eight Australian plants.

1791

George Vancouver discovered King George Sound in Western Australia, and the botanist on board, Archibald Menzies, made extensive plant collections.

The French sent out an expedition to search for La Pérouse, who had been missing since he left Botany Bay. On board were botanist Jacques-Julien Labillardière and gardener Felix Delahaye. Both made extensive collections in Australia.

1792

Thomas Watling, the first trained artist to be sent to the colony, arrived at Port Jackson, NSW and was assigned to make natural history drawings for John White.

The Flower Chain

1793

Louis XVI executed.

Louis Née and Thaddeus Haenke, sailing on the Spanish voyage of exploration led by Alessandro Malaspina, were the first trained botanists to visit the Port Jackson colony. They made substantial collections of Australian plants.

A Specimen of the Botany of New Holland, by James Edward Smith, the first book exclusively devoted to Australian flora, was published in England.

1795

John Hunter, the second governor of the Port Jackson colony, arrived and made extensive drawings of the natural history.

1800

Governor King replaced Hunter.

The British issued passports to a French expedition led by Nicolas Baudin to chart Australia's coast.

1801

Matthew Flinders, commanding the *Investigator*, left England on a voyage to circumnavigate and chart the coastline of Australia. On board he had: Robert Brown, botanist; Ferdinand Bauer, natural history artist; William Westall, landscape artist; Peter Good, gardener.

1802

Flinders and Baudin expeditions coincide at Encounter Bay.

1803

Felix Delahaye went to work for The Empress Josephine at Malmaison.

1804

Napoleon became Emperor of France.

The Royal Horticultural Society held its first flower show.

Labillardière published the first major work on the botany of Australia.

1
The Flower Chain Begins

Convict chains are associated with the early British settlement of Australia, but there were also lighter chains in those grim days. Chains of flowers and seeds to be grown and classified stretched across the oceans from Botany Bay to Europe, looping back again with plants and seeds of the Old World that were to Europeanise the landscape and transform it forever. This book looks at the links in that chain, the discovery, identification, appreciation and cultivation of Australia's plants, together with the sea captains, botanists, artists, gardeners, laymen, books and drawings, which contributed to the slow introduction of the Australian flora to Europe and the rest of the world. For slow indeed it was, and this book also examines the reasons for the delays in the dissemination of knowledge about Australia's unique floral heritage.

Australia has an exceedingly rich and diverse flora. *Eucalyptus*, *Acacia*, *Correa*, *Anigozanthos* (kangaroo paw), *Prostanthera*, *Camelaucium* (Geraldton wax), *Brachyscome* (Swan River and everlasting daisies) are all Australian and are now grown everywhere from California to the south of France. The top-selling house plants in Europe are two Queensland rainforest trees: stunted versions of *Ficus benjamina* and the long-suffering *Schefflera actinophylla* (umbrella plant), churned out by propagation businesses in southern Spain and elsewhere. The number of native vascular species alone in Australia — ignoring the non-vascular plants such as algae and lichens — is estimated at 25 000, and 90 per cent of these species are endemic. Only a small number, though, provide sustenance for a stranger on foreign soil. It was patient foraging, day after day, mainly by women and children, that provided the non-flesh portion of Aboriginal diets. For the white sailors who did not know the secrets of the native plants, Australia was the 'scurvy coast'.

Despite its novelty and potential, the flora of Australia was largely disregarded for 150 years after European discovery. From the time of the first documented European landfall in Australia — by the Dutch in 1606 — until the early nineteenth century, the collection of plants was intermittent and uncoordinated. The earliest known botanical specimens from Australia, probably collected in 1697 by the Dutch captain Willem de Vlamingh, were misidentified for over 200 years. Collected in the Swan River area near Perth, they are fragments of *Synaphea spinulosa*, and *Acacia truncata*. Only the *Synaphea* is still known to be extant, in the herbarium of the Conservatoire et Jardin Botanique, Geneva. It is the sole botanical souvenir from more than a century of Dutch exploration of the coasts of Australia. A few cycad seeds were also bought back to Holland, but they were not filed in any herbarium.

Although the Dutch made over twenty voyages to Australia, they left scant records of its flora and no collections. The Flower Chain really begins with Somerset-born William Dampier, buccaneer and author, picking *Swainsona formosa* (Sturt's desert pea) in the west Australian bush in 1699. Dampier was shipwrecked in the Atlantic and subsequently court-martialled. Despite this, he managed to get this flower, dried and pressed along with over twenty other specimens of Australian plants, back to England and into the hands of one Dr Woodward. These plants are now preserved in the herbarium at the Department of Plant Sciences, University of Oxford. Nine were

The Flower Chain

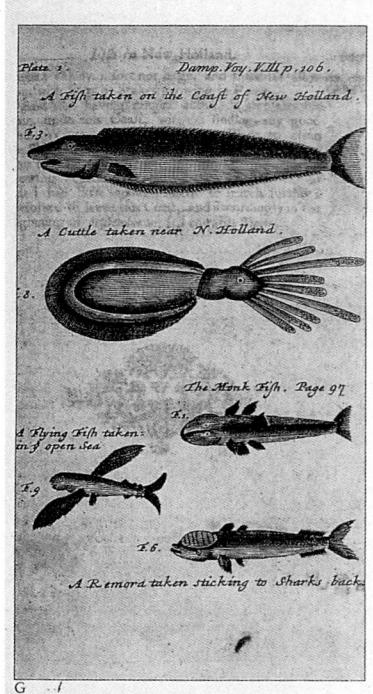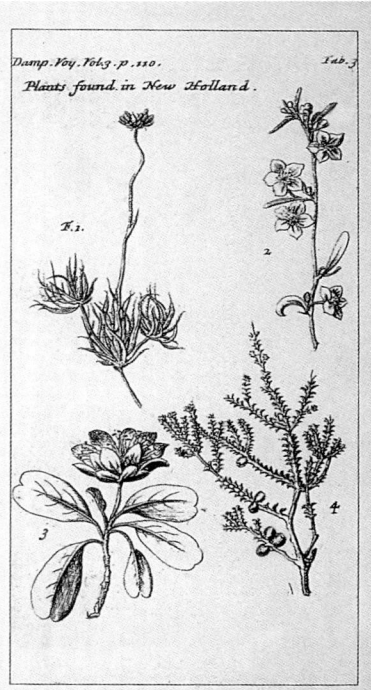

William Dampier made observations and collections of its natural history on his second voyage to New Holland and illustrated his findings. These are the first published illustrations of Australia's flora. (Linnean Society collections.)

illustrated in Dampier's best-selling account of his adventures, *A Voyage to New Holland*, which went into several editions in his lifetime. The plants at Oxford form the earliest extant collection of Australian plants, yet in the botanical literature of the time, they merited only an appendix and a few inadequate descriptions.

Sixty years after Dampier's dried specimens were deposited at Oxford, Joseph Banks arrived there from Eton to spend three years studying botany. We do not know whether he saw Dampier's plants, but he certainly had Dampier's books on board Cook's *Endeavour* in 1770 when, with Daniel Solander, he made the first extensive botanical collection in Australia. This groundbreaking voyage produced a massive haul of botanical specimens. Banks initially planned a splendid publication illustrated with life-sized engravings of the highest quality — a florilegium of the plants of the places visited. Despite many years' work, and the expenditure of a small fortune preparing the illustrations, the book was never finished. Even the exquisite illustrations were destined not to be published for nearly two centuries. The consequences of this non-publication were far-reaching.

When the British Government sent the First Fleet to establish a penal colony in New South Wales, the convicts, marines and officers sailed knowing nothing about the vegetation of Botany Bay. In the seventeen years between Banks' brief visit in 1770 and the departure of the First Fleet, the British had made no inspection of the site. Not only was there no reconnaissance, but information that might have helped settlers was still awaiting completion in the London home of Joseph Banks. The precious specimens collected on his first landfall — the reason for its being christened Botany Bay — languished unpublished in Banks' herbarium cabinets. The First Fleet arrived in 1788 magnificently equipped, but lacking four essentials — a trained botanist, a gardener, a farmer, and information on the soils and flora of this new and alien land that they were to farm. Settlers found that the soils that Banks had described as fertile were in

THE FLOWER CHAIN BEGINS

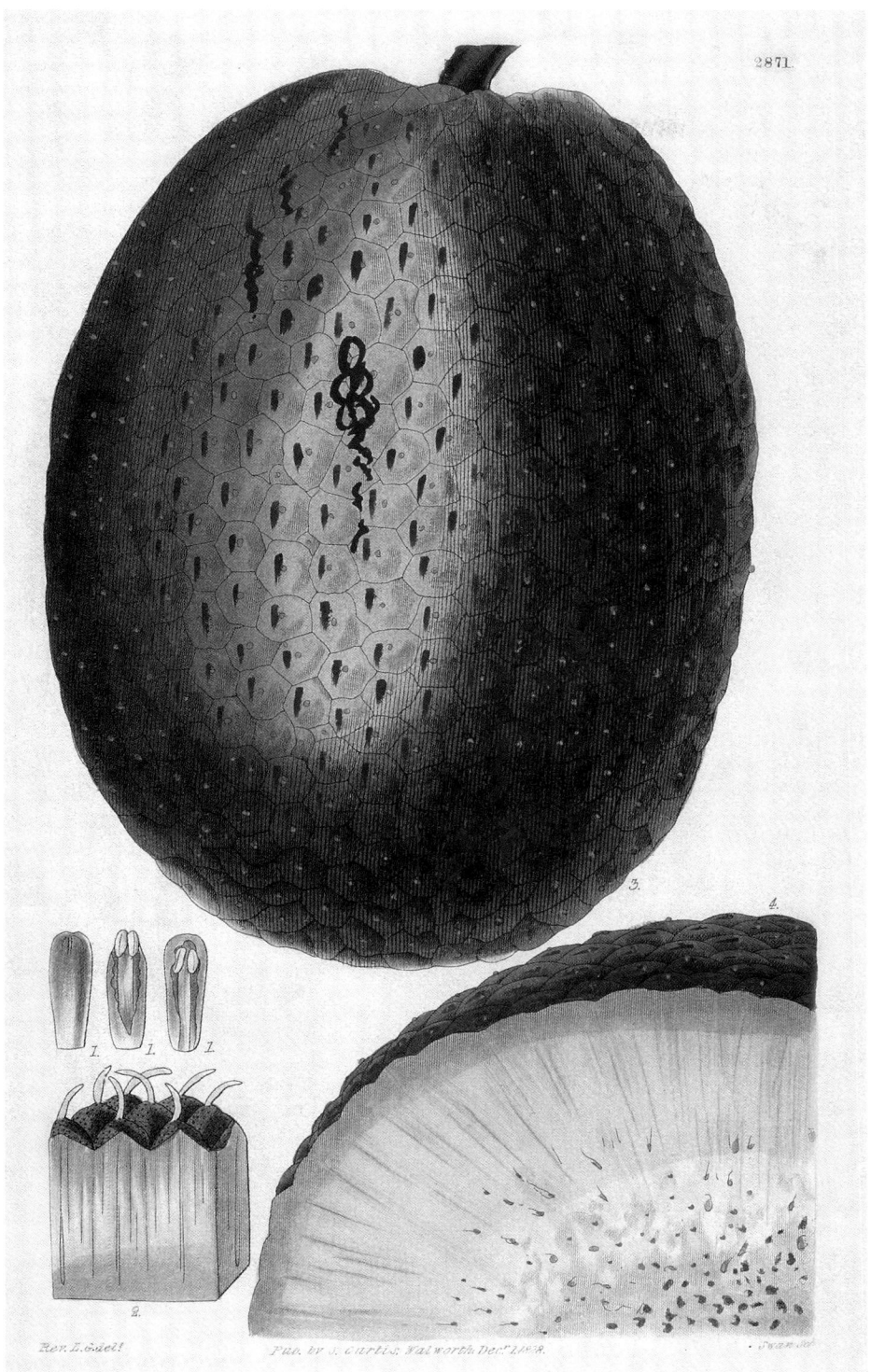

The starchy fruit of the breadfruit tree, *Artocarpus altilis*, was a dietary staple throughout the islands of the Pacific. This illustration is from *Curtis' Botanical Magazine*.
(Linnean Society collections.)

The Flower Chain

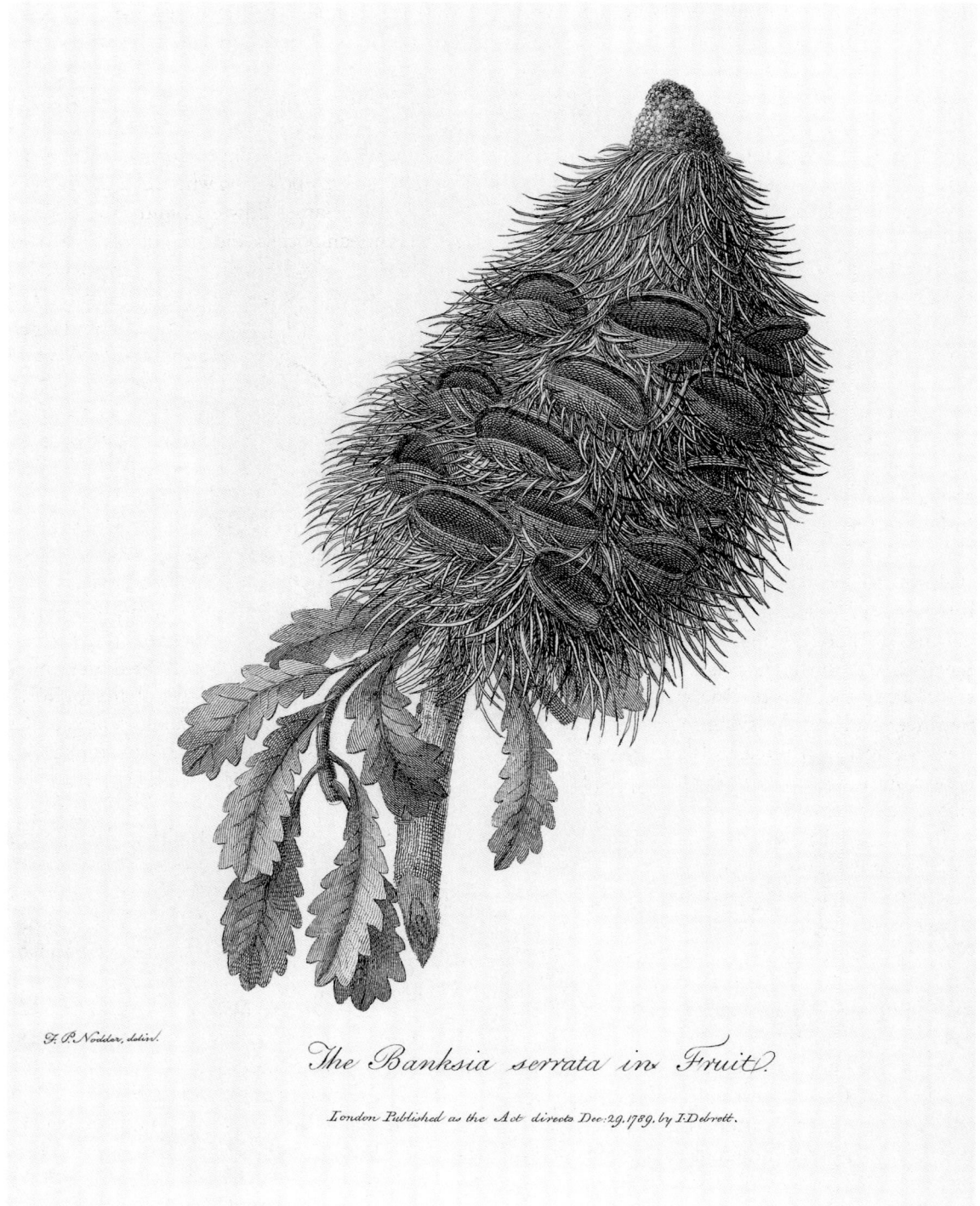

Some of the first published images of banksias, such as this *Banksia serrata* in fruit, appeared in John White's journal, expertly engraved by Frederick Polydore Nodder. (Illustration from collections in the London Library.)

THE FLOWER CHAIN BEGINS

fact marshy, thin or sandy. Without any expert to assess it, they found Australia's unique flora nutritionally and economically worthless. One of the many consequences of this disregard by eighteenth century settlers was the perception of the land as *terra nullius* — belonging to no-one. The repercussions of this perception reverberate today in the issue of Aboriginal land rights.

Initially, it had been planned that two ships of the First Fleet would continue on from Botany Bay north to Tahiti. Here they would collect hundreds of breadfruit tree seedlings and take them to the West Indies to be grown as food for slaves on sugar plantations there. Shortly before the fleet departed London, Banks, who had been intimately involved in the preparations, altered the plans: there would be a separate and independent expedition to Tahiti and the Caribbean led by William Bligh. Both David Nelson, a Kew-trained gardener — who had briefly visited Tasmania on Cook's last voyage — and his assistant, William Brown, who were to have sailed with the First Fleet, were diverted to the *Bounty* and Tahiti. One would be a willing mutineer and end up laying the foundations for the settlement on Pitcairn Island — instead of New South Wales. The other, staying loyal to Bligh, was destined to die in Timor.

In the crucial early days of the colony, the vital task of studying and using indigenous plants of New South Wales was left to amateurs, busy surgeons — and the Spanish and the French. Nobody qualified to study the newly discovered plants resided in the colony. Australian vegetation would have seemed so different to the first settlers, full of diversity and novelty. The greatest number of characteristic Australian species live in the poorest soil, indeed, the poorer the soil, the more varied the vegetation. In contrast to the water-retaining cactus and cactus-like perennials of the dry regions of America and Africa, Australian dry areas have few perennial succulents. Instead, woody plants, such as the banksias, hakeas, mulga and acacias predominate.

No British expert systematically assessed the flora on-site; no-one studied it or fitted it into the developing world system of families, genera and species, until Robert Brown arrived with Matthew Flinders on the *Investigator* in 1801. The colony was then thirteen years old. Brown remained in Australia for three years and collected an amazing 3400 species, of which more than 2000 were previously unknown. In the early years plants had to be sent to Europe to be named and classified by botanists who hadn't even been to Australia. James Edward Smith, the founder of the Linnean Society, did most of the early work on these Australian plants in England. He published *A Specimen of the Botany of New Holland*, and later *Exotic Botany*, describing, illustrating and giving notes on the cultivation of many Australian plants including the waratah and a *Boronia*. Many of these had been sent to England by John White, the chief surgeon of the colony who had his own account of the first six months of settlement published in 1790.

Early settlers found the land and its wild food either non-nourishing or completely alien. Much of the vegetation was treated with aversion, fit only for clearing with the saw or the axe. Apart from the potential of the magnificent timbers and eucalyptus oil, there was no real attempt to look for commercially attractive plants for horticultural, medicinal or pharmacological uses. Of course, some of the officers, to counter scurvy, attempted to find remedies in locally growing wild berries and plants, but this was done in a haphazard, amateur fashion. Although there was also a steady stream of plants sent to England, such as the waratah and Norfolk Island pines sent by Phillip Gidley King to Joseph Banks, little useful information filtered from the experts back to the colonists.

Why was no botanist sent to assess local resources? For over forty thousand years the Aboriginal people had lived off the land. Although their good health was obvious to the new settlers — their wounds healed quickly and they had strong white teeth — the depth of Aboriginal culture and their knowledge of the land were vastly underestimated. Typical of their time, settlers did not seriously consider trying to glean knowledge from native Australians. Some attempted to find out about the native flora, but their efforts were uninformed and generally unsuccessful. The colony as a whole preferred instead to rely on imported foodstuffs and crops

The Flower Chain

Author of *Flora Australiensis*, the first attempt at a complete account of Australia's plant life, George Bentham was widely regarded as a genius. He spoke 14 languages and also made learned contributions in the fields of philosophy, logic and law. (Linnean Society collections.)

grown from imported seed. As a consequence, the settlers nearly starved while they watched their European crops struggle in the alien, nutrient-poor soils, and fall victim to the vagaries of New South Wales weather. And all the time their supplies were dwindling.

As the French Revolution exploded in France, two French botanists and a gardener landed in Tasmania and Western Australia on an expedition looking for the lost ships of the explorer La Pérouse. One of the botanists was Jacques-Julien Houtou de Labillardière who had studied Banks' Australian plants in London. La Pérouse's ships were not found, but Labillardière collected thousands of botanical specimens. These became the basis of the first major book on the Australian flora, and some were grown in the Empress Josephine's private garden at Malmaison, outside Paris. Even before the gardener who had travelled to Australia with Labillardière started working for Josephine, she raised the first expatriate eucalyptus from seed — as well as bottlebrushes, acacias and *Leptospermum*, all of which were to be immortalised in paintings by Pierre-Joseph Redouté.

By 1800, across the English Channel at the Royal Gardens, Kew, 170 plants had been introduced from New South Wales. Kew, with Sir Joseph Banks as its unofficial director, developed links with Australia that it retains to this day. Their Australian plant collection became so extensive that it later had its own Botany Bay glasshouse built, but in New South Wales itself the emphasis was on establishing agriculture based on introduced crops and animals. There has always been a reluctance to grow Australian native plants commercially in Australia, despite the economic potential.

The Flower Chain can be followed to the publication of the first comprehensive flora of Australia, *Flora Australiensis* by George Bentham in the 1870s. Bentham managed this massive work in seven volumes without leaving England, without ever setting foot on Australia. He used mainly herbarium specimens from collections in London, Paris and Melbourne. For the thirty years leading up to this, the chain was gradually changing from a single thread into a web of connections. The lone collectors visiting from Europe were replaced by a network of botanists, including for the first time residents of the new country. Information from the past string of botanists and plant collectors and from these new resident experts, particularly Ferdinand von Mueller, was amalgamated by Bentham into his magnum opus. To tell the story of the plant collectors up to this point in the 1870s would require more pages than this book allows, so we leave the Flower Chain in the early years of the nineteenth century. We focus on 1804, the year Napoleon crowned himself Emperor, the year Robert Brown, the first professional British botanist to work in the colony collected around Sydney, and the year of the publication in Paris of the first serious attempt to give an account of Australia's flora as it was then known. Weighing a hefty six and a half kilograms, and including 265 black and white illustrations and 242 pages of text, *Novae Hollandiae Plantarum Specimen* by Jacques-Julien Houtou de Labillardière, made an uncomfortable contrast with the shameful lack of British effort. It was over a hundred years since the first official English voyage of exploration to the continent — that of Dampier — and sixteen years since the English had established a colony; yet they had neglected the serious collection and study of the flora, and the publication of anything of significance on the subject. Even Robert Brown's ambitious attempt to produce a Flora on his return from Australia in 1805 was doomed to failure. He only published the *Prodromus*, the introduction, in 1810. This was received so poorly he never completed the work. Yet today, Brown's *Prodromus* is regarded as the most important single contribution to the study of Australian plants, and its publication marks the end of the exploratory period. If it had been granted recognition at the time, the story of the discovery of Australia's flora would have been very different.

In contrast to the lack of success with either the cataloguing or exploitation of Australian plants, is the ruthless triumph of the exploitation of the breadfruit tree. Its story — despite the loss of well over fifty lives and two naval ships in five years — runs parallel with the early connections the British had with Australia and embraces five of the same protagonists: Dampier, Cook, Banks, Bligh and Flinders.

It is now nearly 400 years since the European discovery of the Australian continent — the quatercentenary is 2006 — but it was not until 1979, after a painfully long gestation period, that the Federal Minister of Science launched a twenty-year project to produce a definitive *Flora of Australia*, funded by the federal government in Canberra. The task is still proving monumental and looks set to exceed its original twenty-year estimate for completion.

The lack of regard for the Australian flora has been no temporary setback, it has lasted well into the twentieth century. Most of the Australian plants sold in world markets are grown in other countries. The Australian native plant movement is growing in strength, and many Australians are truly proud of their plant heritage, but as the distinguished botanist Alex George says in Volume I of the *Flora of Australia*, 'the Australian flora is still far from being adequately known'. He continues:

> Few parts of Australia have been fully explored botanically. New species and records continue to be turned up, even close to civilisation, and there are very large areas — thousands of square kilometres — where no work at all has been done. This applies especially to parts of the north and to Western Australia.

It has been estimated by John Yencken, Melbourne-based nursery industry consultant

A statue of Carolus Linnaeus, surrounded by Australian cultivars — kangaroo paw, Geraldton wax and blue gum — presides in the library of the Linnean Society in London. (Linnean Society collections.)

and author of a 1994 paper 'The Australian Wildflower Industry — A Review', that less than 1 per cent of the plants grown in domestic gardens in Australia are native. Five years ago, Israel exported nearly 17 million stems of Australian native waxflower to the flower auctions in the Netherlands; Australia's contribution was a mere 500 000. Little has been done to create a healthy domestic market in native plants for vases or gardens, although Australian plants can be bought in Covent Garden flower markets. Sales of Australian native cut flowers worldwide amount to about A$440 million annually, but only an estimated 10 per cent are actually exported from home territory. Apart from Israel, they are widely grown in South America and the south of France. In Australia, only a tenth of the total value of the domestic retail cut-flower industry is from Australian natives. Compared to roses, carnations, chrysanthemums, gerberas and other exotics, the number of native species grown for commercial sale is insignificant. Globally, the cut-flower industry is gigantic — a turnover of about A$22 billion a year. Yet Australia, with one of the largest floral gene-pools in the world, contributes less than 1 per cent to the global trade.

The dismissive attitude of the early settlers towards the country's flora continued into the twentieth century, only changing with the work of individuals such as Lindsay Pryor, who encouraged the planting of native trees and shrubs. In 1956 the City of Brisbane chose the showy red poinsettia from Mexico as its floral emblem instead of a native flower. Canberra, although the capital city of Australia, was built around exotic trees, mostly those found in English parks: millions of oaks, elms, beeches, birches, North American firs, cottonwoods and Mediterranean cypresses. Australian trees do not change to autumn colours as they do not lose their leaves in winter, but the thousands of northern hemisphere trees in Canberra mean that there is an autumn spectacle of oranges and browns. This book hopes to make Australians aware of the need to redress the balance.

Over two hundred years after Linnaeus' favourite pupil, Daniel Solander, made the first major collection of Australia's flora with Joseph Banks — and other botanical followers of Linnaeus studied the plants sent back to England — this book was researched in the Linnean Society of London's library. From these researches came the inspiration for Flora-for-Fauna, a campaign that aims to combine aesthetic horticulture with scientific botany by encouraging gardeners, local authorities and farmers to grow native plants to encourage native wildlife. Emphasis is placed on promoting regional native plants, to make gardens an increasingly important food source for birds, butterflies and other creatures. Cultivated plants are essential to human survival. Now cultivation of wild plants is becoming crucial for wildlife. Flora-for-Fauna was launched in Britain at a reception in the Temperate House of the Royal Botanic Gardens, Kew. For three years it was a special fund within The Linnean Society of London, and although it is now independent, it still maintains its close links with The Linnean Society, the Natural History Museum in London and the Royal Botanic Gardens, Kew.

Flora-for-Fauna was first established in Britain, but like the Flower Chain, it now links back to Australia. Publication of this book coincides with a campaign by the Nursery Industry Association of Australia to introduce native regional plants into garden centres under the banner of Flora-for-Fauna. The nursery industry has formed a special Flora-for-Fauna marketing company and provided over a quarter of a million dollars to start it.

2

Terra Australis Incognita

Australia escaped detection, let alone description, for centuries. Leaving aside the lichens, grasses and mosses of Antarctica, Australia's flora was the last of any continent to be discovered, appreciated or classified by Europeans. Large but sparsely peopled, and protected by its remoteness, this island continent, lying between the Pacific and Indian oceans, remained uncultivated for thousands of years. Considering the soil erosion, pollution and damage caused by agriculture and grazing, it is certain that if Australia were a living entity, it would not have minded waiting a few thousand more years to be disturbed by the plough, axe and hoofed animals such as sheep and cattle.

Great buildings had been built in India, Asia, Africa, Europe and the Americas, but until 1788, Australia, the smallest, flattest and driest of the continents, had never had a permanent house built on it, never been trodden by a hoof, never had a wheel roll across it. The tenure of the land by the Aboriginal people was marked not by ruined temples or palaces but by rock paintings and engravings, middens of shells, and a land permanently altered by fire. Appearing on maps before white seamen ever sighted its shores, a great continent in the southern hemisphere was imagined and rumoured in Europe for centuries. These maps were conjectures of Greek philosophers and Chinese sailors, Arab traders and Christian missionaries, and of scholars who misinterpreted Marco Polo.

Five hundred years before the birth of Christ, Pythagoras proposed that there must be landmasses to the south of the known continents to counterbalance them — there was no concept of hemispheres at this time. Claudius Ptolemy of Alexandria (AD 90 – c.168), refined this idea, postulating that the world was saved from wobbling because of a huge landmass south of the equator that balanced Europe and Asia. This vast expanse of dense soil and rock, he said, gave stability to the Earth which, he explained, was suspended in the centre of the universe; the landmass prevented the Earth from colliding with the stars and other celestial bodies.

It is likely that Chinese explorers and traders knew about Australia very early on. India and China traded with each other even before Buddhism was introduced to Burma, Japan and Java. Huge Chinese junks manned by up to 400 oarsmen, and swift Indian ships, bartering all over the Orient, ranged as far as Java and Timor, just a few hundred kilometres from the north coast of Australia. If they did reach the continent, however, no evidence survives; but then without the lure of profitable spices, the traders had no incentive to return or to record their discovery.

Much later, Christians debated whether rain fell up in the Antipodes. Did people stand on their heads? Did trees grow downwards? St Augustine (AD 354 – 430), however, scorned 'that fabulous hypothesis of men who walk a part of the earth opposite to our own, whose feet are in a position contrary to ours, and where the sun rises when it sets with us'.

Eventually scholars of the thirteenth century, including Roger Bacon (c1214 – c1292), who dreamt of horseless carriages, flying machines, explosives and optical instruments, reasoned that the southern hemisphere did exist. It even featured in *La Divina Commedia* of Dante Alighieri (1265 – 1321). In his fictional journey, Dante travelled with Virgil, through the Inferno, through the centre of the earth. As Easter Day dawned he emerged from the gates of Hell into

Purgatory, a mountain surrounded by the waters of the southern hemisphere (the Pacific), opposite Jerusalem. Dante probably got his inspiration from an Arab globe as the Arabs, who had observatories at Baghdad and Damascus, knew every sea from Spain to China.

The Europeans began to join the Arabs, Indians and Chinese in the Southern Seas and lands, often in the hope of bringing back tons of the brown pebble-like seeds (nutmeg) so prized in European cuisine. Ships ranged further to fetch the spices from where they grew, instead of bringing them along the trade routes of old. By the sixteenth century the galleons of Portugal's Prince Henry the Navigator were following the coast of Africa southwards. The oceans became highways between the continents. The supremacy of the camel trains as cargo-carriers was challenged by the swiftness of sea-borne ships. With more information coming back to Europe via these trading vessels, the web of knowledge about the southern hemisphere grew.

Ptolemy's *Geography* was updated by Renaissance mapmakers to take account of this new information, showing the Indian Ocean and the Americas. But although these later geographers knew more of the world than Ptolemy, they still did not dispense with the need for a great southern continent. Abraham Ortelius' world map, *Theatrum Orbis Terrarum*, published in Antwerp in 1570, shows a massive *Terra Australis Nondum Cognita* enveloping the south polar area. Ortelius included Tierra del Fuego and a large peninsula reaching up towards Borneo marked as 'Beach' and 'Lycach' in his Unknown South Land. This peninsula was actually part of the north coast of Australia. The Great Southern Continent was to appear again and again, along with the names Luchac, Laach, Maletur, Malaiur, Boeach and *Terra Australis Incognita.*

Between 1530 and 1570, six maps of the southern hemisphere were made by the expert school of cartographers in Dieppe. With each

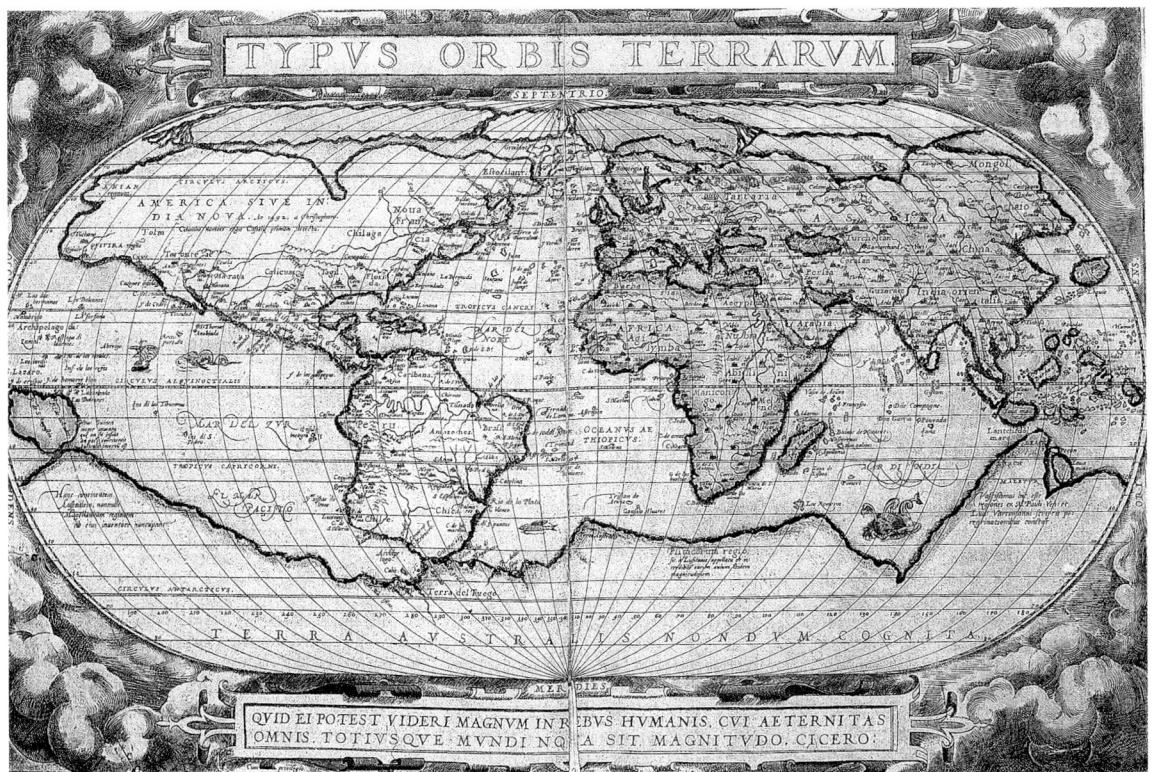

In his 1570 map of the world, Abraham Ortelius depicted a vast continent, *Terra Australis Nondum Cognita*, over the South Pole to balance the landmasses of the north. He included parts of the newly discovered coastlines of Tierra del Fuego, north and western Australia and New Guinea in his continent. (Linnean Society collections.)

successive map Australia's boundaries expanded, contracted, crept upward to the equator and down to the South Pole. Most show the Tropic of Capricorn running through the continent, and in all it is located south of Java. In some, it is broken into islands; in others, Australia is not represented at all.

Java-la-Grande was the name given to a continent-sized landmass drawn on the Dieppe maps to the west of Australia's actual position. It mysteriously disappears from maps drawn after about 1566. The mapmakers themselves claimed that the information about the island, whose shape bore a striking resemblance to the actual continent of Australia, was gained from the Portuguese. It is assumed that the information for these maps came from visits by caravels from Portugal's colony at Ternate, in the Moluccas (Maluka), into Australian waters. This is not surprising as the continent is hundreds, not thousands, of kilometres from the Spice Islands, then Portugese territory. Australia is a big target and when the Spice Islands drew ships from every maritime nation of the world, sailors would have been aware of the continent just under 500 kilometres beyond Timor. Rumours of the wreck of a Portuguese caravel, known as the Mahogany Ship, near Warrnambool off the western coast of Victoria have persisted, despite the failure of archaeological expeditions to bring up evidence. Twenty-seven people independently sighted it before it disappeared beneath shifting dunes at the end of last century.

Did the Portuguese know about Australia before the first authenticated Dutch landfall of 1606? In one of the earliest atlases still in existence, the *Boke of Idrography*, presented to King Henry VIII in 1542, the author, Jean Rotz, depicts a 'Land of Java', apparently Australia, giving names to places on the east coast similar to those they bear today. The hazardous Great Barrier Reef is the Coste Dangereuse, Botany Bay is Coste des Herbiages, the Bay of Inlets is Baye Perdue and the Bay of Isles is De Beaucoup d'Isles. These seem not to be fanciful names applied to hypothetical maps but actual localities. Rotz states that 'All this I have set down as exactly and truly as possible, drawing as much from my own experience as from the certain experiences of my friends and fellow navigators'.

The following description appeared in an exquisitely engraved book of 200 pages and nineteen maps published in Holland by Cornelius Wytfliet in 1597, *Descriptionis Ptolemaicae Augmentum*. An English edition was published in the same year:

> The Australis Terra is the most southern of all lands and is separated from New Guinea by a narrow strait. Its shores are hitherto but little known, since, after one voyage and another, that route has been deserted, and seldom is the country visited, unless when sailors are driven there by storms. Australis Terra begins at two or three degrees from the Equator, and is maintained by some to be of so great an extent that, if it were thoroughly explored, it would be regarded as a fifth part of the world.

The evidence for a continent grew. A seventeenth century map clearly shows a landmass south of Java, with a coastline bearing a striking similarity to the north coast of Australia. It is annotated with the information that this land, known as 'Eendracht' by the Dutch, was discovered by the Portuguese in 1601, five years before the first Dutch landfall. There is a huge and controversial literature on the supposed pre-Cook discoveries of eastern Australia.

As the sixteenth and seventeenth centuries progressed and Portuguese and Dutch traders probed south and east on their voyages to the East Indies, coastlines and continents that might, or might not, have been Australia appeared and disappeared on contemporary maps. The desire to find *Terra Australis Incognita* persisted. Eventually, successive Dutch voyages delineated the west and much of the north coast of Australia. Was this land, called 'New Holland' by its discoverers, *Terra Australis Incognita*? Even after Tasman sailed around much of Australia in 1642, proving that New Holland was nothing like the size of the old Great Southern Continent portrayed on the maps, the myth persisted. However, as the jigsaw of Australia's coastline was gradually pieced together it became obvious that if there were a *Terra Australis Incognita*, Australia was not it.

3
The Plant Hunters

Moving plants to improve agriculture, and later scenery and gardens, began with civilisation, and nothing illustrates this plant exchange better than the English garden. Most of the shrubs, flowers and trees now seen in England originated from other countries. Before the arrival of the Romans, the British landscape was dominated by birch, oak, Scots pine and hazel. There was little choice of vegetables for the Celtic pot — nettles, berries, dandelion leaves and a few root crops. It was the Romans who, in the first century, changed the British flora forever. Off their galleys came bags of seeds and pots of sprouting trees: plane, chestnut; fruits such as pears, cherries, damsons, quinces, peaches, mulberries and figs; herbs such as sage, thyme, rosemary, parsley, mint and shallots; celery, spinach, leeks, onions, radishes, lettuces; and those cottage garden favourites, lavender and roses. Yes, even the English rose is not English. The ancestors of today's cultivated roses spread throughout western Europe as the Arabs moved from Persia, conquered in the seventh century.

The English apple is an import, as is the London plane. The oaks, with their massive trunks and acorns are, perhaps, the most associated with Britain. Yet only two of the species growing today are indigenous — the English oak, *Quercus robur*, and *Q. petraea*, which is also widespread in Europe. The holm oak, *Q. ilex*, red oak, *Q. rubra*, and turkey oak, *Q. cerris*, have all been introduced in the past few hundred years. It is even doubtful that the so-called English elm, *Ulmus procera*, is a native of England. More likely it came from the continent.

Some carnations — *Dianthus* — probably came to England with William the Conqueror in 1066. The jasmine, pomegranate and the cedar of Lebanon returned with the Crusaders. The cornflower, *Centaurea cyanus*, arrived from Turkey in the seventeenth century. Both the marigolds (*Tagetes erecta* and *Calendula officinalis*) came from America, as did nasturtiums and dahlias, while chrysanthemums originated in the Orient.

J. C. Loudon, author of the *Encyclopaedia of Gardening*, 1822, estimated that before 1700 the number of exotic plants in Britain was probably less than a thousand. In the following century another 5000 species were introduced. So many foreign plants have been growing wild and self-seeding for so many centuries in Britain that they are accepted as native. By the time Britain began acquiring its empire, it had gained a rich, varied and commercially significant non-native flora. It would have no qualms about redistributing that flora to its empire, nor about bringing more plants back to the Mother Country.

THE NAMING OF PLANTS

In Europe, scholars have laboured at naming and identifying plants, pigeonholing them into families, genera and species. The first three major Western scholars of botany — Plato, Aristotle and Aristotle's pupil, Theophrastus, all lived in fourth century BC Greece. They laid the foundations of botanical classification that was to be followed for centuries. In his *De Historia Plantarum*, Theophrastus attempted to understand the minutiae of plant structure, as well as plant habitats and uses. He also described plants from India and Persia brought back to

Greece by Alexander the Great's warriors. The generic names *Anemone* and *Asparagus* were first used by Theophrastus, and the names crocus, cyclamen, delphinium, gentian, lily, peony, rose, violet and narcissus have been in use since the days of Ancient Greece and Rome.

Many of Theophrastus' observations on plant structure were not superseded until the advent of the microscope, and until molecular biology arrived his books were still thought worth recommending to students of elementary botany.

Although the Roman scholar Pliny the Elder, writing five centuries after Theophrastus, said much about plants in his thirty-seven volume *Historia Naturalis*, most of it was summarised from other sources and is quite uncritical. Accordingly, its readers had to try to separate fact from fiction. Eight volumes dealt with medicinal plants, with such hints as using tannin-rich blackberry leaves for treating 'affections of the mouth'. The Greek physician Pedanius Dioscorides, also working in the first century AD, compiled his famous *De Materia Medica*, in which the medical uses of 600 plants were listed.

The writings of these classical scholars, particularly Dioscorides, were still being followed in Europe centuries later, and formed the basis of the plethora of European herbals that appeared with the advent of the moveable-type printing press in the sixteenth century. Among the most renowned of these were Jerome or Hieronymus Bosch's *New Kreüterbuch* (1539) and Otto Brunfels' *Herbarum Vivae Eicones* (1530). Other workers in Germany, such as Leonhard Fuchs and

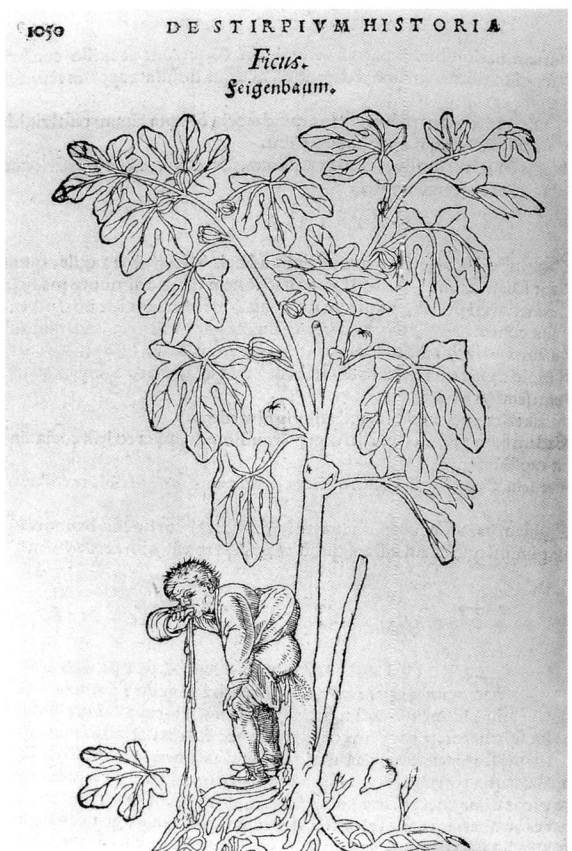

A graphic depiction of the purging effects of the fig — an illustration from a sixteenth century herbal by Hieronymus Bosch. Herbals became popular with the advent of the moveable-type printing press that made the production of books easier.
(Linnean Society collections.)

Valerius, as well as Rembert Dodoens, Charles de l'Ecluse and Matthias de l'Obel in Holland, and William Turner and John Gerard in England, also published substantial works.

THE FIRST PLANT COLLECTORS

Botanical knowledge expanded further when travellers began bringing plants back to Europe from far-flung corners of the globe. Plant collectors in the New World began to realise that the works of the classical scholars, based on the plants of the Mediterranean region, had little relevance to the myriad new plants being found in the Americas. Explorers and collectors were returning from the New World with so many different species of plants and animals that if pairs of them all had been carried on Noah's Ark it surely would have sunk. The numbers were so great that it raised doubts about the immutability of species and the biblical version of creation. How could God have made all these animals and plants on earth in just four days?

Scholars and collectors experienced increasing difficulty in naming newly discovered species, resorting either to using familiar names — hence mountain lion for puma — or native names, such as tobacco and potato. By doing this, they were not challenging accepted wisdom, but it gradually

The Plant Hunters

Transporting plants by sea was a haphazard business in the early days. Resourceful plant collectors often resorted to the strangest of receptacles to ensure a safe passage for their botanical trophies. (Linnean Society collections.)

became clear that new classification systems were needed. This realisation marks the emergence of botany as a study separate from medicine, with which it had previously been intimately connected. New systems, such as that based on morphology developed by Andrea Cesalpino in Bologna, attempted to show the relationships and affinities between different plants, and to describe variation and its relation to habitat. These new ways of thinking about classification paved the way for great thinkers such as Darwin to postulate their theories of evolution.

England's involvement in serious plant collecting began in the seventeenth century when John Tradescant — later to become gardener to King James I — returned to England with plants from his travels in Russia, Alicante and Algeria, collected for Robert Cecil. Tradescant's son later brought more from North America. Zeal for botanical exploration spread, like Christianity. The missionaries, especially French priests, who travelled far to win souls, returned with a cornucopia of new species, a few of which survived to adorn gardens and parks.

The chase for plants from the far corners of the world was a quest for something new, and an attempt to understand the connections between living things. Scientists set out to catalogue everything from the smallest insect to the largest fossil, from the most delicate flower to the tallest tree. Ships ventured further in the expectation of finding riches in yet-to-be-discovered lands. The rewards could be high with sponsors of successful voyages becoming rich beyond belief. The wealthy also wanted exotic new plants to grace their gardens. They had leisure to study and many became patrons of scientists, gardeners and artists. While there was no official government sponsorship of botanical exploration, there was a host of private individuals from captains to adventurers, ship's surgeons to humble ratings who were interested enough to collect and study plants on voyages, either on their own account or for their patrons.

Quarterdecks of ships could be cluttered with uprooted plants in tubs or sawn-off wine casks, but casualty rates among these plant passengers were high. Tubs were washed overboard; some were secretly jettisoned by thirsty sailors competing for water rations; others perished if sea spray was not washed off leaves; rats and cockroaches ate them; the ship's dogs and cats urinated on them; some were scorched by the equatorial sun or drowned by tropical storms. Seeds went mouldy or were eaten by weevils.

Ships' captains often had instructions from their wealthy sponsors to collect plants — dried or preserved in spirits — for botanical study, and also seeds or living plants for gardens or cash crops. Even ordinary seamen would hide seeds and plants, knowing that such souvenirs might mean quick cash at the end of a voyage. Plants travelled in straw and mats; in wicker baskets with moss around their roots; in soil over broken shells and stones for drainage; in potatoes; or in an old woollen sock filled with dirt. Acres and acres were transplanted by pocket, sock or barrel.

For a plant to be on sale in England, it had to withstand two main hazards: the long sea voyage and acclimatisation on arrival. But first, the plant had to be found and collected. Carrying live plants back to base could be awkward, although smaller plants could be transported in ox bladders tied to saddles. Men might have to forego water rations so water could be sprinkled on a plant, or suffer the sun when a hat was used to cradle a delicate bloom.

The main peril was the return voyage. 'The difficulty of carrying plants by sea is very great', read the instructions given by Joseph Banks (years later) to one plant collector:

> ... a small sprinkling of salt water, or of the salt dew which fills the air even in a moderate gale will inevitably destroy them if not immediately washed off with fresh water ... it is necessary that the cabin be appropriated to the sole purpose of making a kind of greenhouse ... Every precaution must be taken to prevent or destroy the Rats ... and as poison will constantly be used to destroy them and cockroaches, the crew must not complain if some of them that die in the ceiling make an unpleasant smell.

THE DEVELOPMENT OF CLASSIFICATION

The ordeal of obtaining plants was equalled by the struggle to get them over the seas to an expert for identification. Was it related to known plants? Was it new? What should it be called?

At the beginning of the eighteenth century the system of naming and classifying flora and fauna was confused. Aristotle's legacy to biology: classifying according to form or structure and degrees of 'perfection' was still current. A different method of nomenclature was used by each botanist and each country. Which name to which plant? It varied from place to place. The appearance of the first truly methodical book on botany in 1548 — William Turner's *Names of Herbes* — had not untangled the chaotic mass of names in loose and meandering Latin, and there was still no agreed concept of genera and species.

By this time the interest in plants as an economic resource and as items of trade was greater than ever before. It was more and more necessary to be able to name and classify plants, and the science of botany rapidly developed to meet that need. During the previous century botany had begun to move away from its traditional association with medicine to be regarded as a science in its own right. The world of scientific inquiry was changing. In England, an august group began meeting in the panelled room at Gresham College, 'for improving Natural Knowledge by experiments', the Royal Society. Started in 1660 and gaining the patronage of Charles II in 1662, the Society soon attracted intellectuals such as Sir Christopher Wren, Sir Isaac Newton and Robert Boyle. As well as mathematicians, chemists and physicists, it also numbered botanists among its fellows, signalling that this study was moving into the realms of conventional science.

One Society fellow, arguably the most influential figure in English botany of the time, was John Ray (1627 – 1705). Ray came from humble origins, being the parson son of an Essex

The Plant Hunters

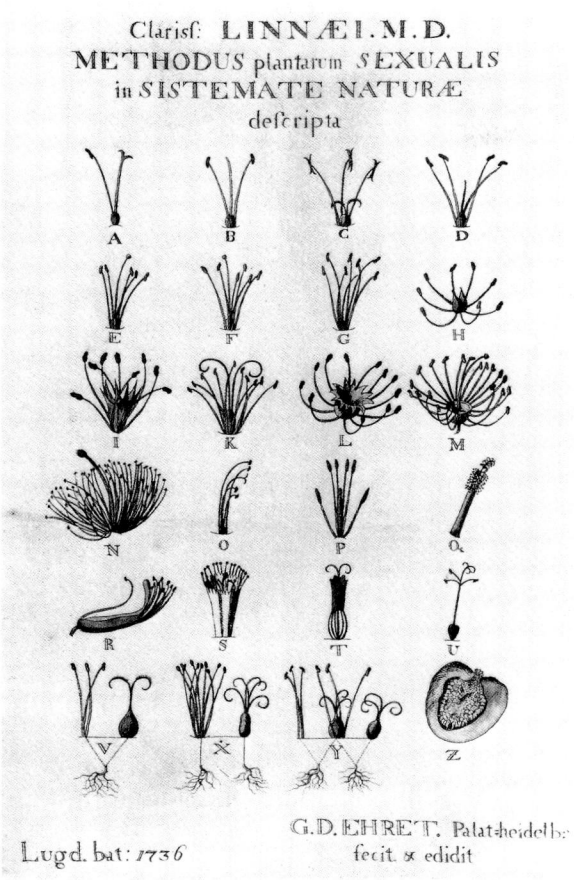

Carl Linnaeus' system of botanical classification by the structure of sexual organs, illustrated here by George Ehret, the famous natural history artist. (Linnean Society collections.)

blacksmith. He may well have got his passion for botany from his mother who was a herbalist. Ray organised his unique collection of flora and fauna into groups of mutual fertility and confined the term species to a group of animals or plants capable of interbreeding. He also originated some of the basic higher taxa of plant categories: cryptogams (which includes algae, fungi, lichens, mosses, liverworts and ferns); monocotyledons (plants with a single seed leaf such as grasses and lilies); and dicotyledons (plants with two seed leaves).

The value of reproductive structures in plant classification was well established by John Ray, and the concept was to be further developed by Carl Linnaeus. Ray expounded his use of flower structure to classify flowering plants in his magnum opus, the three-volume *Historia Plantarum Generalis* (1686 – 1704). This work has particular relevance for Australian botany. Included in an appendix were eleven plants from 'New Holland', collected by the pirate-adventurer William Dampier in 1699. These were the first plants then known to have returned to Europe from Australia.

Although an improvement on what had existed previously, Ray's system was still inadequate. The idea that living things, including plants, could be sorted in a hierarchical manner into smaller and smaller groups right down to an individual species, was not new. What had not been standardised (and some would say still hasn't) by the mid-eighteenth century, were the characters on which this classification should be made. In addition, there was no consistent way of naming species.

It took the analytical mind of a Swedish doctor to provide a system that botanists worldwide could use to name and classify plants. Carl Linnaeus' method was a beautifully simple one, similar in concept to Ray's, that grouped plants on the structure of their sexual organs. This was essentially an artificial system and did not, at higher levels, reflect actual relationships in the natural world. It has since been superseded by several more 'natural' systems, but at the time it provided a much-needed framework that everyone could use — an information retrieval system into which new plants could be fitted. Even more significantly, Linnaeus used Latin as a lingua franca, so that naturalists worldwide could understand each other no matter what their native language. Linnaeus also introduced the use of a Latin binomial system to identify species. Before this, scientific names had actually been long Latin descriptions. Linnaeus developed a shorthand system in which every plant is given a unique name consisting of just two elements — genus and species. The generic name grouped the plant with its nearest relatives while the specific name described the fundamental taxonomic unit. Essentially, members of the same species can interbreed. No matter what local name a plant might have, the Latin (or Latinised) binomial would uniquely identify it. Latin binomials were extended to the animal world and this system is still used today.

THE ESTABLISHMENT OF BOTANIC GARDENS

The term 'botany' was certainly in use by 1660 to describe the study of plants, particularly by physicians and apothecaries. Medical practitioners used physic or apothecaries' gardens to grow medicinal plants and teach students. It was to these gardens, which later expanded into growing non-medicinal plants, that newly discovered species were sent. There were hundreds of botanic gardens in Europe by the end of the eighteenth century; some private, some royal, some ducal, all vying for anything new. Many of these centres of scientific research would receive Australian plants from voyages of exploration, and the continent's new settlements, through the course of the eighteenth and nineteenth centuries.

The Jardin des Plantes in Paris was founded by Louis XIII in 1635, originally as a physic garden. By the time of the French Revolution, when its name was changed from the Jardin du Roi, it was a museum, a menagerie, a centre for research and education, and an influential sponsor of scientific expeditions.

The physic garden of Charles de Lécluse in Leiden, Holland, had expanded in the sixteenth century to include extensive collections of flowering bulbs — the foundation of tulipomania. Until the end of the Dutch East India Company in 1795, herbarium specimens and seeds were sent annually to the gardens in Amsterdam and Leiden.

The Royal Botanic Garden at Edinburgh began in 1670 as a small private garden owned by two physicians. In England, in 1722, the grounds of the Chelsea Physic Garden, established the previous century, were leased at a nominal rent by Sir Hans Sloane (1660 – 1753) to the Society of Apothecaries. The garden had two aims, to grow medicinal plants in London for its members and to be an instruction centre for the Society's apprentices. Sir Hans, like John Ray, was a giant of English botany. In his twenties, as physician to the Duke of Albemarle, he accompanied the newly appointed Governor of Jamaica, and collected 800 botanical specimens, which he classified and published according to Ray's system. His library, manuscripts, natural history

Augusta, wife of Frederick Prince of Wales, took a great interest in the landscaping and developing of the garden he bought for her at Kew. The royal family would have a formative influence on Kew throughout the eighteenth and into the nineteenth centuries. (Linnean Society collections.)

specimens, antiquities and curiosities formed the basis for the establishment of the British Museum.

The foremost botanical garden in the United Kingdom, at Kew on the south bank of the Thames, was originally the garden of Sir Henry Capel, a keen horticulturist. The grounds were purchased by Frederick, Prince of Wales, for his wife, Princess Augusta, in 1730. After Frederick's death in 1751, Augusta, with the assistance of Scottish courtier Lord Bute, chief minister and mentor to her son George III, transformed them. Part was turned into a physic garden and the rest was landscaped in a variety of styles. Bute, who reputedly became Princess Augusta's lover, was a man of immense intellectual ability, who initiated an exchange of knowledge about plants with other European botanical institutions. It is usually forgotten that it was he who laid the foundations of Kew, greatly enlarging its plant

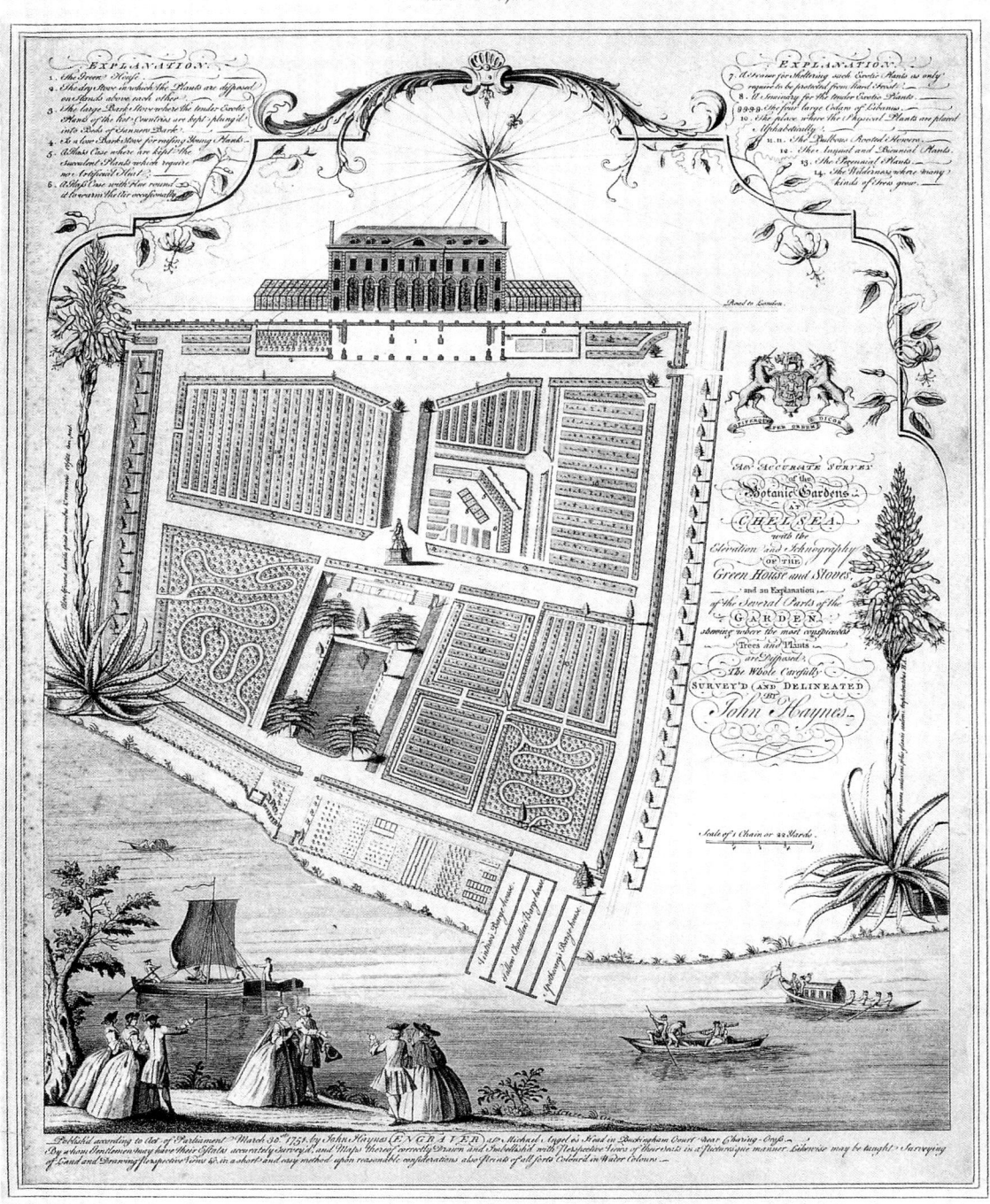

Chelsea Physic Garden — here depicted in 1751 just two years before the death of its benefactor and leading botanist Sir Hans Sloane — would become an important centre for the cultivation of Australian plants in the eighteenth century. (Linnean Society collections.)

collections and prompting the botanist Peter Collinson to describe it in 1766 as 'the paradise of our world, where all plants are found, that money or interest can procure'.

The establishment of botanical gardens spread to the colonies. At enormous effort they were maintained to perfect plants for agriculture, to experiment with cheap raw materials for the home country and to grow edible tropical crops. The Dutch East India Company had established a garden at the Cape of Good Hope in 1652. France's first colonial botanic garden was established in 1735 on the Isle-de-France (Mauritius), the gateway to the Indian trade routes. Attached to the grand 'Mon Plaisir', home of the Governor, it changed its name often over two centuries, eventually being known by the same name as the district in which it lies — Pamplemousses (which coincidentally means grapefruit). Although the spices propagated there never fulfilled their intended purpose of bringing wealth to the colony, the several varieties of sugar cane on which the fortune of the planters was founded were bred in the garden.

Britain set up its first colonial botanic garden in 1764 on the island of St Vincent in the West Indies, for the purpose of introducing tropical crops, such as cinnamon, cloves, nutmeg, camphor, vanilla, pepper, coffee, tea, spices, cotton and sugarcane to their possessions in the Caribbean. Others followed: Jamaica, in the same year; Calcutta, the main garden for acclimatising tea plants from China to grow in India, 1786; Penang, Malaysia, 1796; Ceylon (Sri Lanka), 1821; and Singapore 1859. The acquisition of raw materials was a prime consideration in England.

Spain, too, started botanic gardens abroad. Baron von Humboldt (1769 – 1859), the German naturalist and explorer, wrote:

> No European government has laid out greater sums to advance the knowledge of plants than the Spanish government. Three botanical expeditions, those of Peru, New Granada, and New Spain ... have cost the state about two million francs. Besides, botanic gardens have been established at Manila and in the Canary Island ... more than four thousand new species of plants ...

But, like *Banks' Florilegium*, the *Flora of New Granada* by José Celestine Mutis, had to wait until the 1980s to be published and the first of a multi-volume *Flora of Central America* is only now appearing.

THE ECONOMICS OF PLANT COLLECTING

By the mid-eighteenth century the world was being combed for botanical specimens that could be grown to make money in new colonial possessions, or which would grace the gardens of the gentry. Moving plants was a flourishing trade. English gardeners, with their eclectic tastes and passion for densely planted beds and borders, encouraged nurseries which vied for new varieties of flowers. An eager clientele awaited the strange and exotic plants which were hurried from ships to London nurseries. In west London alone there were ten enterprises, together covering well over forty hectares. An establishment which pioneered many Australian plants was James Lee and Lewis Kennedy's 'Vineyard' nursery in Hammersmith.

Private London nurseries such as these were the sorting houses of foreign trees and flowers. By the time the English had settled Australia, moving plants in sailing ships around the world had become a trade. Until colonisation Australia had been secluded from invasion by foreign seeds. It was as if a glass cage had enclosed the continent, keeping it in a time capsule, preserving the extraordinary vegetation from destruction or contact. But when the settlers came, instead of the flora being valued, much of it was replaced, without being studied, evaluated or appreciated.

4
Fire and Flora — The Origins of Australia's Plants

Even the earliest commentators on Australia's flora remarked on its strangeness, compared to what they knew in Europe. In the eighteenth century, botanists working on Australian flowers noted similarities with South African plants. Further similarities were found with South American plants and later with the fossil flora of Antarctica.

The reasons for these similarities can be found in the earliest origins of Australia's plants, some 140 million years ago in the Cretaceous period. At this time Australia, Antarctica, India, South America and Africa were joined in one massive landmass called Gondwana. Flowering plants evolved in the regions of this supercontinent which are now Africa and South America, and slowly spread across the rest of the landmass. The shared origins of these plants can be seen in families that are common to the southern continents, such as the Proteaceae which has members in both Australia and Africa. Then, around 90 million years ago, by a process known as plate tectonics, Gondwana began to split into the continents we know today; Africa, India and South America drifted northwards, while Australia and Antarctica remained locked together in the south. Finally, they too split apart and Australia began its long, isolated journey north. It carried with it animals and plants that were to be separated from most of the rest of the world for the next 50 million years. The uniquely Australian elements of the continent's wildlife evolved during these years of isolation.

On its slow drift northwards to its present position, Australia kept pace with a changing world climate. There has been a worldwide cooling trend over the last 40 million years which Australia largely avoided as it moved towards the equator, enjoying instead a long period of climatic stability. Australia also remained generally free from other physical traumas that affected most of the rest of the world during this period, such as glaciation and continental collision, and it only experienced volcanism in the far north-east. But this stability had its downside — glaciation and volcanism are essential contributors, in the long term, to the recycling of minerals and the renewal of the soil. Consequently, Australia has the poorest soils of all the continents, containing, on average, only half the levels of nutrients, such as nitrates and phosphates, of similar soils in other areas of the world.

ADAPTATION

As Tim Flannery pointed out in *The Future Eaters*, nutrient conservation is a major theme running through the evolution of Australia's flora, forcing 'some unusual adaptations in its plants'. There is a high number of carnivorous plants in Australia, for instance, including pitcher plants and more than half the world's species of sundews. These obtain nutrients lacking in the soil from their insect prey. Another adaptation to nutrient deficiency — rather than to aridity as previously thought — is 'scleromorphy' where plants are generally small, slow growing, and have small, rigid or spiny leaves with waxy or hairy surfaces. Scleromorphy can be seen in many unrelated but typically Australian plants, such as banksias, eucalypts and acacias.

Scleromorphy also fits these plants for the rigours of life in Australia's arid zone. Larger than any other desert region south of the equator, comprising one-third of the continent, Australia's desert areas are augmented by extensive semi-arid regions. Unlike other parched regions of the world, Australian dry areas are dominated by these scleromorphic, woody plants rather than perennial, succulent, water-retaining, cactus-like plants that often characterise the dry regions of America and Africa.

FIRE AND MAN

Related to Australia's aridity is the relatively high incidence of fire which is a major formative agent of the Australian environment. Some native plants not only survive burning, showing specific adaptations to counter its effects, but actually require fire to complete their life cycle. Some banksia seed cones, for instance, do not open to release their seeds until burnt. Recent research suggests that their subsequent successful germination is also a chemical response to compounds in smoke. It seems a strange adaptation to have, but the tightly closed pods protect the seeds until the plant is burnt, and then release them when the fire has passed into an environment enriched by ash, increasing the chances of successful germination and growth. Fire is also one way, albeit an inefficient one, of recycling nutrients, especially in a nutrient-poor environment.

Some eucalypts also have fire adaptations, although a number are fire sensitive and do not survive burning, only regenerating from seed. Fire-resistant species possess wood that is tough and durable and resists the ravages of fire. After burning they put out sprouts from buds protected in their inner bark. The bark, leaves and branches of many eucalypt species are constantly shed, creating fuel for bushfires. The oil of eucalypts is also highly flammable so during a fire the oil creates a gas which ignites and forms fireballs, but these blazes are quick as the easily available fuel is soon spent.

The adaptation of such a large group of plant species to nutrient deficiency, aridity and frequent burning is unparalleled in the rest of the world and there has been much debate as to how this unusual ecology developed. Fire-tolerant species evolved in Australia's dry, very nutrient-depleted heathlands where natural fires, such as those ignited by lightning, were frequent. Many heathland plants eventually adapted to burning, not only surviving it, but in some cases, actually taking advantage of it.

Archaeologists have found evidence from some ancient pollen deposits that Australia's vegetation changed dramatically around forty thousand years ago in favour of these fire-tolerant plants. Before then, they suggest, there were many more areas of fire-sensitive plants, such as broad-leaved forests, than today. It has long been thought that the arrival of Aboriginal people at about this time, and their introduction of 'firestick' farming — burning the countryside — accounted for this spread of fire-tolerant species. The increase in charcoal in the archaeological record suggests a widespread increase in the occurrence of fire, but dating of these deposits is inconclusive, with some giving ages for the charcoal that predates the arrival of humans by fifty thousand years. The story is not a simple one, with several factors probably having an effect, particularly climatic change. During this period the earth was going through the last ice age and although Australia was spared the rigours of glaciation because of its high latitude, its climate was still affected, becoming much dryer and colder than previously. This would undoubtedly have had an impact on the vegetation, which might have been further affected by human action after colonisation of the continent around forty thousand years ago.

One theory suggests that Aboriginal people did have a marked influence with their use of fire, particularly locally, but did not embark on a systematic burning of the continent immediately on their arrival — that would come later, in response to another possible consequence of their actions. When they first colonised Australia, Aboriginal people found a land dominated by large animals: giant kangaroos, wombats, lizards and flightless birds ruled Australia. These provided easy prey for the new,

Acacia decurrens, described here under its old name of Mimosa and painted by Pierre-Etienne Redouté. Acacia is a typically Australian genus. (Linnean Society collections.)

Right: Carl Linné, or Carolus Linnaeus, the Swedish doctor who revolutionised plant classification and nomenclature. He introduced the Latin binomial, and a classification based on the sexual organs of plants. (Linnean Society collections.)

Below left: Australia boasts many beautiful plants which can be cultivated under the right conditions. *Blandfordia nobilis* for instance was among the first Australian plants to be successfully grown in Britain. James Edward Smith, one of the most enthusiastic proponents of the cultivation of non-native species, stated in his *Exotic Botany*, from which this illustration is taken, that there were living *Blandfordia* plants in existence in England in 1804. (Linnean Society collections.)

Below right: Grevilleas, such as this *G. refracta*, drawn by Ferdinand Bauer in 1802, along with haekeas, banksias and others, are Australian members of the family Proteaceae. This family is also found in South Africa, South America, India, Madagascar and New Guinea, providing botanical evidence for the existence of the southern supercontinent Gondwana. (Olde P. Marriott N. *The Grevillea Book.* Kangaroo Press, 1994.)

clever hunters, too easy perhaps, for before long they became extinct, although whether this was due to over-hunting or to other factors is still being debated. Whatever the cause, it has been suggested that there was an unforeseen consequence of their disappearance. These large herbivores had played a vital role in the ecology of Australia by consuming vast quantities of vegetation and by recycling nutrients via their dung — especially in the fire-sensitive broad-leaved forests. Without these animals to clear the dead vegetation, the standing fuel-load increased and the areas became vulnerable to burning. Once consumed by fire they could not regenerate, leaving the way open for colonisation by fire-tolerant plants from the arid heathlands such as eucalypts, hakeas, banksias and acacias.

The loss of large tracts of broad-leaved forest, whether through human action or climatic change or a combination of factors, would have left the way open for colonisation by hardy sclentropics. Such change would also have had further effects on the local climate. The broad-leaved vegetation absorbed rainfall, returning moisture to the atmosphere. But the open structure of the eucalypt woodland that replaced it allowed much more rainfall to reach the ground and drain away. Consequently it returned less water to the atmosphere, resulting in less rain. Dry Australia got dryer, already nutrient-poor soils became more impoverished and the eucalypts and mulgas took over. In the increasingly arid continent, fire began to take hold.

With the structure of the vegetation irreparably changed, and the risk of fire ever present, the development of firestick farming could have been one strategy used to lessen the likelihood of intensely destructive major bushfires. Controlled fires had to be brief, as excessive burning-off can be fatal even to fire-tolerant plants. In many cases burning would have been infrequent, perhaps with intervals as long as twenty-five years between fires in areas that required a long period to recover. Too-frequent burning could completely destroy vegetation and habitat but the right amount of burning produced ash, providing nutrients, and cleared the combustible undergrowth creating the right environment for rapid plant regeneration. Aboriginal burning was therefore highly selective. Certain areas would be kept regularly burned to attract game or to facilitate easier travel, while some were infrequently burned and yet others that supported fire-sensitive food plants such as yams were not burnt at all.

DOMINANT PLANT GROUPS

The Australian landscape is dominated by two genera — *Eucalyptus* and *Acacia*. These sclero-morphic groups radiated across the continent and adapted to seasonal and sometimes perennial drought, low nutrients and fire, leading to extraordinary diversification. *Acacia*, one of the most widespread and numerous of all Australian genera, is also found in Asia and Africa, but the greatest number of species is found in Australia. Worldwide, *Acacia* has about 1100 species, of which at least 900 are indigenous to Australia with more yet to be described, and they thrive from the coastline to the arid centre.

It is the eucalypts, however, that are most identified with Australia. They belong to the Myrtaceae, a family with tough resinous foliage and showy brush-like flowers which includes the bottle-brushes, Geraldton wax, honey myrtle and Melaleuca or paperbark. With some 600-plus Australian species, eucalypts characterise forests across the continent. Their narrow, pendulous leaves let light filter through to the ground beneath, thereby quickly drying the leaf and bark litter, providing fuel for fires and giving a walk through the Australian bush the distinctive sound of crushing leaves.

Eucalypts have become a major world source of hardwood, as their growth and yield can be spectacular. The jarrah of Western Australia, *Eucalyptus marginata*, is so dense, heavy and strong that it was used last century to support paving beneath the streets of London and Melbourne. The erroneously named mountain ash, *E. regnans*, is one of the tallest known species, matched only by the Californian redwood. But whereas *E. regnans* grows to 300 feet in as many

THE FLOWER CHAIN

years, the redwood takes 3000 years to achieve the same height.

Financially, the most important trees in Australia are the quick-growing hardwoods, *E. grandis* and *E. globulus*. In temperate areas the yield of wood from these two species can surpass that of pines, although from a plantation point of view, the exotic pines, although producing soft timbers, are still the most economically viable and widespread. *E. globulus* and *E. grandis* are now so widely planted everywhere from Morocco to Brazil, even in quite cool climates, that few people realise that they all originated in Australia. It is the irregular, stately shape of the eucalypt which dominates Australian forests. The giant gums of Tasmania and Victoria, the karri and the jarrah forests of Western Australia, the twisted, gnarled white gums of the sandstone, stringybark, the ironbark and box of the open forests, the tallow-wood and spotted gum of the coast and the mallee scrubs of Victoria all give the Australian landscape its distinctive character.

Two other characteristic groups of Australian flora are the banksias and the casuarinas. Banksias, those most typical of Australian plants, named by the younger Linnaeus after Joseph Banks, belong to the Proteaceae, a family which has some of its most spectacular members in Australia such as waratahs, grevilleas and hakeas. In the early days of settlement the gnarled trunks of banksias with their thick, rough bark, were favoured as fuel. Later, because of their attractive grain, some were used for furnishings. Banksias are one of the groups that confirm the link between Australian and Gondwanan flora. The family Proteaceae occurs most notably in South Africa where it is represented by spectacular proteas. Another link with Gondwana is the desert rose of western Queensland and central Australia, which is related to the South American

Some 750 *Acacia* species are known in Australia and they often display scleromorphic adaptations such as narrow, waxy leaves. Many early workers placed them in the genus *Mimosa*. This example, collected and described by the French botanist Labillardière, is now known as *Acacia saphorae*. (Linnean Society collections.)

Eucalypts typically produce pungent oils. John White, surgeon to the First Fleet, likened the smell of this species, *Eucalyptus piperita*, to peppermint and it was described by James Edward Smith and illustrated in White's published journal in 1790. The oils have the effect of making eucalypt forest very flammable, but some eucalypts have adapted to survive burning. (Illustration from collections in the London Library.)

cotton plant, a thirsty species. The CSIRO (Commonwealth Science and Industrial Research Organisation) has embarked on a program to improve the strain of this American cotton, commercially grown in Australia, by cross-breeding it with the desert rose to make a new variety with lower water consumption.

Casuarinas are hardy trees found throughout the continent. With their characteristic long, drooping branches, all but two casuarinas are unique to Australia — the widely distributed *Casuarina equisetifolia* and *C. cunninghamiana* are also found on Pacific and Indian ocean islands. The genus has recently been reclassified and some are now known as *Allocasuarina*. They are commonly known as she-oaks. 'She' was used by timber-men to indicate inferiority of timber — as in she-beech or she-pine — because the timbers of these trees, although like their namesakes, are not as good as the real thing.

Australia is not all dry sclerophyll forest. Tropical rainforest and mangroves are found along the north and north-eastern coasts. The rainforests in the wet tropics have the highest concentration of primitive flowering plant families of any area in the world. Of the nineteen families classed as the most primitive in the world, thirteen are found in these rainforests; two, *Austrobaileyaceae* and *Idiospermaceae*, are endemic to Queensland.

CULTIVATION OF AUSTRALIAN PLANTS

Despite the fact that Australia has a range of climates, the myth has grown up that Australian plants can only survive in tropical or hot climates. This is not true. Many gardening books give minimum temperatures for Australian plants which are higher than those of a freezing winter in Australia's capital city, Canberra. Australia is thought of as a continent of sunshine and surf, but snow falls regularly all along the mountains of the east coast from Tasmania to the Victoria–New South Wales border.

When Australian plants do not prosper abroad it is usually because of factors such as poor soil drainage (which can be overcome in raised beds), low levels of light, and perhaps short days in the winter months of northern Europe. Soil acidity is another important factor — many native Australian plants are lime-haters and need a reasonably acidic compost or soil. Many are adapted to a low-nutrient environment, and over-fertilising can prove fatal to plants such as banksias. Some plants will thrive in foreign areas but may need to be acclimatised first. Tasmanian blue gum, *Eucalyptus globulus*, normally grows in the British Isles if the seed is gathered from a parent tree growing at high enough altitude. Spinning gum, *Eucalyptus perriniana*, grows around London. Plants will often survive if there are windbreaks and a good dark mulch to keep soil temperature up. If plants are located near sunny walls they endure bad weather more easily.

Australian plants can be cultivated in England and other temperate climates, although some, if in inappropriate situations, will never bloom. The Tasmanian waratah, *Telopea truncata*, in the rock garden at the Royal Botanic Garden, Edinburgh, although over forty years old, is still only sixty centimetres high due to its exposed, windy situation, where it is occasionally cut back by frosts. At Wakehurst Place, Sussex, there is a tree of the same species, over seven metres high, flowering freely and regularly setting seed. Here all its needs are met: an acid soil, plenty of moisture and shelter from wind.

Australian gardeners can be frustrated in their attempts to cultivate native plants, despite the fact that these same plants have been growing in Australia for millions of years. An unjust reputation has spread that native plants prosper only in the bush. Many suburban gardens, dug with much enthusiasm by home-owners, produce spindly, disappointing native plants. This is because land was often cleared of all trees and topsoil when areas were developed for housing and sometimes topsoil was replaced by excavated subsoil. To compensate, the ground was enhanced with fertiliser but this only gave nourishment to non-indigenous shrubs and trees, killing many native plants. Also, many Australian native plants, unused to daily rainfall, are literally drowned by deluges from automatic watering systems.

The Flower Chain

ISOSTYLIS INTEGRIFOLIA Britten.

This engraving of a *Banksia integrifolia*, collected by Banks and Solander, shows the bud, flower and an old seed cone on the same branch, something that is also observed in the wild. The cone is extraordinarily hard and robust, and only opens, as shown here, after exposure to fire. (Linnean Society collections.)

Many modern gardeners fail to propagate seeds of plants such as banksias and hakeas as splitting the testa, or seed coat, and germinating the seed can be problematic. By observing how seeds are now propagated one can see the value of the brief and brisk Aboriginal fires. Some gardeners mistakenly put seeds in very hot ovens that actually kill the embryo; some soak seeds in water, which can also kill the germ of the embryo. There are various ways to duplicate the effects of a brisk fire: scarifying the seeds by rubbing them on sand on a hard surface; pouring boiling water over them for some seconds — one expert insists on counting to ten then plunging the seed in icy cold water until a sharp crack is heard; putting seeds in a wire basket and holding them briefly over a gas flame; setting fire to the banksia cone with a small wood fire; dousing the fruit with methylated spirits and setting it alight; a few sheets of crumpled newspaper set alight on a concrete floor with the banksia cones at the centre of the blaze; all are usually sufficient for the nuts to open. These latter methods are likely to be the most effective if the latest research,

Fire and Flora – The Origins of Australia's Plants

which indicates banksia seeds germinate in response to the chemicals in smoke, is true.

It is perfectly possible to grow native plants in Australian gardens, but cultivators need to be sensitive to the specific conditions required for them to thrive. If more native species were grown, the benefit to native fauna could be dramatic. Insects, small marsupials and birds could be encouraged into suburban gardens. However, it is not just habitat and food loss that is adversely affecting native fauna. It is also much at risk from depredation by domestic cats and dogs. Encouraging the cultivation of Australia's unique flora is only part of the story.

5

The Scurvy Coast

For the white man who did not know the secrets of its plants, Australia was the 'Scurvy Coast'. The flora of Australia is exceedingly rich in beautiful species, but only a small number of plants provide sustenance for a stranger. By contrast, for the Australian Aboriginal people, the continent could be a land of plenty with all manner of plants contributing to their diet, but they had tens of thousands of years of experience behind them. The exact date of human colonisation is unknown, but most authorities now agree that they probably arrived, from South-East Asia, between forty and sixty thousand years ago.

Civilisations elsewhere were founded on grain culture, on the harvesting of huge crops including wheat, oats and rice, which provided basic nutrients but required a settled population to tend them. It demanded planning ahead, ploughing and planting in cleared areas, and harvesting each autumn. Nomadic life ceased, tribes settled. Cereal production around the Mediterranean started before 7000 BC and in China around 5000 BC. Cultivation of crops and civilisation were simultaneous; man no longer had to chase food so he devoted energy to other pursuits — what we might call leisure or culture. Daily bread led to other aspects of civilisation: the development of writing, literature, science and sophisticated music and art.

In contrast, the survival of the Aboriginal people in Australia was reliant on daily foraging and hunting for a varied diet of animals, insects, plants, fruits and fungi. Farm the land they did not, but set fire to it they did — with zeal and persistence. Before the merchandising of spontaneous combustion matches at the beginning of the nineteenth century, arguably no other race on earth ignited and manipulated fire as skilfully as the Aboriginal Australians.

Fire has always been one of man's constant tools providing heat for warmth, cooking and the smelting of metals. Use of fire was, and is, common practice among hunting people of the world, particularly in Africa. Early man used slash-and-burn as a basic clearance technique. Even in modern farming, burning has become a common practice in arable areas. The burning of straw and stubble after harvests to clear the fields of weeds and infestations is a common sight. But the Aboriginal peoples used fire to maintain the productivity of the land.

Fire prompted the regrowth of shoots and the germination of seeds; in some areas it suppressed the growth of woody shrubs in favour of grass. This burning regenerated the vegetation not just for the people themselves; it also had the consequence of providing sustenance and habitat for their main prey — the smaller marsupial herbivores.

Agriculture, with its settled lifestyle and material possessions, was always inappropriate to native Australians. There were no beasts of burden to till the land — all indigenous animals had paws (e.g. kangaroos and wombats), or webbed feet (the platypus), and many hopped on two feet; picture a kangaroo pulling a plough. In the tropical north the abundance of wild food meant that people had no need to adopt laborious gardening and farming practices. There was little point in producing food surpluses when hot temperatures throughout much of the year, combined with high seasonal rainfall in the monsoon areas, presented problems with long-term preservation of food, so only rarely was this undertaken. When it was, methods were invariably simple: bunya pine nuts buried in bags, sliced palm nuts dried in the sun and then wrapped in paperbark or left in a grass-lined trench before being covered with dirt.

Within a few thousand years of their occupation of Australia, the Aboriginal people had established a way of life that was to remain virtually unchanged until 1788. They had neither written words nor grain sprouting out of furrows, but they had a civilisation and a spiritual sense of being. Stories about trees and plants were handed down through rock drawings, corroborees and storytellers. Knowledge, such as the uses of plants, was passed on verbally and by demonstration from parent to child and grandchild. Little disturbed the isolation of the continent from other influences. There may have been visits by Chinese voyagers and, from the end of the sixteenth century, European boats came and went, but never lingered. Unlike the brisk pace of American history, Australia has an interminable list of European discoverers before colonisation. A gap of 182 years stretches from the first recorded landing to white settlement.

This is in contrast to the attention the Americas received. Just a year and a day after Christopher Columbus crossed the Atlantic in 1492, he returned to the Caribbean with over a thousand immigrants. In American history, there is a close connection between its discovery and settlement and the appreciation of its flora, as is seen by the introduction of its magnificent flowers into the Renaissance gardens of Europe. After Columbus, the yucca, nasturtium, lobelia, passion flower, swamp cypress and goldenrod were shipped to Spain and later grew there and in England. Imported plants became important crops — potatoes, tomatoes and pumpkins from the Americas rapidly became part of European cuisine. Fabulous trading in pineapples began after one was admired by Columbus in Guadeloupe in 1493. Tobacco was grown in plantations, and smoking became a popular European relaxation.

Australian discovery and settlement was a much more hit-and-miss affair. Its history is studded with discoveries, but it is uncertain when its shores were first sighted from a European ship. There was no world-shattering moment, comparable to 1492, when 'Columbus crossed the ocean blue'. There is some evidence that the Portuguese may have landed along the north coast but the first authenticated landfall was by the Dutchman Willem Jansz in 1606. From then on, Australian history tells of sailors coming, leaving and never coming back — even Captain Cook never returned to the mainland.

The first ships that arrived on the coasts of Australia showed no curiosity to venture beyond the mangroves, sand dunes, coastal plains and eucalypt forests. Although the shores were reached, the bush with its characteristic scent — seafarers can often smell the resin from the eucalypts before catching sight of the land — remained unexplored. Early voyagers to Australia complained that they could make few landfalls because of the difficulty in finding likely ports among the mangrove swamps, cliffs, or sandy beaches with rolling surf. When they did get ashore water was scarce and there were no recognisable fruits and vegetables, nothing obviously edible, nothing similar to what they were used to. They preferred the nearby Pacific islands with bananas, breadfruit, spices, coconuts and sweet potatoes. Ironically, it was the trade in the edible plants of the lush East Indies — nutmeg, cloves and cinnamon — which led to Australia's European discovery by traders anxious to find new sources of spices.

Thus Australia was neglected for a variety of reasons: distance, a coastline inhospitable to sailing ships, insufficient fresh water and green vegetables or fruit to relieve the tedium of ship rations. Captains were eager for fresh food to keep sailors free from scurvy, the major cause of death at sea. Scurvy results from the absence of vitamin C found in fresh vegetables and fruits. This substance was not actually identified until the twentieth century, but seafarers gradually became aware that fresh provisions went some way to ameliorating or preventing scurvy. In the 1790s 'lime juice' (actually lemon juice) became part of normal navy rations.

The first sign of scurvy is a debilitating cold followed by dizziness, infirmity, aching legs and bleeding and ulcerated gums causing teeth to fall out. Death is usually imminent when relentless diarrhoea, internal bleeding and gangrene of the lungs occur. The disease is not confined to sailors — many people on land suffered, and continue to suffer, from various levels of the affliction. It has now been postulated by medical historians that Henry VIII's ill health was caused by early scurvy brought on by a meat-rich diet eaten to the exclusion of vegetables and fruit.

Although Europeans who made landfalls on the Australian coast failed to find anti-scorbutic plants, scurvy was virtually unknown to Aboriginal people until they were deprived of their means of subsistence by white settlers. The land did provide sufficient sustenance for the population it already supported. The difference was, they knew where to look.

Aboriginal people subsisted in Australia because of a well-developed knowledge, gained from thousands of years of experience, of how to find, use and cook what was growing wild. The belief that native Australians adapted to the vegetation without increasing food supplies is mistaken; they increased yields through their use of fire, achieving a half-way house to agriculture. They also practised domiculture — the random cultivation of plants. For instance, when they ate yams, they ate only the lower portion and replanted the top. Also, they would spit out various seeds, especially fruit tree seeds and those of the pandanus nut, into the debris of fish remains and shells in refuse heaps at the edge of a camp. These midden soils with their compost of decaying organic matter and lime from shells provided an ideal environment for certain plants to grow. So consistent was this practice that archaeologists can now identify prehistoric sites by the groves of native fruit trees. An equilibrium with food supply was also maintained by not increasing the population. In parts of Queensland, for instance, unwanted pregnancies were terminated with a drink made from poisonous red gidee-gidee beans.

Immediately before white colonisation, the continent was inhabited by between 300 000 and 700 000 Aboriginal people, divided among 500 to 600 tribes, subdivided into clans and families with intricate relationships. Tribes had distinct boundaries, languages and territories. Many tribes were semi-nomadic, their movements dependent on the seasons, eating ripe fruit and edible flowers and roots. Each tribe was restricted to clearly

An Aboriginal man demonstrates how nectar can be obtained from grevillea flowers. Aboriginal burning of the land provided regrowth food plants for both people and smaller marsupials.
(Photo: P. Olde & N. Marriott *The Grevillea Book*. Volume I, Kangaroo Press, 1994.)

defined territories, delineated by natural features such as rivers and hills. Lands never changed hands; ownership was communal, fixed and immutable. The emphasis was on eating what was fresh and in season at that moment.

Every forest, every river, every bay, every beach was someone's territory. Just as now, the coastal fringe was more densely populated than the interior. Journals of foreign ships before settlement describe seeing smoke and fires along the coasts, even when they had no sightings of people.

These Aboriginal people's tenure of Australia is the longest of any group of humans of a significant land area anywhere in the world. After white settlement, their numbers were reduced dramatically by diseases such as smallpox and measles which came with the new settlers and swept across the continent because the people had no natural immunity. In a community with no written language, where knowledge was handed down verbally from one generation to another, such epidemics resulted in a huge loss of wisdom, not least regarding the uses of plants.

Botanical knowledge, essential for human survival in pre-European settlement Australia, resided mainly with the women, the chief food collectors. Food gathering was a daily practice, the men were the hunters, the women the foragers. Men provided for their parents, women for their husbands, but the distribution of food was complex. The sex roles were well defined and women spent long days with their children collecting a wide range of both vegetable and animal foods such as honey ants and witchetty grubs. When fresh food was scarce they ate unpalatable nuts, fibrous roots and leaves, briefly chewing them for any goodness, then spitting out the fibres.

The white arrivals, used to beef, beer, bread, butter and bacon, did not adapt to 'bush tucker' — the term they bestowed on Aboriginal food. In the eighteenth century some schools of philosophy, like that of Rousseau, admired the natural life of the savage state; others, such as James Burnet, Lord Monboddo, favoured progress. He believed that in the savage state man was scarcely distinguishable from a brute. There was an inbuilt feeling of superiority in the British, rulers of the most powerful Christian empire in the world, over nomadic tribes who had not progressed from the hunter-gatherer stage to the making of leavened bread. Bush tucker represented this primitive state and was generally rejected. There were times, however, when it was eaten out of necessity and a few of the Aboriginal food-plants did indeed creep into the diet. In the outback, the quandong *Santalum acuminatum*, a small, bright-red fruit, a third of the size of an orange but with twice its vitamin C content, was popular. Confusingly, the bright-blue fruits of *Elaeocarpus angustifolia* are also called quandongs. These were used in pies, jams and jellies as the raw fruit tastes rather tart. Pigweed, *Portulaca olearacea*, was eaten by early settlers to ward off scurvy, but research has since shown that it has only small traces of vitamin C. With its thick, green watery leaves it was cooked and used as a vegetable, or eaten raw.

The novelist Anthony Trollope, who visited Australia in the nineteenth century, expressed the colonists' attitude when he wrote that:

> The country ... produced almost nothing ready to the hand of the first comers ... There were no animals giving meat, no trees giving fruit, no yams, no breadfruit trees, no cocoa-nuts, no bananas. It was necessary that all should be imported and acclimatised.

In addition, Europeans found that Australian native plants were generally unpalatable. Many of them are, in fact, poisonous, not only to man, but to sheep and cattle. Unfortunately, the whites were ignorant of Aboriginal ways of rendering toxins in certain plants inactive by heating and cooking, by soaking (sometimes for weeks at a time), or by pounding or grating the plant.

Their ignorance led to European repugnance of native food. The distinguished nineteenth century botanist, Sir Joseph Hooker, later director of Kew, expressed British culinary reserve when he wrote that Australian edible plants were 'eatable but not worth eating'. Until recently, most food on sale in Australian supermarkets, apart from odd examples such as the macadamia nut (*Macadamia integrifolia*, *M. tetraphylla*), came from foreign seeds, although there are other nuts used by the Aboriginal peoples, such as species of *Athertonia* which could also have become a cash food crop. There is now an increased interest in native foods. In the last decade gourmets, restaurants, TV producers and journalists from glossy magazines have gone off in four-wheel drives searching for bush tucker — bunya nuts, quandongs, Kakau plums, wattle seed, Illawarra plums and sharp-tasting leaves. Australia does have palatable alternatives to common European fruits, which are, at last, proving their commercial potential.

Trials in Africa by Australian aid agencies have shown that the seeds of *Acacia holosericea* — a common dryland plant in Queensland possessing distinctive bright-yellow flower spikes — can provide a nutritious and popular food, much higher in protein and fats than wheat and rice. The protein content is 17 to 25 per cent. The seeds can be roasted, boiled like lentils, or steamed. Although this was one of the foods collected by Joseph Banks and Daniel Solander near Endeavour River, it has taken 200 years for the Aboriginal use to be copied.

Out of the hundreds of species of *Eucalyptus*, the Aboriginal people used the ones with the most leaf oil as an inhalant cure for colds, sinus problems and rheumatism, just as it is used all over the world today in vapour rubs, antiseptics, inhalants and embrocations. Only three species of eucalypt — *E. globulus*, *E. sideroxylon* and *E. citriodora* — have oil in sufficient quantities to make extraction commercially viable in countries with high labour costs. Many other Australian plants, though, yield valuable oils. *Melaleuca alternifolia* — the source of tea-tree oil — is already a million-dollar industry, rapidly getting bigger, as is the trade in boronia oils.

As the importance of both the use and preservation of our natural resources is becoming recognised world-wide, perhaps at last the Australian flora will be examined and appreciated for the contribution it can make to providing timber, foodstuffs, medicines and other substances in a sustainable global economy.

6
The Dutch — Australia Seen but Forsaken

The oldest surviving botanical link between Australia and Europe is probably a faded dry plant fragment, now nearly 300 years old. This little trophy, an object of curiosity, is to be found in a collection in Switzerland — the Herbarium of the Conservatoire et Jardin Botanique, Geneva. After it was collected it was lost to the world for almost a century, misidentified and ignored, its significance unknown.

Distinguished as the first of thousands of Australian plants to be examined and named in Europe, this specimen is from a small woody shrub with yellow flower spikes, *Synaphea spinulosa*, a member of the Proteaceae. It also appears to be the sole known extant specimen from over a hundred years of Dutch exploration of the coasts of Australia.

Botanists this century have combed Dutch archives and have come up with nothing apart from this *Synaphea* and references to a specimen of *Acacia truncata*, which seems to have been collected at the same time and, apparently, went to the Geneva herbarium, although its whereabouts today are unknown. This lack of floral evidence from Australia comes as a considerable surprise for a nation famed and admired for its rich horticultural history. To add insult to injury, both specimens were misidentified for years as Javanese ferns.

Conjecture surrounds whether these neglected specimens, or the collection of Englishman William Dampier, also made in Western Australia, should be regarded as the first Australian plants to have been preserved. If collected by de Vlamingh in 1696 they pre-date Dampier's 1699 specimens by three years, but Dampier's specimens were in flower and taken immediately to Europe, whereas the Geneva specimens languished for decades in Java. However, assuming the *Synaphea* was collected by de Vlamingh, it certainly wins the race as the oldest extant specimen, and it, and the missing acacia, were the first to receive modern binomials — even if it was mistakenly as ferns.

The story of these specimens shows the casual attitude of early Dutch expeditions to the continent. They may have discovered Australia, but they did little about the country itself. The magnitude of their disregard — their indifference, their lack of enthusiasm — is revealed when the number of their voyages covering a period of nearly a century and a quarter is examined. During that time Dutch trading ships passed close to the shores of Australia many, many times a year. But the continent was simply not commercially important to the Dutch East India Company, the all-powerful and immensely wealthy Vereenigde Oost-Indische Compagnie (VOC), without whose support further exploration was simply not possible.

The story of the lost flowers almost certainly began with a Dutch captain, Willem de Vlamingh, commanding the *Geelvinck*. The identity of the sailor or officer who dried and pressed these botanical specimens is unknown; perhaps it was de Vlamingh himself. No record has been found of their provenance, but all evidence points to them being collected during this voyage as it was the only ship that sailed to the Fremantle region at that time, which is the only place where the *Synaphea* grows naturally. We do know that Nicholaas Witsen (1641 – 1717), the renowned Dutch botanist, burgomaster of Amsterdam and one of the VOC's directors, asked de Vlamingh to collect plants and other curiosities for his private collection. Were the *Synaphea* and the

Synaphea spinulosa, misidentified in Nicolas Burmann's *Flora Indica* as *Polypodium spinulosum*, a fern from Java. The original specimen from which this drawing was made is now in the herbarium of the Geneva Botanic Garden. (Linnean Society collections.)

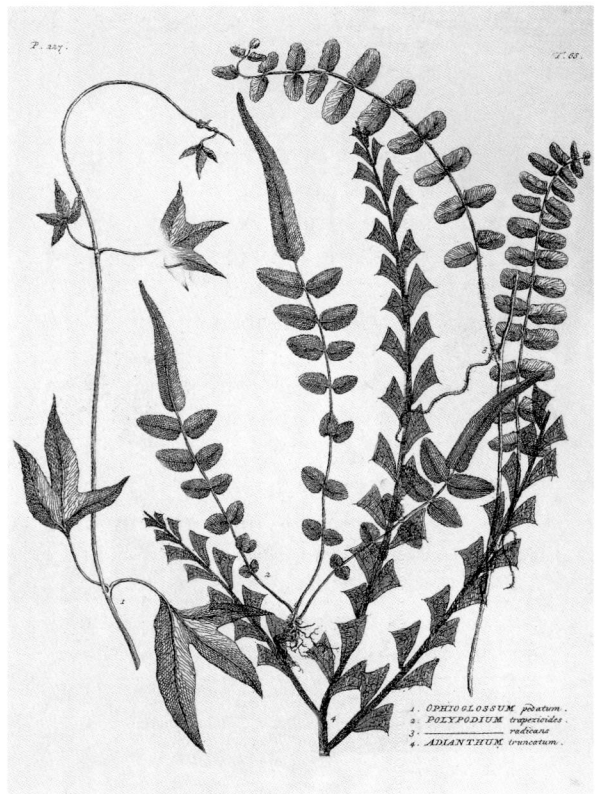

Another misidentified New Holland plant from Burmann's *Flora Indica*. *Adianthum truncatum* was later correctly identified by Jonas Dryander as *Acacia truncata*. (Linnean Society collections.)

acacia intended for him? If so, why did they end up in Java? Another mystery is why the *Synaphea* was picked and not the more sensational banksia, also a member of the Proteaceae, which is abundant in the area. It seems incredible that someone walked through this wonderland of beautiful flowers and came back to his ship bearing just these two unspectacular specimens. Perhaps they were part of a much larger collection that has since been lost.

The *Geelvinck* returned to Batavia where the specimens were filed away. Nearly seventy years later, in 1768, they made their debut in an impressive book, *Flora Indica* by Nicholas Burmann, Dutch physician and botanist. The *Synaphea* is illustrated at Tab. 67 with an entry on page 233 saying that it is *Polypodium spinulosum*, a Javanese fern. Two pages later *Acacia truncata* appears, also identified as a fern, *Adianthum truncatum*, apparently sent from Kleinhof's botanical garden in Batavia and described 'ex Java D. Kleinhof. Habitat in India'.

Acacia truncata is one of Australia's endemic species of wattle. Wattles are so numerous and so spectacular when in flower that one species, *A. pycnantha*, has become Australia's national floral emblem. How *A. truncata* could be confused with a fern is a puzzle, especially as acacias are found in Asia and Africa and should have been a familiar genus to Burmann. Perhaps it was because, unlike most acacias in the world, many Australian wattles do not have distinctive prickly spines or thorns. Or perhaps because it was not in flower, and the leaves of this Australian species were different from those of acacias from other parts of the world.

The wattle and the *Synaphea* were finally correctly identified by two botanists in London at the beginning of the nineteenth century. Jonas Dryander, working in Joseph Banks' extensive herbarium, realised that the *Acacia truncata* was falsely identified after seeing another specimen of acacia from Australia. A decade later Robert Brown, also working in Banks' herbarium while he was preparing his famous 1810 paper on his new family, the Proteaceae, recognised in Burmann's illustration of the other Javanese fern yet another mistaken classification. He included it in this new family, called the new genus *Synaphea*, and described four species, having collected three others during his own three-year sojourn in Australia between 1802 and 1805. Despite this flurry of interest, *Synaphea* remained until recently one of the last Australian genera to be fully investigated. In his book on the Proteaceae, John Wrigley states:

> The genus *Synaphea* is probably the most poorly known of all Proteaceae genera. The Western Australian Herbarium recognises nine species, and at least six other undescribed species exist. The whole genus is confined to south-west WA.

The genus has now been revised and the new *Flora of Australia* recognises fifty species.

The disregard the Dutch seemed to have for the Australian flora is, perhaps, unexpected. The Dutch have been botanists and florists since time immemorial. Their passion for flowers can be seen in the astonishingly lifelike, still-life oil paintings of bouquets in vases that they produced in the late sixteenth century. Previously in European painting, flowers had appeared only as symbols, decoration, foreground filler, or as crude botanical illustrations, not as the actual subject.

The Dutch led the way with commercial flower growing and selling in Europe. Always astute in seizing opportunities for new enterprises, they could claim to have invented the business of floriculture. It is an irony that in the seventeenth century, when Australia bore the name New Holland, they ignored the now celebrated foliage and blooms in the florally rich western coast of Australia, as in modern times they have led the way in Europe in hothouse growing of Australian flowers such as kangaroo paws and banksias. Admittedly, the Dutch explorers were Company men and sailors, not botanists, and some visited New Holland when most species were not in flower. The coastal vegetation which they would have seen is floristically poor compared to farther inland. Yet, even so, the uniqueness and interest of the plants was not lost on that other famous explorer of the Western Australian coast, William Dampier. Perhaps in times past, the subtlety of silvery and dark shades, the dull greens of many of the leaves and the different shapes and colours of the Australian blooms, were overshadowed by the Dutch passion for gaudy, brightly coloured tulips.

Tulips had found their way to Europe in the diplomatic bag of Ghiselin de Busbecq, the Viennese ambassador to the Turkish Court of Suleiman the Magnificent. Mid-seventeenth century Holland was swept by tulipomania. Homes, estates and industries were mortgaged as bulbs were purchased and promptly resold for higher and higher prices: sales and resales were sometimes effected without the bulbs ever being dug from the ground. One Viceroy tulip bulb was exchanged for: '2 loads of wheat; 4 loads of rye; 4 fat oxen; 8 fat pigs; 12 fat sheep; 2 hogshead of wine; 4 barrels of 8-florin beer; 2 barrels of butter; 1 000 lbs. [450 kg] of cheese; a complete bed; a suit of clothes and a silver beaker'. The boom crashed in 1637 with results as spectacular as the Wall Street Crash almost three hundred years later.

There was to be no such interest in Australia's plants. The Dutch, or more specifically, the VOC, found nothing of value in Australia and had no interest in its natural history. Their contribution to knowledge about Australia was minimal compared to that of the lands it found commercially important such as South Africa and Java.

The absence of a firm date on which to chart ascension of white interest in Australia, prior to colonisation, has resulted in giving importance to the Dutch arrivals. Apart from Abel Tasman's voyages, when he charted the coasts but never significantly explored the mainland, voyages were frequent but inconsequential. When trade with the Spice Islands drew the ships of every maritime nation in the world into southern waters, an area as vast as Australia, it might be imagined, would be mapped and colonised.

The Dutch arrived on the East Indies scene in 1595, overwhelmed the Portuguese, and began trading first in Java, then in Sumatra. The Dutch East India Company was founded in 1602 and established trading posts and settlements with its headquarters at Batavia (Djakarta), the centre of a Dutch colonial empire in the east. The nearest of these islands of the East Indies, Timor, is only about 500 kilometres to the north-west of Australia, so it would not be surprising if adverse winds, treacherous currents — and occasional curiosity — took ships there.

In 1606, the first Dutch ship sailed into the waters between New Guinea and the north-west tip of Australia. Captain Willem Jansz sailed from Java on the 61-tonne pinnace *Duyfken*, 'little dove', destined for New Guinea. They reached the coast then ran a south-easterly course, eventually sighting land again, which they still thought to be New Guinea. In fact, it was the Cape York Peninsula. They continued southwards, surveying the coast. At each attempted landing they came across Aboriginal people who bravely defended their territory. Eventually Jansz anchored north of Duyfken Point, near the red cliffs of Weipa, on the Cape York Peninsula. Driven by lack of water and provisions, and having found no spices or precious metals, he turned north at Cape Keerweer ('turn about'). His is the first record of Europeans retreating from Australia because they did not find nourishment — or anything of commercial value. Ironically, Jansz had come to one of the world's greatest deposits of bauxite.

At Port Musgrave, the mouth of the Wenlock River, Jansz anchored again, sending some sailors ashore in a rowing boat. About eighteen kilometres upstream they clashed with a party of Aboriginal men who, with spears and boomerangs, killed nine Dutchmen. Jansz reported that the new land was 'for the greater part uncultivated, and certain parts inhabited by savage, cruel black barbarians'. He never returned.

By the mid-seventeenth century, ships sailing from the Dutch port of Cape Town in South Africa to the East Indies skimmed along on a highway of waves. Low in the southern hemisphere, between the South Pole and latitude 43 degrees, a steady draught of air from the west blows ceaselessly round the globe, never sinking below a stiff breeze, rising often to a gale. Nearly 1600 kilometres broad, designated as a quick route from Africa to Asia ever since it was discovered, this impressive highway of sea constantly rolls round the earth from west to east, and has brought ships towards Australia, their canvas sails full before the wind.

Once in this fast-moving water, ships sailed east for about 8000 kilometres, then turned sharp north for the East Indies. A miscalculation of longitude meant they could sail over 9000 kilometres and hit the west coast of Australia. Although none of these ships brought back souvenirs of plants, a few ships' captains did give descriptions of them. Finding no gold, no water and no provisions, they left quickly, except for those that were wrecked in the *Batavia* in 1629, the *Vergulden Draeck* in 1656, the *Zuytdorp* in 1712, and the *Zeewijk* in 1727.

In 1623, Jan Carstensz, when sailing with the *Pera* and the *Arnhem* round Cape York Peninsula, landed several times and encountered hostile natives. On 8 May he went ashore to be met by 200 Aborigines. After the Dutch fired, killing one and scattering the rest, Carstensz offered his sailors a reward of ten pieces-of-eight for every man captured.

'We did not see one fruit-bearing tree, or anything that man could make use of', wrote Carstensz, adding that the country lacked water. The land, he noted, was 'flat and fine countryside with few trees, good soil for planting and sowing, but as far as we could see and observe with no fresh water at all'. He reported despondently that this was 'the most arid and barren country that could be found in the whole world'. Also, 'the pitch-black, thin of body and entirely naked' inhabitants had no knowledge of precious metals or even nutmegs, cloves and pepper. The land contained 'no metals, nor any precious woods such as sandalwood, aloe or columba'.

The incomplete outline of Australia was slowly filled in but voyage after voyage had no impact; and no real connection with Europe was made. The maps themselves, though, were invaluable for later explorers such as Dampier, Cook, Flinders, d'Entrecasteaux, Baudin and Dufresne, who often could not have navigated so successfully along various Australian coasts without this initial groundwork.

The Dutch traders, owners of the early ships, received reports that the shores of New Holland were monotonous and inhospitable, but these north-western and western coasts that were visited are the least watered coasts of the least watered continent on earth, where nothing flaunts itself. The more visually appealing east coast was not discovered until much later by James Cook.

If the Dutch did see the west coast's now famous wildflowers, they overlooked them. The sandy scrub produces colourful flowering shrubs, such as the superb orange-coloured *Nuytsia floribunda*, the Christmas tree; the little *Calythrix flavescens* covered with yellow flowers; the mauve flowers of the Swan River daisy, *Brachyscome ibiridifolia*. In spring, visitors from all over the world now come to feast their eyes on the rainbow of colours carpeting the south-western corner of Australia.

The discouraging reports led to a lull in Dutch exploration — apart from the ships that arrived by mistake — until Anthony van Diemen became governor general of the East Indies. He received many requests from the directors of the VOC to make further surveys. In 1636 he dispatched Commander Pool but the results were disappointing. Three years later he sent Abel Janszoon Tasman to search for riches beyond Japan — fabled islands of silver and gold. Not surprisingly, the islands were not found, but the voyage increased Dutch knowledge of the Pacific and a satisfied van Diemen sent Tasman out again in 1642 to establish a southern route into the Pacific.

Taking a wide sweep of the known coasts, Tasman, with the vessels *Heemskerck* and *Zeehaan*, sailed around part of the coast of

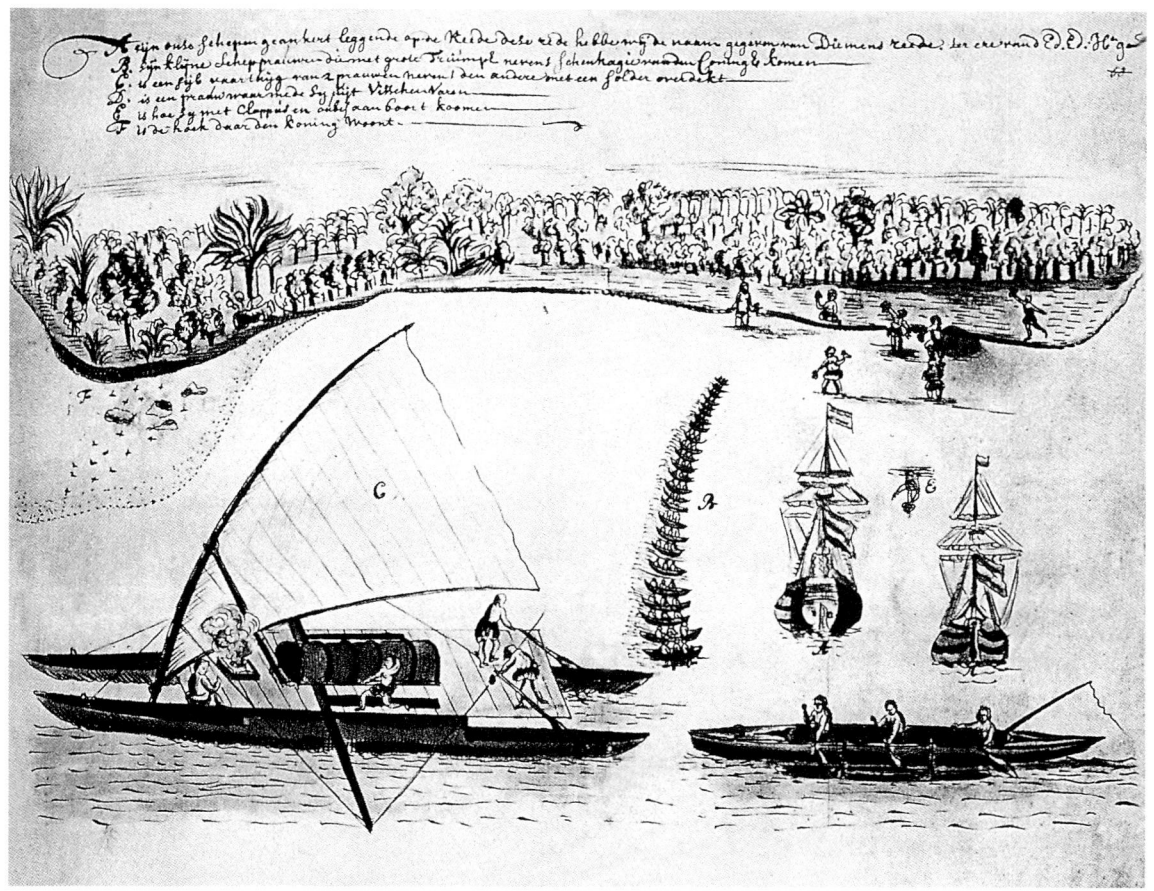

The account of Tasman's voyage was illustrated with crude engravings. Note the stylised representation of the vegetation in this drawing comparing Dutch ships with native canoes in Tonga. (Linnean Society collections.)

present-day Tasmania, which he named Van Diemen's Land in honour of his sponsor. Here the only landing on Australian soil was made, at Blackman's Bay on the south-eastern coast. Tasman was not in the landing parties but his men saw 'in the interior, a large number of trees ... which had been burnt deep inside, above the roots, while the earth had become as hard as flint because of the continual effect of the fire'.

Tasman also reported that the men found:

> Two trees about two to two and a half fathoms [3 – 4 metres] in thickness, about sixty-five feet [20 m] high under the boughs, with notches carved into the trunk ... in which trees gashed with flints and the bark was peeled off (thereby to climb up and gather the birdsnests) in the shape of steps Each being measured fully five feet [1.5 metres] from one another so that they presumed, here to be Very tall people or that these Same by some means must know how to climb up said trees.

As they were instructed to 'find out what commodities (as of fresh water supplies, timber and otherwise) might be available there', the sailors returned bringing:

> ... various samples of greens which they had seen growing aplenty some not unlike certain greenstuff which grows at Cape of Good Hope and suitable to use as pot-herbs, another being long and salty which has not a bad likeness to sea-parsley.

The 'long and salty' plant collected by Tasman's men was probably samphire, *Sarcocornia quinqueflora*, a small saltmarsh herb similar to European samphire. Some excrement, presumed to be from quadrupeds, was also brought back on board, as well as a small quantity of fine gum that had dripped from the trees and resembled gum-lac.

The seas were rough and unwelcoming the next day, so Tasman, abandoned another attempt at taking a boat ashore, ordering the ship's carpenter to swim to the beach with a pole marked with the company's name and a 'prince flag' to claim the land for Holland.

Tasman sailed on to discover New Zealand, Tonga and Fiji, before returning to Batavia. His employers were far from pleased; he had not explored inland nor reported anything useful on the people or its products, he had only drawn maps. Yet he had done them well so they gave Tasman a second chance in 1644 with three ships, the *Limmen*, *Zeemeeuw* and *Bracq*. Sailing closer to the coast this time, when he returned he reported barren country, adding that the people were 'very numerous and threw stones at the boats sent to the shore. They appear to live very poorly; go naked; eat yams and other roots.'

Globes and maps from Tasman's voyages were made within a few years of his return, but nothing else was published until 1671 — nearly thirty years after the first visit. Featuring in Arnoldus Montanus' *De Nieuwe en Onbekende Weereld*. The account also appeared incompletely in an appendix entitled 'The Unknown South-Land' in John Ogilby's *America* published in 1671:

> On the twenty fifth of November [1642], he [Tasman] discover'd a barren Shore, against which the Sea beat very furiously; and Steering along this Coast, he found a convenient Inlet but was forc'd by the hard Weather to stand to Sea again; yet not long after approaching the Shore, he saw great hollow Trees, and round about them abundance of Mussle-shells, and from the Wood heard a shrill noise of People Singing ...

The Royal Society in London printed seven pages of Tasman's journal in 1682, which contained the first description of the vegetation. Another version appeared in 1694 and Sir Joseph Banks had a full translation made and published in the third volume of James Burney's work on Pacific exploration in 1803.

The last significant Dutch voyage to Australia, and the one most likely to have produced the *Synaphea* and acacia specimens now in Geneva, was undertaken by Willem Hesselsz de Vlamingh, who sailed from the Netherlands in 1696 with three ships to search for a shipwreck near the mouth of the Swan River.

De Vlamingh arrived in December at an island off the west coast which he first named Fog Island and described as 'delightful above all others that I have ever seen'. He later renamed the island Rottnest (rat's nest) after the profusion of small rat-like marsupials (quokkas) that live there. De Vlamingh 'found there the finest wood in the world, from which the whole land was filled with

Members of the family *Myrtaceae*, such as this *Angophora floribunda*, along with acacias, dominate Australia's forest areas. *Angophoras*, of which there are seven species in Australia, are closely related to eucalypts, and this example was originally classified along with other eucalypts in the genus *Metrosideros*. (Linnean Society collections.)

It was marsupials the size of these banded hare wallabies, here painted by Charles Alexandre Lesueur, artist on Nicolas Baudin's voyage, that thrived in the newly burned areas created by Aboriginal firestick farming. (Badger G. *Explorers of the Pacific*. Kangaroo Press, 1996.)

Sea parsley, *Apium prostratum*, was used by sailors as an antiscorbutic. It appears in the writings of the Dutch explorers of the seventeenth century. This illustration is from Ventenat's Jardin de la Malmaison. (Linnean Society collections.)

In the 1980s Editions Alecto, in cooperation with the Natural History Museum, published a stunning colour edition of *Banks's Florilegium* plates of which this *Dillenia alata* is an example. The colour was applied directly to the surface of the engraved plates using a specially designed soft pad. The work was painstaking but the results were far more spectacular than Banks could ever have imagined. His vision was that the engravings should appear in black and white. (Badger G. *Explorers of the Pacific*. Kangaroo Press, 1996.)

THE DUTCH – AUSTRALIA SEEN BUT FORSAKEN

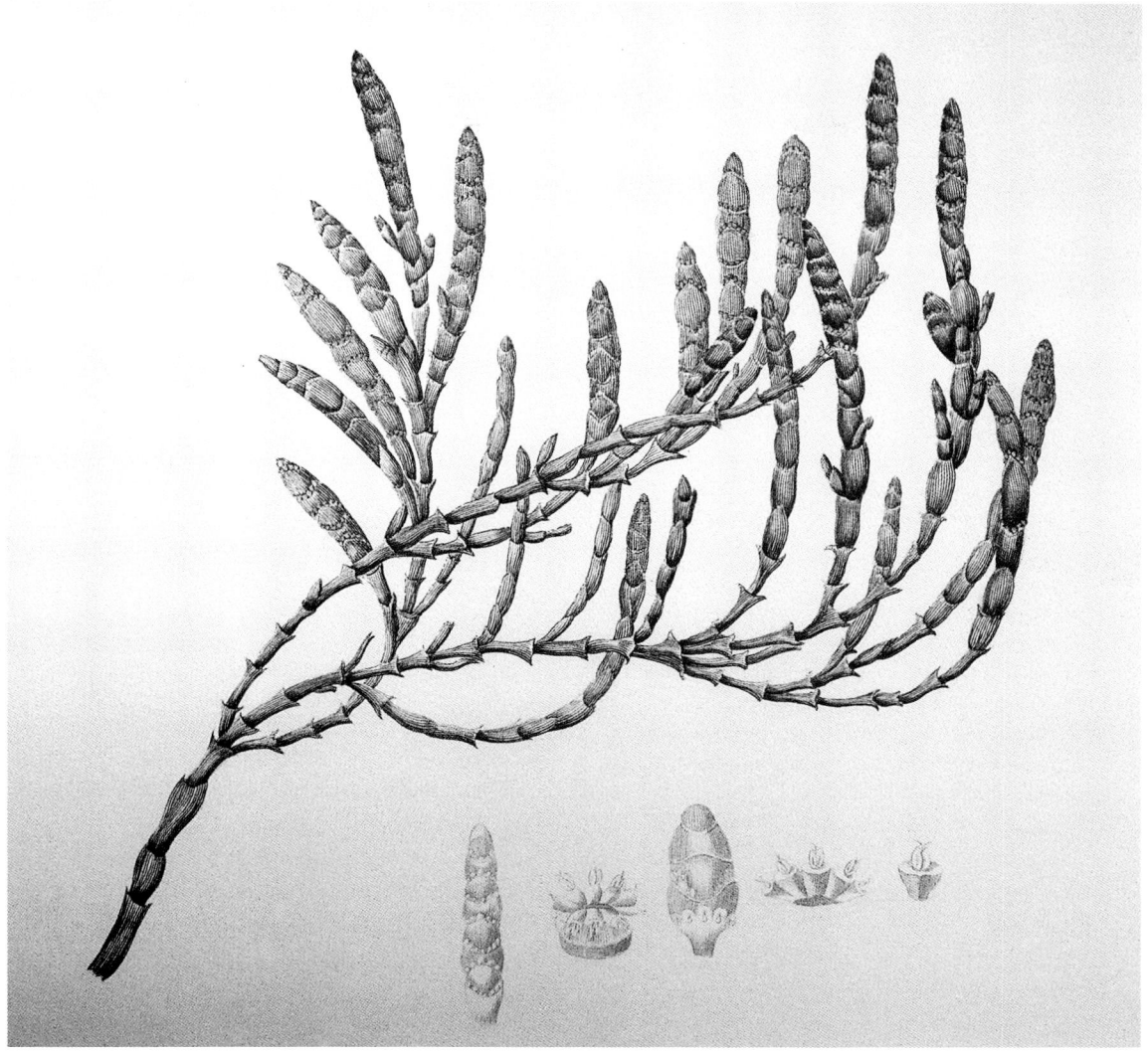

One of the Australian plants used by the Dutch for edible greens was probably *Sarcocornia quinqueflora*, a sort of samphire. This example is from a specimen collected by Banks on the *Endeavour* voyage. (*Banks' Florilegium*.)

a fine pleasant smell'. He cut a sample of the wood and pressed it for its oil. On the mainland his crew also found some trees that they described as very 'gummy'; thus the eucalypt made its debut. On de Vlamingh's return, Nicholaas Witsen, wrote up some of his descriptions in *Noord en Oost Tartarye*, published in Amsterdam in 1705:

> A pleasant smell as of roses was noticed in this island, which emanated from the trees, as can be observed from a few branches or pieces of wood brought to me from there. A fragrant oil can be extracted from this wood ... On the mainland coast they found unknown red trees, mainly in the south, which produce a great deal of reddish-brown coloured gum which drips from the heart of the tree and falls down in drops like little balls, a sample of which having been brought here, being the bark of a tree to which this resin or gum is still attached, is in my keeping.

De Vlamingh then went to the mainland and rowed about thirty kilometres up the Swan River. If the acacia and *Synaphea* specimens originated from this voyage, it was probably on this excursion that he, or some member of the crew, did the collecting. Certainly de Vlamingh's crew picked up seeds of the beautiful cycad *Macrozamia riedlei*, which is prized by Aboriginal people as an important food source (but only after they have been vigorously washed, soaked and leached for several days). This elaborate preparation is necessary to remove the highly toxic compounds which cause poisoning in both humans and animals. Witsen described them in his book as looking like:

> ... our local scarlet beans, the colour being between yellow and white: these beans contain a nut which is not unlike the chestnut and is not unappetising, but causes a vertigo in the head which resembles madness, for the mariners who tasted of them crawled on the ground and made senseless gestures, which lasted for two days.

De Vlamingh himself also fell violently ill:

> They brought me the nut of a certain fruit tree ... having the taste of our large Dutch beans; and those which were younger were like a hazelnut. I ate five or six of them ... but, after an interval of about three hours, I and five others who had eaten these fruits began to vomit so violently that we were as dead men.

De Vlamingh returned to Holland with:

- 1 phial of oil, extracted from wood brought from the South Land
- 1 small box with shells from the South Land
- 1 bundle of wood from the South Land, which is marked as fragrant and from which the aforesaid oil has been extracted
- 1 pewter plate found on a post in the South Land
- 1 old damaged piece of hide, stitched together in several torn places, also brought from the South Land ...

But Witsen was unimpressed by the results of the voyage and disappointed in the commander. He wrote to Gilbert Cuper in 1698 that there had 'not been very much done because the commander, too much addicted to drink ... nowhere stayed longer than three days'. In another letter he added:

> Nothing has been discovered which can be any way serviceable to the company. The soil of this country has been found very barren, and as a desert; no freshwater rivers have been found ... There were found many fine smelling trees and out of their wood is to be drawne oyl smelling as a rose, but for the rest they are small and miserable trees.

In a final damnation he wrote to the Governor General of the Indies 'it has proved to be nothing but a barren, dry wasteland'.

Thus ended the first brief appearance of Australia's flora in Europe. The next major collection, by the Englishman William Dampier, was to fare little better.

7
William Dampier — The Botanical Buccaneer

William Dampier picked the vibrant *Swainsona formosa* — Sturt's desert pea — in the Western Australian bush, and took it back to England. This spectacular plant, with scarlet petals and a glossy black centre, flowers throughout the dry interior of the continent as well as the mountains, plains and sandhills and the semi-arid coast of Western Australia. When the deserts bloom after the rare rains, the dry earth bursts into carpets of these red and black flowers. They are now the floral emblem of South Australia.

Dampier was an unlikely candidate for the first collector of Australia's flora. Born in East Coker, Somerset, England in 1652 he lost both his parents before finishing grammar school at Crewkerne, and went to sea while still a teenager. He worked his way up to being commander of his own ship via a colourful career that included buccaneering, managing a Jamaican plantation and writing two best-selling books about his travels.

It was Dampier's vivid accounts of his two voyages to New Holland that made Australia a reality for the British. He was, for instance, the first person to apply the term 'gum-tree'. In the bush of Western Australia Dampier collected flowers and plants which he found beautiful, unusual or fragrant, and 'for the most part unlike any I had seen elsewhere'. Around twenty of the plants, brought back to England after a hazardous journey, introduced the Australian flora to Britain. Although dried nearly 300 years ago, some of these specimens survive and are remarkably well preserved, pressed in paper in a black leather folder tied with cotton ribbon, in the herbarium of the School of Plant Sciences at the University of Oxford.

This little collection is the beginning of the scientific collection of Australian flora, yet its importance continues to be underestimated. Dampier, too, is often overlooked as the person who officially brought the British flag to Australia, seventy-one years before Cook. Dampier was the only Englishmen to visit Australia twice before settlement — the second time in command of his own ship.

The year Dampier first visited Australia, in a hijacked ship captained by Englishman John Read, saw a series of events connecting Dutch, British and Australian history. It was 1688, the year of the Glorious Revolution in Britain, marked by the accession to the British throne of the married first cousins, William of Orange and Mary, the daughter of James II. William forsook the position of Stadtholder of the United Provinces in Holland in order to become King of England, Scotland and Ireland. By coincidence, when he left Holland, the Dutch also lost their monopoly on Australian exploration.

The same year that William crossed the English Channel, the *Cygnet*, a British ship sailing figuratively, if not actually, under the Jolly Roger — the skull and crossbones — arrived on the coast of arid north-western Australia. The *Cygnet* had originally been on a trading mission commanded by Captain Swan. Swan drove his crew to breaking point by dallying for six months on the island of Mindanao in the Philippines. His crew which included Dampier, frustrated by waiting for their debauched and idle captain, eventually took matters into their own hands, 'we left Captain Swan and about 36 men ashore in the city, and six or eight that had run away; and about 16 we had buried there', wrote Dampier as they took control. One of the mutineers, John Read, assumed command.

This portrait of William Dampier, by Thomas Murray, was painted the year before Dampier's departure on his second voyage to Australia. It depicts him more as the sophisticated man of letters than the buccaneer explorer. (National Portrait Gallery, London.)

The brotherhood were soon back at their old trade — 'our business was to pillage'. In February 1687, eight leagues outside Manila, they took a Spanish barque. Two days later they took another Spanish vessel laden with rice and cotton-cloth. Having put their prisoners ashore they sailed with their prizes to islands off the coast of Cambodia to 'wait for the Acapulco ship that comes about that time'. In the event, however, fearing bad weather and that they might encounter Dutch or British ships, they changed their plans and decided to head south 'intending to touch at New Holland, a part of Terra Australis Incognita, to see what that Country would afford us'.

Read, at the helm of the *Cygnet* crewed by pirates, sighted Australian land on 4 January 1688 (old calendar). One hundred years later almost to the day, Captain Arthur Phillip, with the First

WILLIAM DAMPIER— THE BOTANICAL BUCCANEER

Fleet of convicts, got his first glimpse of what would become Australia when he sighted Tasmania, just a few days' sailing from their goal, Botany Bay. Although the bicentenary of European settlement in Australia was celebrated in 1988, the fact that it was also the tercentenary of British discovery by Read was largely overlooked. So was the coincidence that the earliest British ship of discovery and the first British settlement ships both carried felons — the former at liberty, the latter convicted.

There was also an earlier British voyage to Australian waters that deserves mention here. In 1622 the *Tryal*, sailing eastwards across the Indian Ocean, overshot the point at which to turn north to the East Indies and hit the reefs near Barrow Island off the west coast of Australia. Survivors filled casks with rainwater during their seven-day stay on one of the Monte Bello islands, before sailing to Batavia. Master John Brooke wrote a report, but as he did not mention the vegetation or go near the mainland, it is discounted here as the earliest British ship of discovery.

John Read and William Dampier have always been overshadowed by James Cook and the discovery of the east coast of Australia. As the British Empire developed, so did a new epoch of imperial image-making. Into this context Cook, as explorer/hero/scientist, readily fitted. Cook's journals and journeys became books of adventure for children, inspiration to boost the new spirit of the British Empire. Cook became a hero of British imperialism. A pirate such as Dampier did not fit this image. Yet, if Dampier had been to the continent twice, how could Cook have discovered Australia? The only time the British government resurrected Dampier's journeys, in the nineteenth century, was to counter French claims to the western half of the continent based on François Alesne de St Allouarn's brief exploration of the west Australian coast in March 1772.

But Read and Dampier preceded this by more than eighty years. In early January 1688 the *Cygnet* finally reached a 'pretty deep Bay ... good hard sand, and clean ground', and was careened in what is now King Sound, near Broome. Dampier gave an excellent description:

> The Land is of a dry, sandy Soil, destitute of Water, except you make Well; yet producing divers sorts of Trees; but the Woods are not thick, nor the Trees very big. Most of the Trees that we saw are Dragon-trees as we supposed; and these too are the largest Trees of any there. They are about the bigness of our large Apple-trees, and about the same height: and the Rind is blackish, and somewhat rough. The Leaves are of a dark colour; the Gum distils out of the knots or cracks that are in the Bodies of the Trees. We compared it [the resin] with some Gum Dragon, or Dragons Blood that was aboard; and it was the same colour and taste. The other sorts of Trees were not known by any of us. There was pretty long Grass growing under the Trees; but was very thin. We saw no Trees that bore Fruit or Berries ...

This is the first undoubted description of a eucalypt, probably the bloodwood kino, whose gum, a potent Aboriginal medicine, was used to stop blood flowing from spear wounds and to treat abrasions, sores and burns.

Dampier made the first English description of Australia's native people. Like so many after him, his lack of understanding caused him to draw an unflattering picture:

> The Inhabitants of this Country are the miserablest People in the World. The Hodmadods of Monomatapa [in the western half of South Africa], though a nasty People, yet for Wealth are Gentlemen to these; who have no Houses, and skin Garments, Sheep, Poultry, and Fruits of the Earth, Ostrich Eggs, &c as the Hodmadods have: and setting aside their human Shape, they differ but little from brutes. They are tall, straightbodied and thin, with small long Limbs ... They have no Houses, but lie in the open Air without any covering; the Earth being their Bed, and the Heaven their Canopy ...

Mistakenly, Dampier added:

> For the Earth affords them no Food at all. There is neither Herb, Root, Pulse nor any sort of Grain, for them to eat, that we saw: nor any sort of Bird or Beast that they can catch, having no Instruments wherewithal to do so.

He had, however, come to the barren north-west coast, to a lonely, unknown inlet, near present-day Broome, Cygnet Bay in the Pilbara. 'The land

THE FLOWER CHAIN

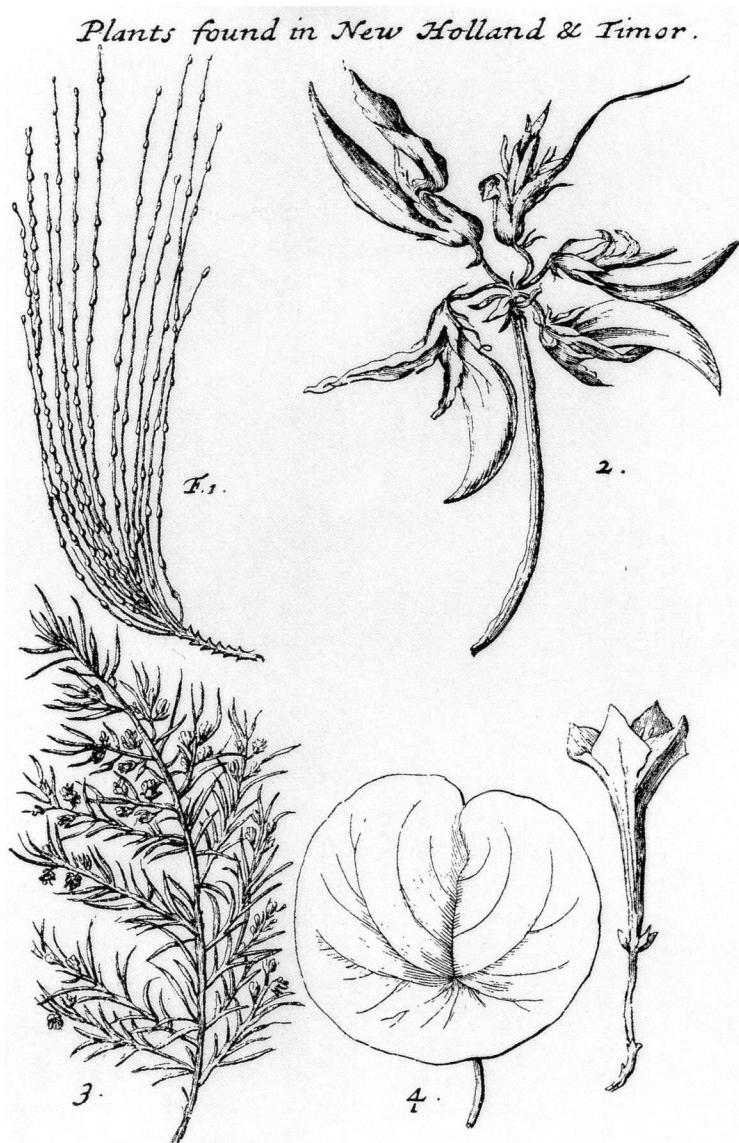

Figure 2 of this engraving from Dampier's *A Voyage to New Holland*, shows Sturt's desert pea, *Swainsona formosa*, one of the first plants to be collected by Dampier in Western Australia. The dried specimen from which this drawing was made, along with Dampier's other extant Australian plants, is now in the herbarium of the Department of Plant Sciences at the University of Oxford.
(Linnean Society collections.)

is dry, rocky and barren,' he reported, 'there is no water unless you make wells for it, and inland, as far as man can see, is just stony, empty desert.'

After nine weeks, on 12 March 1688, the *Cygnet* departed from the west Australian coast for the island of Nicobar where Dampier abandoned the 'mad crew' and deserted ship. He returned to England after a circuitous journey around the world, which took yet another two years. All the time, the precious manuscript about his travels remained rolled up in a piece of bamboo, stopped at both ends with wax, to keep out water and insects.

This manuscript was to form the basis of his famous book, *A New Voyage Round the World*. Because Dampier wrote up this adventurous journey of the *Cygnet*, it is often forgotten that it was actually John Read who commanded the voyage — the first by the British to mainland Australia — albeit as a pirate. As Dampier would later captain his own ship, the *Roebuck*, to New Holland he is sometimes erroneously credited with being commander of both voyages. Dampier dedicated his account of the *Cygnet* voyage to Charles Montague, Earl of Halifax, the hot-tempered and malicious politician and sometime President of the Royal Society, who had just helped found the Bank of England.

The book was first published in London in 1697, went through three editions in just over a year and was in its sixth edition after Dampier died in 1715. It has been in print ever since not only because it contains the first description of Australia by an Englishman, but because it is a fabulous pirate story of survival on the Spanish Main and the Pacific islands. Vivid descriptions tell of people, animals, sea-creatures, battles for gold, exotic potentates and trivia — even how mango chutney was made — and such human touches as the grief of the crew when the captain gave the ship's dog to the ruler of Guam.

Also in Guam, Dampier made the first description of the breadfruit tree and how the fleshy pulp of its large fruits forms a staple in the diet of the natives of tropical regions. This handsome, quickly maturing tree, with a dense foliage of large, lobed leaves, grows in humid tropical lowlands with a high rainfall. So much was said in its favour that the myth of the breadfruit was born; people thought that in the Pacific free loaves of bread grew on trees, just waiting to be picked off the branches and baked. Dampier wrote:

> The breadfruit (as we call it) grows on a large Tree, as big and high as our largest Apple-Trees. It hath a spreading Head full of Branches, and dark Leaves. The Fruit grows on the Boughs like Apples: it is as big as a Penny-loaf, when Wheat is at five Shillings the Bushel. It is of a round shape, and hath a thick tough Rind. When the Fruit is ripe, it is yellow and soft; and the taste is sweet and pleasant. The Natives of this Island use it for Bread: they gather it when full grown, while it is green and hard; then they bake it in an Oven, which scorcheth the rind and makes it black: but they scrape off the outside black Crust, and there remains a tender thin Crust, and the inside is soft, tender and white, like the Crumb of a Penny Loaf. There is neither Seed nor Stone in the inside, but all is of a pure substance like Bread: it must be eaten new, for if it is kept above 24 Hours, it becomes dry, and eats harsh and choaky; but 'tis very pleasant before it is too stale. This Fruit lasts in season eight Months in the Year; during which time the Natives eat no other sort of Food of Bread-kind. I did never see of this Fruit any where but here. The Natives told us, that there is plenty of this Fruit growing on the rest of the Ladrone [Mariana] Islands ...

Read's voyage would have been unrecorded had it not been for Dampier's book. With its vivid descriptions of the breadfruit and the continent of Australia *A New Voyage Round the World* also provided the background for two of the most significant British voyages into the Pacific of the next century; Bligh's breadfruit voyage and the establishment of a convict colony in Australia.

Through Montague, Dampier was introduced to the First Lord of the Admiralty. Being an ex-buccaneer — albeit a famous one — was apparently no drawback to advancement. Dampier was elevated to Royal Navy captain and in 1699 was given his own ship, the *Roebuck* and a crew of fifty, ready to sail to the South Seas. He seldom used the Spanish misnomer 'Pacific' which he thought too flattering an image for the many hazards and currents of that tempestuous ocean.

But Dampier soon encountered problems. The ship was in poor condition and her crew was mutinous; neither was fit to battle the high and perilous waves of the Cape Horn route, so he sailed around the southern tip of Africa. At the end of July 1699, six months after leaving England, Dampier arrived on the west coast of New Holland. Here they went ashore on an island to look for water but found none. Undaunted, Dampier turned his attention to the flora:

> There grow here two or three Sorts of Shrubs, one just like Rosemary; and therefore I called this Rosemary Island. It grew in great Plenty here, but had no Smell. Some of the other Shrubs had blue and yellow Flowers; and we found two Sorts of Grain like Beans: the one grew on Bushes, the other on a Sort of creeping Vine that runs along the Ground, having very thick broad Leaves, and the Blossom like a Bean Blossom, but much larger, and of a deep red Colour, looking very beautiful ... The stones were all of a rusty colour, and ponderous.

Dampier unwittingly described the dark red, heavy iron ore in the rocks. If only a geologist had scrutinised his journals perhaps the greatest mineral riches of Australia would have been discovered sooner, for Dampier's rocks indicated

THE FLOWER CHAIN

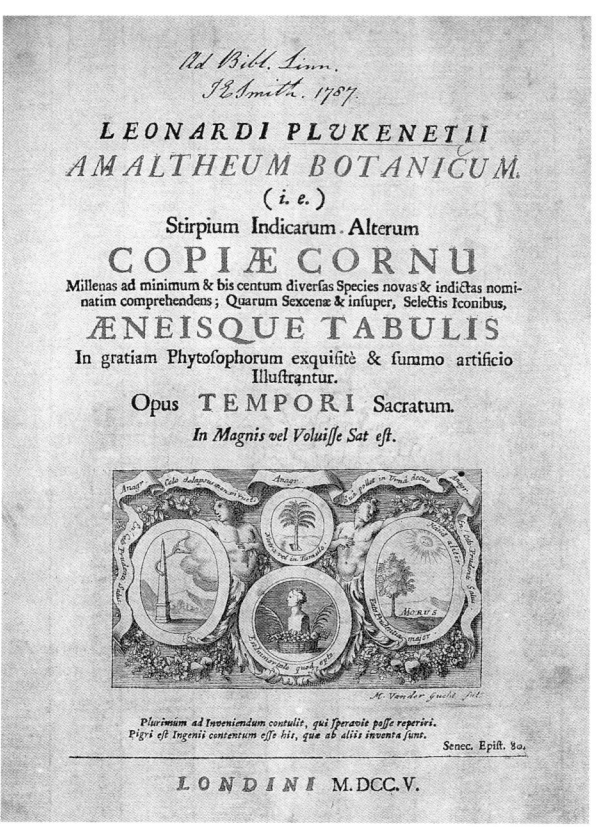

Leonardi Plukenet described some of Dampier's New Holland plants in his *Amaltheum Botanicum* of 1705. Eleven of Dampier's Australian plants also appeared in an appendix in John Ray's *Historia Plantarum*.
(Linnean Society collections.)

Further examples of plants collected by Dampier in Western Australia and illustrated in his book.
(G. Badger, *Explorers of the Pacific*, Kangaroo Press, 1996.)

the presence of one of the world's richest iron deposits.

Dampier collected plants on Rosemary Island (now one of the Lewis Islands) and on Dirk Hartog Island and the mainland around Shark Bay. Although not trained in botany, Dampier had an eye for the distinctive or curious. He saw 'some very small flowers growing on the ground, that were sweet and beautiful and for the most part unlike any I had seen'. He also noted that, 'the Blossoms of the different Sort of Trees were of several Colours, as red, white, yellow, &c. but mostly blue'. Almost as if to contradict the general opinion that the foliage of the continent was dull, he collected spectacular plants such as the Sturt's desert pea, *Swainsona formosa*, now universally admired for its splendour.

Among the other plants he gathered are the well-known *Casuarina equisetifolia*; one of the species of wattle, *Acacia rostellifera*; and the rounded shrub *Myoporum acuminatum*, which has clusters of small white flowers that fruit into berries.

After about a month and 'having ranged about a considerable time upon this Coast, without finding any good fresh Water ... and it being, moreover, the Heighth [sic] of the dry Season and my men growing Scorbutic for want of Refreshments', Dampier left. It was the old story: his men could not find enough palatable greens or fruits growing wild. Setting course for Timor, he jogged on from island to island, taking on fresh food and water, restoring his men to health. Planning to investigate the eastern coast of New Holland, Dampier rounded the northern coast of New Guinea and ran eastward, reaching as far as the island he named New Britain. Leaks in the boat worsened; the boat's planking was deteriorating badly. It was time to head home, via the easier African route.

They made the Cape safely, but the onward voyage was a nightmare. The *Roebuck* could hardly be kept afloat; even with all hands on the pumps with 'some drams to comfort them', the ship still took in water. Dampier had holes in the timbers plugged with salt beef, deeming this to be all but impenetrable! Eventually, in February, 1701, fifteen months after they had left the west Australian coast, the crew abandoned ship close to Ascension Island in the South Atlantic. They made a raft 'to carry the men's chests and bedding ashore', and managed also to land water and bags of rice, but Dampier lost many books, papers and all the strange sea shells he had collected.

Miraculously, he managed to salvage both journal and botanical specimens, safeguarding them throughout a perilous five weeks ashore where he and his men slept in caves, living on goats, birds and turtle and drinking water high on a mountainside. This site is still called Dampier's Drip. At last, two British ships saw Dampier's beacon fires and he and his crew were rescued.

Dampier returned to England with the clothes he wore, his journal and his collection of dried plants — and to a court-martial for extreme cruelty to one of his officers, Lieutenant Fisher. Dampier reported unfavourably on the west coast of New Holland saying that it was 'unsuitable for colonisation', but he did urge that the English send an expedition to the east coast, which should prove more fertile. Seventy years later Cook — armed with Dampier's books — was able to confirm this prediction.

Dampier's second book, *A Voyage to New Holland*, also delighted the public, although this naval voyage did not cause the same sensation as his first as a pirate. The two voyages, eleven years apart, meant that Dampier spent a total of three months on the west Australian coast. He knew it well and his books, frequently reprinted, separately and in collections, were 'in every gentleman's library'. They were much-quoted in subsequent works on the Pacific and its natural history.

The theme of these books, and of other contemporary voyages, is parodied in Jonathan Swift's *Gulliver's Travels* which appeared in 1726. Gulliver himself is a traveller in the same mould as Dampier, an adventurer who responds to the Royal Society's requests to voyagers to collect and record data on the flora and fauna of far-off lands. Gulliver soberly sends up pedants, cranks and parvenus while relating the projects of the Academy, that is, the Royal Society, for 'extracting sunbeams out of cucumbers', 'softening marble for pillows and pin-cushions', 'reforming language by abolishing words'. Swift based some ventures on actual scientific proceedings at the Royal Society.

The parody of Dampier is carried through, even to the name of Gulliver's ship and dates. Gulliver sails on the *Antelope* in 1699; he is shipwrecked off Van Diemen's Land; the map showing the position of Lilliput corresponds to the south-west coast of Australia and is copied from Dampier.

In 1755, ten years after Swift died, John Hawkesworth, a literary and religious friend of Dr Johnson, edited Swift's works and in his introduction wrote about both Dampier and Swift. By an irony worthy of the pages of Swift himself, Hawkesworth was soon to write about the land visited by Dampier — Swift's Land of Lilliput — again. When Cook returned to London in 1771 after the *Endeavour* voyage, the Admiralty handed Hawkesworth Cook's journal, together with the journals of Joseph Banks — and, rumour has it, a thousand pounds. He was to write an account of the voyage from the combined journals. On four occasions in the South Pacific narrative, Hawkesworth compares Cook's and Banks' observations of the flora with those of Dampier — so the strands of the Flower Chain were linked, although gossamer thin.

But what of Dampier's precious collection of plants? In his preface to his second book, *A Voyage to New Holland* he states that the 'Plants themselves are in the hands of the Ingenious Dr Woodward'. Woodward showed eleven of these strange specimens of casuarina, wattle, grass and gum-tree leaves to his friend, the botanist John Ray, who was then finishing his famous three-volume *Historia Plantarum*. Ray included these Australian plants in an appendix. Woodward showed a further six specimens to Leonardi Plukenet, who described and illustrated them in his *Amaltheum Botanicum*, so they have been on record for every scholar of botany in the world ever since. In 1710 Woodward passed Dampier's collection, along with the rest of his own herbarium, to William Sherard, founder of the Sherardian Chair of Botany at the University of Oxford. Here they remain today in the Department of Plant Sciences, minus two of the specimens listed by Ray and three by Plukenet. In all, twenty-three specimens that were collected by Dampier in New Holland survive today.

Strangely, when George Bentham came to compile his massive *Flora Australiensis*, in the late nineteenth century, he did not include Dampier's plants. Whether this was a reflection of the general downgrading of Dampier's importance in the known history of Australia, or whether the collection was not made available to Bentham, is debatable.

Dampier died in 1715. His resting place seems not to have been recorded, but perhaps he lies in some London churchyard; all we know is that he died when he was sixty-five. His name, however, is commemorated in a string of placenames in Western Australia, including the port of Dampier from where the iron ore from Dampier's stones of 'a rusty colour, and ponderous', mined in the nearby Hamersley Range, is transported round the world.

Also, there is Dampier Land, Dampier Island and the genus of flowers, *Dampiera*, which has sixty-six species. These herbaceous plants are usually blue but can also be purple, pink, white or, in the case of one species, yellow, with spectacular flowers. *Dampiera* belongs to the Goodeniaceae family, which is almost exclusively Australian; a fitting tribute, to the man who first brought Australia's unique flora to the attention of the outside world.

8
Joseph Banks and the *Endeavour*

Sixty years after Dampier collected plants on the west Australian coast, a man who was to have a pivotal role in the history of Australia and its flora, Joseph Banks, went to Oxford to study botany. Just a few years later, Banks would accompany James Cook on his first voyage round the world — his only voyage to mainland Australia — on board the *Endeavour*.

In 1760 all that was still to come. Banks would remain in Oxford, on and off, for the next three years. Did he examine Dampier's Australian plants in the Botany School Herbarium during that time? And if he did, might they have aroused his curiosity about New Holland? He certainly made no surviving mention of them, although he referred to Dampier's observations in his *Endeavour* journal. It's hard to believe Banks did not know about these plants because there were records of them in places of great botanical importance. Eleven were in the Appendix of John Ray's *Historia Plantarum*, essential reading for any botanist; six more were described and illustrated in Plukenet's *Amaltheum Botanicum*. Banks' Professor of Botany was Humphrey Sibthorp whose son, the brilliant and famous John (1758 – 96), later annotated Dampier's herbarium sheets.

Banks was the only son of a wealthy Lincolnshire landowner. His great-grandfather, the first Joseph Banks, was an attorney in Lincolnshire and member of parliament. At one point the first Joseph Banks had wisely bought 1200 hectares of marsh in the fens. The family got richer as these were drained and became profitable as agricultural land. Advantageous marriages brought more money into the family and by the time Joseph Banks IV was born, in London in February 1743, the Bankses were becoming ensconced in the upper echelons of society.

Rich they might have been, but they were only on the edge of the gentry until Banks' maternal aunt, Eleanora Margaret, a famous beauty, married the Honourable Henry Grenville was one of the 'cousinhood' of the political trio of Grenvilles, Temples and Pitts, joined in opposition against Sir Robert Walpole. The only child of this union, Louisa Grenville, Banks' first cousin, married the third Earl of Stanhope. Banks' great-aunt on his mother's side, Hannah-Sophia Chambers, married the eighth Earl of Exeter, a member of the famous Cecil family.

Although no aristocrat himself, Banks and his only sister, Sarah Sophia, had a place in society through two splendid aunts. Banks found he could get away with being slightly eccentric, self-indulgent and follow his own interests. This he did — with a vengeance.

Banks was the first of his family to gain entry to Harrow, Eton or Oxford. He went to all three, after being educated privately at home — Revesby Abbey in Lincolnshire. But the young Banks was no scholar. As the favoured only son he had the run of the estate and his love of natural history probably had its roots in his country upbringing, where he was allowed to play unsupervised in the countryside with boys from the village. At age nine he was sent to Harrow where, according to his friend Henry Brougham, 'Joe cared mighty little for his book'. Harrow ill suited the unscholarly boy and in September 1756 he was removed to Eton.

The change of scene did little to improve his studies in Latin and Greek — his tutor bemoaned that Joe was a boy with 'an immediate love of play'. It was with some pleasure, therefore that

THE FLOWER CHAIN

Revesby Abbey, Banks' childhood home and country seat in Lincolnshire. Unfortunately this house was demolished in the mid-nineteenth century. (Linnean Society collections.)

he found Banks one day, at the age of fourteen, reading rather than sporting in his hours of leisure. He was not, we may judge, reading the classics. Banks gave his own account of this incident to his friend, the surgeon Sir Everard Home. He had apparently been river-bathing with his friends one summer evening, but had lingered too long and they had gone back without him. As he dawdled back to school by himself along a flowery lane, Home reports that:

> He stopped and looking round, involuntarily exclaimed, 'How beautiful!' After some reflection, he said to himself, it is surely more natural that I should be taught to know all these productions of Nature, in preference to Greek or Latin; but the latter is my father's command and it is my duty to obey him; I will however make myself acquainted with all these different plants for my own pleasure and gratification. He began immediately to teach himself Botany.

Young Shanks Banks, as he was known on account of his height, enlisted the assistance of the local women who gathered herbs for the apothecaries. He paid sixpence for every valuable piece of botanical information he got from them. Home for the holidays, he found in his mother's dressing-room an old and battered copy of Gerard's *Herball*, with its woodcuts of the very plants he knew. He carried it back to school in triumph, 'and it was probably this very book that he was poring over when detected by his tutor, for the first time, in the act of reading,' concluded Home.

In 1760, aged seventeen, he was entered at Christ Church, Oxford, as a gentleman-commoner where his record as a poor scholar in Greek and the classics continued. But his love of natural history in general, and botany in particular, persisted. He found that Humphrey Sibthorp, the Sherardian Professor of Botany, did

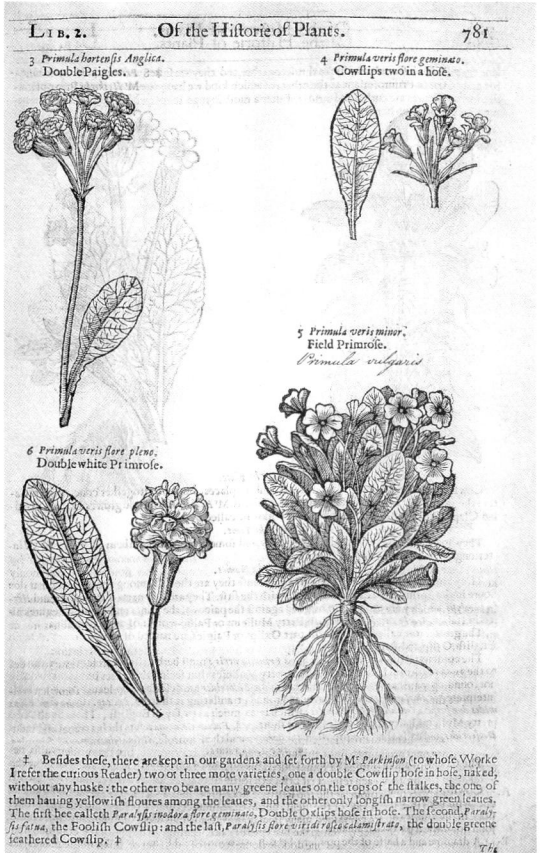

Banks found his mother's copy of Gerard's *Herball* an invaluable source of information on the plants about which he was so keen to learn.
(Linnean Society collections.)

JOSEPH BANKS AND THE *ENDEAVOUR*

Britten of the British Museum (Natural History), writing at the turn of the twentieth century, commented that Banks 'had much more botanical knowledge than was at one time supposed. This seems to have been recognised by his contemporaries.' We can assume, therefore, that he was certainly competent and throughout his life must have acquired a broad knowledge.

While her son was at Oxford, Banks' mother bought a London house in Paradise Row (now Royal Hospital Road) near the Chelsea Physic Garden. A neighbour, Lord Sandwich, although twenty-five years his senior, became Banks' firm friend. Then First Lord of the Admiralty, Sandwich was frequently attacked for corruption, and in private life criticised as a profligate gambler and rake, but his friendship with Banks was to prove very advantageous to the ambitious young botanist.

It was around this time, the early 1760s, that Banks met Daniel Carl Solander (1733 – 82), who for eighteen years, until he died at forty-nine (probably of a stroke), was his closest friend. Always called the favourite pupil of the illustrious Linnaeus, Solander had come to London in 1760, initially at the request of such luminaries of botany as Peter Collinson, to teach English botanists the Linnaean system of plant classification. He catalogued the plants in Collinson's garden and herbarium and helped John Ellis with work on zoophytes — tiny aquatic animals that live in plant-like colonies. Solander never returned to his native Sweden, taking a post as assistant librarian at the newly established British Museum. He was much liked and esteemed everywhere he went, and four years after he arrived in London was elected a fellow of the Royal Society.

Banks became Solander's patron and employer as well as friend and their closeness is demonstrated by sentiments in a letter he wrote after Solander's death in 1782:

> Through his death I have suffered a loss which will be impossible for me to fill even if I should find another person as learned and as noble ... it is not possible for my heart to replace the impression which twenty years ago it took as easily as wax and which now will not be effaced until the heart itself dies.

not do any actual teaching. So, with Sibthorp's permission, he hired the services of Israel Lyons, a botanist from Cambridge, to give a series of lectures. Banks finally left Oxford without taking his degree, a common enough occurrence at the time. In addition, his responsibilities suddenly changed in his second year with the unexpected death of his father. Although this meant that at twenty-one he would inherit the family fortune, he now had to spend much of his remaining time at Oxford under the supervision of his uncle Banks-Hodgkinson, learning how to manage his estates.

Much has been made of Banks' lack of academic qualifications and supposed lack of botanical knowledge. However, at a time when qualifications could be bought or acquired with little effort, it is difficult to judge what his real abilities were. Certainly contemporaries were rarely critical of his botanical skills and James

THE FLOWER CHAIN

Although from a modest, middle class background in Piteå, Sweden, Solander's charm, and the fact that he was Linnaeus' pupil, gave him entry to grand and aristocratic circles. The work of Linnaeus, and in particular the principle of his system of nomenclature — that all plants should bear just a two-word Latin name — allowed a greater understanding of the subject. Both scientists and private individuals could think of no higher honour than to send an unknown plant to be named and classified by Linnaeus in Sweden. Enthusiasts ventured forth to locate and list all the living things rooted to the earth, and to find places where they could be transplanted and multiplied to bring revenue to the Europe.

Between the mid-eighteenth and the early nineteenth centuries science became intensely fashionable. In 1746 Peter Collinson said that works on natural history 'sell the best of any books in England'. George III's mother, Princess Augusta, was busy creating her Botanic Garden at Kew, aided by Lord Bute; the Duchess of Portland was accumulating a vast collection of shells; and Capability Brown was transforming the gardens of the landed gentry to reflect the forms of nature. But it was botany that was in vogue among the aristocracy, becoming a tasteful pursuit of the leisured and cultured.

Although not yet a member of the aristocracy, Banks certainly followed this trend, even to the point of eschewing the usual grand tour of Europe undertaken by young men of his class. He preferred to embark on a collecting tour to Newfoundland on HMS *Niger*. He organised this through an old friend from Eton, Constantine John Phipps, the future Lord Mulgrave, and it was on this expedition, primarily a fishery protection patrol, that Banks learnt how to cope with the rigours of shipboard life and the problems of transporting plant specimens by sea.

When Banks returned from Canada, he bought a house in New Burlington Street — later to be exchanged for the grander 32 Soho Square — and began to set up a library and herbarium. In his absence on the *Niger* he had been elected to fellowship of the Royal Society. Unlike today, fellowship did not require excellence in a given

On his father's death, Banks' mother moved to a small house in Paradise Row overlooking Chelsea Physic Garden. These gardens, and their superintendent Phillip Miller, were to provide further sources of knowledge for Banks, the young student of botany. (Linnean Society collections.)

scientific discipline. Fellows were elected as much for their social standing as their scientific knowledge. Banks offered the attractive combination of youth, wealth and an obvious enthusiasm for the natural sciences. He would never shake the world with his scientific studies nor even produce a large corpus of scientific publications, but, in the words of his contemporary, Humphry Davy:

> ... he was a good-humoured and liberal man, free and various in conversational power, a tolerable botanist, and generally acquainted with natural history. He had not much reading, and no profound information. He was always ready to promote the objects of men of science.

But Banks had his bad points too. Davy went on to accuse him in later life of requiring 'to be regarded as a patron' and that he 'readily swallowed gross flattery ... and made his house a circle too like a court'.

On his return from Newfoundland, Banks began to establish himself in the London scientific world and his home certainly did become a centre for scientists and the exchange of ideas. His convivial breakfast and dinner gatherings were famed as meeting places for such eminent naturalists of the day as Thomas Pennant, John Ellis, John Lightfoot and the nurseryman James Lee. Lee had translated Linnaeus' book on classification from Latin into English, published the influential *Introduction to Botany* and, with his co-proprietor Lewis Kennedy, would later play a major role in growing and selling of Australian plants at their vast nursery, 'The Vineyard' in west London.

Banks seemed set to enjoy the leisurely life of a rich man, dabbling in science and later politics. But a voyage being planned by the Admiralty and the Royal Society was to change all that. European scientists were preparing for a rare astronomical event — the Transit of Venus — in June 1769. Scientific observers were being sent by the Empress of Russia to Siberia and by Louis XV of France and Charles III of Spain to North and South America. In all, 151 observers stationed in seventy-one outposts were to watch Venus, the brightest of the planets, pass between the Earth and the sun. It was hoped that detailed observation of this event would help in the calculation of longitude — then almost impossible for navigators to determine with accuracy. Captain Wallis, recently returned from a voyage to the Pacific, recommended the newly discovered Society Islands — Tahiti — as an excellent site from which to make the observations. The Royal Society petitioned the King to send a ship, and George III, determined that Britain would not be overshadowed, gave his enthusiastic support to the scheme.

The Admiralty appointed Lieutenant James Cook to captain the expedition vessel. Cook was not unknown to the Royal Society. A talented mathematician, he had made observations about an eclipse of the sun which were read before the Society, causing amazement that a mere warrant officer could report with such scientific accuracy. Cook was the ideal choice. By chance, he had also been in Newfoundland at the same time as Banks, but there is no evidence that they ever met there.

As well as sending Charles Green, the astronomer, the Royal Society recommended that Joseph Banks, who would travel with a staff of eight, equipped and paid for by himself, should also sail with the expedition to make studies of the natural history. Banks' connections with Sandwich undoubtedly tipped the balance in his being allowed to accompany the voyage, albeit at his own expense. Banks later wrote:

> When we were dining at Lady Monson's table and talking about how I had an unmatched opportunity to enrich science and to become famous, Solander all at once excitedly rose from his chair and asked me with intent eyes: Would you like a fellow traveller? I answered: Someone like you would give me untold pleasures and rewards. Then that is it, he said, I'll travel with you.

Thus, Banks' suite included Solander, two artists and an amanuensis, two Negro servants, two servants from his Lincolnshire estate listed as footmen, and two dogs. Little did they realise only four of them would return — Banks and Solander and the two men from Revesby, James Roberts and Peter Briscoe. The two Negro servants, Dorlton and Richmond would freeze to death on Tierra del Fuego in January 1769; Alexander Buchan, figure and landscape artist

THE FLOWER CHAIN

would die in Tahiti in April 1769 and both Hermann Diedrich Spöring, amanuensis, and Sydney Parkinson, natural history artist, would die after contracting a fever, probably malaria or dysentery, in Batavia near the end of the voyage in January 1771.

But in August 1768, it was all excitement. Mr Banks was to bring back things from the earth and sea, Mr Green was to examine the heavens — 'no people ever went to sea better fitted out for the purpose of natural history, nor more elegantly' wrote John Ellis the naturalist. Indeed, the *Endeavour* was a floating observatory and laboratory — with maps of the heavens, telescopes, magnifying glasses, nets, barrels, an extensive library, and even machines for catching and preserving insects. In a letter to Linnaeus, John Ellis confided that 'Solander assured me this expedition would cost Mr Banks ten thousand pounds'.

Although early white visitors recognised that some Australian plants were related to known food plants in Europe, little presented itself as obvious sustenance. *Indigofera australis* is related to peas and beans but it was recorded here by Redouté, from a specimen growing in the garden of Empress Josephine at Malmaison, for its beauty rather than for any nutritional benefit. (Linnean Society collections.)

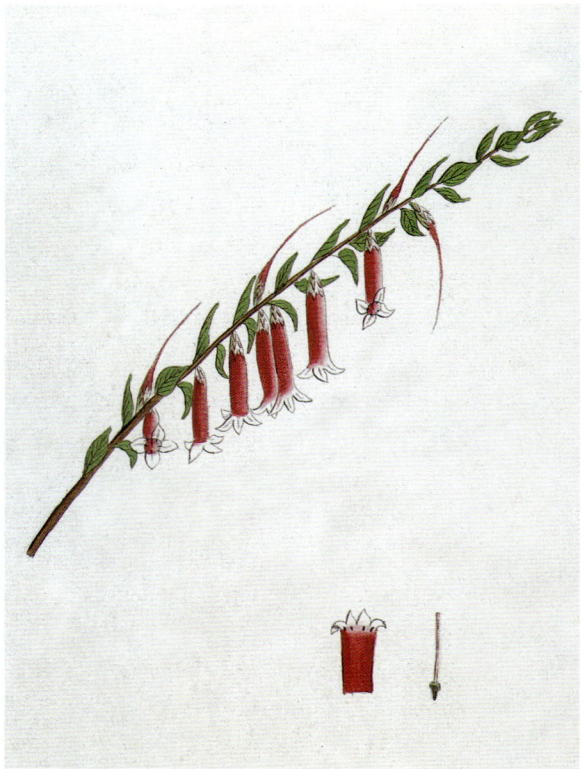

Original drawings of *Epacris grandiflora* (top) and *Melaleuca ericifolia* (bottom), done by Thomas Watling, convict artist in New South Wales, alongside the finished illustrations by F. P. Nodder that appeared in James Edward Smith's *Exotic Botany*. Smith refers in his description of *M. ericifolia* to 'coloured drawings made from the plants in their wild state,' and to this and several other species of *Melaleuca* being cultivated in Cambridge. Smith also hoped that as the 'beautiful' *Epacris grandiflora* had not at that point been grown in England, that this picture would 'excite cultivators to endeavour to obtain some of the seeds'. (Linnean Society collections.)

9

Botanists in Botany Bay

On 25 August 1768, James Cook hoisted a Jack at the fore topmast to signal Mr Banks and party to come aboard. The *Endeavour*, with her complement of scientists and their expensive paraphernalia, set off on her momentous journey from Plymouth at three o'clock in the afternoon. *Endeavour* was well equipped in other ways too; her one-handed cook had superior provisions to most ships. The Victualling Board and the Sick and Hurt Board were attempting to find cures for that curse of seafarers, scurvy. Consequently *Endeavour*'s stores included: portable soup (dried soup cubes), rob (extract) of oranges and lemons, raisins, mustard seeds, 3565 kilograms of sauerkraut and 1450 litres of malt to try as antiscorbutics, as well as the usual unappetising supplies of salted meat (known as 'salt horse'), and weevil-infested flour. To wash it all down there was 5450 litres of beer and 7730 litres of spirits.

Each sailor had only a tiny space in which to sling his hammock. They slept above the rough wooden benches and tables where they also ate, sang and drank. This converted collier, thirty metres in length and nine metres wide, had on board ninety-four people and eighteen months' provisions. It even had a small flock of sheep, some pigs and a nanny goat to provide milk for the 'gentlemen's coffee'. It was the same nanny goat which had travelled with Captain Wallis on the *Dolphin* when he discovered Tahiti in 1767. In all, three officers, including John Gore, one sailor and a goat joined the *Endeavour* from the *Dolphin* for another circumnavigation of the world, and yet another visit to Tahiti.

Cook had a good crew and a sturdy, serviceable ship but he had to face unusual challenges on this voyage. First, he had two very different sponsors to satisfy: the Royal Society and the British Admiralty. The Admiralty had several aims apart from the astronomical observations of the Transit of Venus. It decided to use the *Endeavour* voyage to respond to a revival of interest among scientific and commercial circles about the existence, or otherwise, of *Terra Australis Incognita*. There was no question that there was a landmass in the South Pacific — New Holland, the uninteresting place discovered by the Dutch and visited twice by Dampier — but was there another continent in the vast, as yet uncharted tracts of the Southern Ocean?

Secondly, the Admiralty was aware that France wanted to expand into the Pacific, to compensate for the huge colonial losses imposed upon her by the treaties that ended the Seven Years' War. They also knew that a French expedition, led by Louis Antoine de Bougainville (1729 – 1811), was already in the Pacific before Cook set out. Bougainville visited Tahiti with his two ships, the *Boudeuse* and the *Etoile*, soon after Wallis had left there. An intellectual, and a competent mathematician who had written a paper on integral calculus, Bougainville was a friend of Diderot and Rousseau and actually found the 'noble savage' on Tahiti. Bougainville returned with descriptions of an earthly paradise, flowers from the Pacific Eden, and a living noble savage — Ahu-Toru, a dignified Polynesian. Stories of free love plus the presence of Ahu-Toru, took Paris by storm. The myth of an island paradise started with Bougainville's book describing the voyage, which went into raptures about the islands' innocent sex and beautiful women.

After Tahiti, Bougainville had sailed west

The Flower Chain

Louis Antoine de Bougainville, seasoned explorer and patriot, was the first commander to employ an official naturalist and artists for his Pacific voyage of exploration. (G. Badger, *Explorers of the Pacific*, Kangaroo Press, 1996.)

towards Australia searching for *Terra Australis Incognita* and arrived in the Coral Sea, in waters not previously navigated by any European ship. He sighted a piece of land he thought was the continent somewhere east of today's Cooktown but did not investigate further. He was on the fringes of the Great Barrier Reef and alerted to its dangers by the endless wall of surf. Instead of trying to land he turned north to New Guinea. In the 1770s no kudos could be gained from visiting Australia, a place known by Europeans for nearly two centuries. If Bougainville had decided differently and landed there, he would have preceded Cook by nearly fourteen months as the first recorded European to reach Australia's east coast.

Bougainville's voyage is not just notable for his observations of Tahiti, it also set a precedent for ships of exploration to carry an official naturalist on board. It was not new for ships to carry collectors, naturalists and botanists, such as the eager pupils of Linnaeus, but up until now they had been mere passengers. Bougainville took a naturalist, Philibert Commerson, as part of the expedition. It is fitting, therefore, that Commerson named one of the most beautiful flowering vines in the southern hemisphere, *Bougainvillea*, after this far-sighted captain. Bougainville's voyage was the first that systematically collected, described and classified plants and animals, with shipboard artists drawing the specimens. Unfortunately, the published scientific results were few and Commerson never returned to France to write up his results, dying in the Isle-de-France (Mauritius) in 1783.

As Bougainville headed home, Cook rounded Cape Horn and entered the Pacific — and the annals of history. Already, in the five years since the end of the Seven Years' War, there had been the voyages of John Byron (grandfather of the poet and known as Foulweather Jack), Samuel Wallis and Philip Carteret (who discovered Pitcairn Island and, much to the advantage of its later inhabitants, misplaced it on his map). But Cook's voyage would be far more significant than these precursors.

The *Endeavour* reconstruction, completed in the 1990s, faithfully reproduces the onboard conditions for the crew of Cook's first voyage.

Left: The reconstructed *Endeavour* moored at Greenwich, England, in 1997 during her circumnavigation.

Below: This eating area below decks doubled as sleeping quarters. The crew would sling their hammocks above the tables at night.
(Photos: Julia Bruce.)

THE FLOWER CHAIN

During the seven months to Tahiti — stopping at Madeira, Tierra del Fuego and Rio de Janeiro — Banks and Solander collected avidly. Whenever the ship was becalmed, Banks lowered a small dinghy over the side and went to shoot sea-birds and net marine life. The botanists and artists would then litter the table in the Great Cabin with their trophies: seaweed, barnacles, decomposing fish and fresh and dried flowers. Banks recorded later that:

> Seldom was a storm strong enough to disrupt our usual study time, which lasted approximately from eight a.m. until two p.m. daily. After the cabin lost the odour of food, from 4 or 5 p.m. until dark, we sat at the great table with the draftsman directly across from us. We showed him how the drawing should be depicted and hurriedly made descriptions of all the natural history objects while still fresh ... we finished each description and added the synonyms to the books we had. These completed accounts were immediately entered by a secretary in the books in the form of flora of each of the lands visited.

The Great Cabin on the *Endeavour* was 4.3 metres by 7 metres at its widest, and was also the dining room for Cook and a dozen of the officers and supernumeraries, including Banks and Solander. Traditionally the Great Cabin — the captain's table — was the preserve of the ship's commander, but Cook seemed unfazed by having to share it with the botanists. There is no record of any resentment on his part at having Banks and his suite foisted on him. Tactful as Banks was, we shall never know how onerous it was for Cook, humble and hardworking, born the son of a labourer in a two-room cottage, to live day-by-day with this flamboyant, engaging but spoilt young man with his staff of eight. Cook was forty years old, Banks was twenty-five.

The South Pacific had barely been touched; there was much to collect, much to observe, much to collate and map. There remained a great triangle — formed by Cape Horn, Tahiti and New Zealand — which had never been explored and might contain *Terra Australis Incognita*. While searching, Banks and his team accumulated, drew, described and carefully preserved a treasure trove of natural history specimens.

Nearly eight months after leaving England, on 13 April 1769, the *Endeavour* arrived in Tahiti. Before any of the men went ashore Cook ordered them to line up before Surgeon Moorhouse for examination. All were reported free from venereal disease. The ship's company was enchanted by the magnificent beaches, soaring mountains and dancing young women wearing leis of tropical flowers.

John Gore reaped the benefit of the garden he had planted on his visit with Wallis, finding vegetables, limes, lemons, oranges, peaches, plums and cherries. The leaving of goats and gardens is an old gesture — a gift for the unknown traveller who later treads one's footsteps. On his last visit to Tahiti Cook ate cabbages planted by a Spanish ship — untouched by the Tahitians who considered them disgusting, possibly poisonous. Alexander Selkirk, the model for Robinson Crusoe, survived on Juan Fernandez Island thanks to wild goats left by sailors. In the early days of Australia pumpkin seeds were planted by stockmen outside their makeshift huts, usually near waterholes, for the next travellers coming through.

The sailors 'married their women' and allowed themselves to be tattooed. Banks had a bright design of scrolls and lines tattooed on his arm. On another occasion he was painted black from head to foot, for a funeral ceremony, much to the hilarity of the natives. A few years later at a London dinner party Banks related to Benjamin Franklin how the Tahitians neither rated chastity as a virtue, nor theft as a vice, and how they did not know about kissing with the lips, 'tho' they lik'd it when they were taught'. Banks' descriptions of Polynesian customs in his journal are graphic and colourful, and include accounts of his 'romance' with Queen Oberea, of music, marriage customs and the scenery. A new friend, the Tahitian Tupaia, and his servant, Tayeto, joined Banks' suite and sailed with them when they left, determined to see England. Perhaps Tupaia filled the berth made vacant by Alexander Buchan, the first of Banks' artists to die on the voyage. Sadly the two Tahitians were also to die, probably of malaria or dysentery, before they reached England.

Banks' other artist, Sydney Parkinson, employed at £80 per annum, worked diligently at

Sydney Parkinson, artist on the *Endeavour*. Parkinson was quiet, diligent and prolific. He produced thousands of sketches and finished paintings on the three-year voyage, but sadly died on the homeward leg. (G. Badger, *Explorers of the Pacific,* Kangaroo Press, 1996.)

recording the plants and animals the naturalists collected. The younger son of a well-connected Edinburgh brewer, Parkinson, a Quaker, had started his career apprenticed to a woollen draper. His talent as a botanical artist was recognised and he found commissions easily in London. He taught drawing to the thirteen-year-old daughter of James Lee at the Lee & Kennedy nursery, and Lee went on to introduce him to Banks on the latter's return from Newfoundland. Banks was immediately impressed by him and employed this quiet Scotsman to draw his Canadian specimens. Parkinson had hardly finished them, when he was whisked off to be the natural history artist on the *Endeavour*.

Apart from his technical skill and ability, Parkinson's output was prodigious — almost a thousand drawings and sketches. To save time when inundated by work, and to capture colours before they faded, he developed a routine of painting a single leaf, flower or seedhead, as soon as possible after it was collected. He then wrote detailed notes on the reverse side of the paper with colour guides so the work could be finished when there was more time, either at sea on the return voyage, or back home.

Much to Banks' annoyance, and without his permission, Parkinson's brother Stanfield posthumously published the journal Sydney had kept of the voyage. The journal shows Parkinson to have been a dedicated young man with a keen mind and an eye for detail. In Tahiti he related that the flies crawled over what he was painting, even eating colour off paper as fast as he brushed it on. Stanfield claimed that while the *Endeavour* crew were ashore indulging in sensual gratification in Tahiti, the serious-minded, twenty-four-year-old Sydney gratified 'No other passion than that of a laudable curiosity ... protected by his own innocence.'

After four months in Tahiti, his task in viewing the Transit of Venus completed, Cook weighed anchor. Unlike Parkinson, many of his crew were loath to leave the island that was soon to have the reputation of the most sensual and seductive place in the world. Cook plotted a southward course heading boldly for uncharted waters — and *Terra Australis Incognita*. His sealed orders from the Admiralty, not opened until he got underway, had instructed him to sail south to a stated latitude — 40 degrees — and then, if he had not encountered the Great South Land, to turn south-west for the unknown eastern shore of New Zealand. If he did find land he was to chart it and if it was uninhabited, take possession of it 'in the name of the King of Great Britain'. Cook and crew spent day after day, week after week, standing on windswept decks, climbing the masthead, staring at the horizon, straining for a glimpse of the land that, alas, existed only in myth. For over six weeks the *Endeavour* zigzagged through the Pacific. Finding nothing, Cook turned towards New Zealand, discovered nearly a century-and-a-half earlier by Tasman. It was postulated that this might just be an extremity of the Great Southern Continent, which Banks called 'our Land of Promise'.

Cook spent six months charting New Zealand's coastline while thousands of natural history specimens were collected by Banks and Solander. Twenty months had passed since the *Endeavour* had left England. The land of myth remained a myth. It was time for Cook to go home, time to 'return to England by such route as he should think proper'.

Australia, New Holland as it was then known, did not find a place, even as a postscript, in Cook's instructions; there was no suggestion that he should go there. However, it became a destination on the homeward route because the *Endeavour* was not strong enough to sail in high latitudes via Cape Horn. They would sail home by the Cape of Good Hope route, but 'fall in with the East Coast of New Holland & then to follow the direction ... it may take untill [sic] we arrive at its Northern extremity,' recorded Cook.

Three sides of Australia were now firmly established if imperfectly known; only the east coast was a blank. Cook headed westwards and on 19 April the east coast of Australia was sighted. For ten days Cook followed it northwards, unable to find a landfall among the cliffs, sandy beaches and the 'great surf which beat everywhere upon the shore'.

The sailors saw Aboriginal fires dotting the coast and occasionally the people themselves were glimpsed. Cook wondered if the blackness of the natives was skin colour or clothes. Banks concluded that the people ashore were totally naked, and the women did not 'copy our mother Eve even to the fig leaf'. At daybreak on 28 April, nine days after first sighting the continent, the *Endeavour* was opposite the entrance of what was to become Botany Bay.

Cook was in no rush to land. A man who liked rules and routine, he took lunch, already delayed from midday till two o'clock. At last, at three o'clock, about half the ship's company climbed into rowing boats and went ashore until sunset.

The next day, with great vigour, wells were sunk to collect fresh water; wood was chopped for the galley fire; grass was gathered for the ship's goat and sheep; fish, including many stingrays, were caught; the British flag was unfurled; Banks' pet greyhound, Lady, tried to catch an unidentified quadruped but lamed herself and abandoned the chase; 'Loryquets and Cocatoos' were shot for food. A few Aborigines made gestures of defiance until driven away by small shot: they avoided any close contact and were indifferent to presents offered by Cook and his men.

In the nine days that the *Endeavour* stayed at Botany Bay no contact with the Aboriginal people was made. They opposed the intruders a few times with spears, but vanished into the bush when efforts at close contact were attempted. Even beads and baubles left for them were ignored. Cook wrote: 'All they seem'd to want, was for us to be gone'.

Banks and his staff collected plants for classification, and edible greens for the galley. Cook, vigilant in compelling his men to eat fresh greens to ward off scurvy, subjected them to many bitter-tasting meals. He served up sea celery, *Apium prostratum*, which grows on many Australian coasts, just as Tasman had to his men 150 years earlier in Tasmania.

Banks added to his journal:

> 1st May. The captain, Dr Solander, myself, and some of the people making in all 10 musquets, resolvd to make an excursion into the countrey ... We ... walkd till we compleatly tird ourselves, which was in the evening ... The Soil, wherever we saw it, consisted of either swamps or light sandy soil on which grew very few species of trees, one, which was large, yeilding a gum much like *Sanguis draconis*, but every place was covered with vast quantities of grass.

Banks did not comment on the extraordinary predominance of two types of trees in the landscape, the wattle and the eucalypt. These trees are so typical of the Australian bush that is surprising that the first botanical description of the genus *Eucalyptus*, came not from this voyage, but from a later one to Tasmania. Banks refers to the trees not being very large and standing 'separate from each other without the least underwood' and comments on the large quantity of plants:

> 2nd May. The morn was rainy and we who had got already so many plants were well contented to find an excuse for staying on board to examine them a little at least. In the afternoon however it cleard up and we returnd to our old occupation of collecting, in which we had our usual good success ...
>
> 3rd May. Our collection of Plants was now grown so immensly large that it was necessary that some extrordinary care should be taken of them least they should spoil in the books. I therefore devoted this day to that business and carried all the drying paper, near 200 Quires of which the larger part was full, ashore and spreading them upon a sail in the sun kept them in this manner exposd the whole day, often turning them and sometimes turning the Quires in which were plants inside out. By this means they came on board at night in very good condition.

Also known as New Zealand spinach, locally collected *Tetragonia tetragonioides* was eaten by Cook's crew. Although vitamin C was unknown at this time, Cook was insistent that his men should eat fresh greens whenever possible and was keen to try any remedy for scurvy. (*Banks' Florilegium.*)

The Flower Chain

But there is no further description of what the plants were. If Cook had not named the place Botany Bay — changing it from his original Stingray's Harbour — there would have been no indication of its botanical delight. Banks does, however, make some reference to plants collected for food:

> They found also several trees which bore fruit of the Jambosa kind ... much in colour and shape resembling cherries; of these they eat plentifully and brought home also abundance, which we eat with much pleasure tho they had little to recommend them but a light acid.

These were, it seems, lilly-pillies (*Acmena smithii*). The fruit makes good jam or can be eaten when ripe. Although it was one of the few plants mentioned in the journal — despite the huge haul from Botany Bay — it was not described and named until twenty-seven years later.

Nothing in Banks' journal suggests that this bay would be suitable for colonisation. After a few days he reported that they had exhausted the botanical possibilities of the place. Cook had no interest in staying in Botany Bay either. He ordered the word 'Endeavour' and the date to be carved onto a tree — a gesture of farewell — and weighed anchor. He quickly headed north, sailing past what he called Port Jackson, noting that it 'might prove a safe anchorage'. It turned out to be the dazzling Sydney Harbour. Banks wrote the following gastronomic farewell to Botany Bay:

> Went to sea this morn with a fair breeze of wind. The land we saild past ... again woody and very pleasant. We dind to day upon the sting-ray and his tripe: the fish itself was not quite so good as a scate ... We had with it a dish of the leaves of *Tetragonia cornuta* boild, which eat as well as spinage or very near it.

Although known as New Zealand spinach, *Tetragonia cornuta* is not a true spinach. Looking like a weed, it grows on sheltered sea coasts. Banks and Cook first found the plant growing on the shores of New Zealand. Native to Australia, it is now known as *Tetragonia tetragonioides* and is experiencing a revival as Warrigal greens.

Day and night the *Endeavour* travelled northwards, inshore or some distance offshore, depending on weather and visibility. Many coastal features were overlooked. Cook's haste suggests that he thought of the east coast as an inhospitable coastline, something merely to survey, to record while homeward bound but not to visit. Australia never found a place in Cook's heart — or schedules. Incurious about it before he saw it, once he was there he left it as quickly as his ship and the weather would allow. He never returned. Nor did he suggest that any other ship should return, or that the country should be settled. Nor did Joseph Banks ever come back; nine years would elapse before he would suggest it as a suitable place for settlement — and then just for convicts.

10
Disaster and Home

On 16 May 1770 Cook was off Point Danger — the present southern boundary of Queensland — and began his 100 days on the Queensland coast. It was here, in the tropical north of the continent, that Banks would collect most of his specimens, but as their provenance is given as 'New South Wales' (the whole east coast was known as such until 1859), it is often assumed they came from Botany Bay.

Strong currents slowed progress as Cook surveyed the coast. When he made his first landfall a fortnight after leaving Botany Bay he stayed less than a day. Banks wrote:

> Here [Bustard Bay] we found a great variety of plants, several, however, the same as those we ourselves had seen in the islands between the tropics and others known to be natives of the East Indies ... In these [swamps] ... grew many mangrove trees ... Upon the sides of the hills were many of the trees yielding a gum like *Sanguis draconis*.

The presence of mangroves and pandanus palms, the first they had seen, affirmed that they were in the tropical zone. Banks assumed, incorrectly, that most of the botanical specimens seen from now on would be already known in Europe.

The *Endeavour* continued northwards through remarkably calm seas, with innumerable small islands on her starboard side as far as the eye could see. Once they had crossed the Tropic of Capricorn they were sailing parallel with the Great Barrier Reef, the longest wall of coral in the world. For hundreds of kilometres Cook groped his way through a sea strewn with islets, rocks, shoals and reefs; Keppel Bay, Cape Manifold, Cape Townsend, Pier Head, Thirsty Sound (because no water could be found), Broad Sound, Cape Palmerston, Cleveland Bay, Magnetical Isle (the compass would not function properly when near it) and the Palm Isles where a brief stop was made and more plants were gathered.

Then came Cape Tribulation, so named because, wrote Cook, 'here begun all our troubles'. It was now a month since they had left the quiet waters of Botany Bay, and the ship, progressing by the light of a full moon, struck coral. The crew saw the sheathing boards separate from the hull and float around them; water rushed in. The pumps were manned by every man on board, the captain, Banks and officers not excepted. To lighten the damaged ship Cook jettisoned about fifty tons of supplies and ballast, including six cannon (now in Cooktown, Canberra, Sydney, Greenwich, Philadelphia and Wellington). The calamity occurred because Cook had dared to do something most captains never do (even, as in this case, with the light of a full moon): sail through coral reefs at night.

With tremendous strength, luck and a piece of coral plugging the largest hole, *Endeavour* floated free on a high tide after twenty-three hours caught on the rocks. Cook fothered the hole, sealing it with a sailcloth covered with oakum, wool and sheep dung. *Endeavour* then limped thirty-odd kilometres north-west to a small harbour at the mouth of a river which Cook named after his stricken ship. Banks commented wryly that there was 'nothing but a lock of Wool between us and destruction'.

Here the ship was careened. The ship's complement of eighty-seven spent forty-seven days ashore, their second longest time on land (after Tahiti). Storage tents, a blacksmith's forge, carpenter's workshop and benches, a butcher's shop, and pens for pigs and the few remaining

The Flower Chain

The stricken *Endeavour* careened on the river that now bears her name. The incident gave Banks and Solander an unexpected opportunity to search this area of Queensland for new plant species. (Illustration from collections in the London Library.)

sheep were rapidly set up, and the crew set about making *Endeavour* seaworthy once more.

When the ship was turned on its side plant specimens stored in a metal bread compartment in the aft end of the ship became wet. Sea-water was still in the bilge despite the pumping. Although this meant that there was much extra drying out to be done, even on the first day Banks wrote 'Dr. Solander and myself began Our plant gathering'. In all they collected some 400 specimens here. Banks seemed to have everyone involved in his activities; a few days later he recorded:

> Some of the Gentlemen who had been out in the woods Yesterday brought home the leaves of a plant which I took to be *Arum esculentum*, the same I beleive as is called Cocoos in the West Indies.

Banks was referring to *Colocasia esculenta*, also known as taro, or to the Tahitians cocoyam. He also found wild yams, dense mangrove swamps and evergreen bark trees or cottonwood, *Hibiscus tiliaceus*, which grows throughout the Pacific.

The activities around the boat roused the curiosity of the local Guugu Yimidhirr people who watched from a distance for three weeks before venturing towards the white people. Tupaia's benign influence meant that Anglo-Aboriginal relations were, although restrained, cordial apart from one instance. The contrast in values and expectations between the Aboriginal people and the Europeans came to the forefront in a dispute over twelve large turtles — some up to three hundred pounds each, caught to provide fresh meat for when the voyage resumed. When the Aboriginal representatives saw this catch on deck they objected, regarding it as hoarding. First they tried to take the turtles but were stopped by Cook's men so they jumped ashore, grabbed some fire from under a pitch kettle and set the grass around the makeshift shore camp alight. As Banks and a few others pulled the tent out of the path of the fire, the Aborigines tried to set the washing and fishing nets ablaze. Cook rushed back on board, loaded a musket with smallshot, and hit an offender in the leg. During the fracas a fence was burnt and a piglet scorched to death. That night, when all returned to peace, Banks was enthralled by the kilometres of Aboriginal fires ablaze in the bush making 'the most beautiful appearance imaginable'.

During the commotion a few pigs escaped. The descendants of these feral swine, known now as 'Captain Cookers', are ferocious wild boars and sows, a curse of north Queensland. Until they escaped, the topsoil of Australia, with its delicate plants and grasses, had never suffered the heavy weight of a hard hoof as Australian animals have soft feet or claws.

The few pigs at Endeavour River in 1770 which did not escape had a hard time. Banks remarked that they were hungry and two died after eating cycad seeds. Some pigs and sailors ate the seeds of *Cycas media*, a similar cycad to that which had made de Vlamingh's men ill on the west coast and 'were violently affected by them both upwards and downwards'.

Coconuts were more palatable and Parkinson in his journal listed the Aboriginal word for the 'cocoa-nut shell' as 'Keremande'. Coconuts are a matter of controversy in modern Queensland. Some locals insist they are not indigenous to Australia, that they were introduced, and therefore should not be grown as extensively as they are — especially as, like most popular palms, they provide little food for native wildlife. Parkinson's journal suggests that coconuts certainly were in Queensland before white settlement. Parkinson also gives the word 'Nampar' for bamboo. This is again curious: although it grows widely now in the Endeavour River area, bamboo has long been thought to have been introduced with the first white settlers in the area during the gold rushes in the 1870s. It may be that the term was used rather generally for a whole range of large grasses rather than specifically for bamboo.

The sailors were also interested in the wild animals of the area. Crocodiles were seen and John Gore shot what was described as a kangaroo, which was then eaten. The skin of this animal was taken back to England, stuffed and became the subject of a famous painting by George Stubbs.

Although the repairs to the *Endeavour* were soon finished, it took several attempts to refloat her, and a long wait for the best winds to take her

This engraving, described as a kangaroo, is taken from an oil painting by George Stubbs of a mounted skin. In fact, the animal brought back by Banks and Cook was probably a wallaby rather than a kangaroo. (Illustration from collections in the London Library.)

THE FLOWER CHAIN

out of the river. Banks took the opportunity to summarise the Australian flora. Remarks in his journal are contradictory to those given with his recommendations years later suggesting settlement at Botany Bay. Indeed his descriptions of the flora of Australia make it seem so plain and so inedible, that if his whole journal had been published before settlement there would have been severe doubts as to whether Australia was a suitable site for the new colony.

> For the whole length of the coast which we saild along there was a sameness to be observd in the face of the countrey very uncommon; Barren it may justly be calld and in a very high degree, that at least we saw. The Soil in general is sandy and very light: on it grows grass tall enough but thin sett, and trees of a tolerable size ... upon the Whole the fertile soil Bears no kind of Proportion to that which seems by nature doomd to everlasting Barrenness ... Soil so barren and at the same time intirely void of the helps derivd from cultivation could not be supposd to yeild much towards the support of man. We had been so long at sea with but a scanty supply of fresh provisions that we had long used to eat every thing we could lay our hands upon, fish, flesh, or vegetable which only was not poisonous; yet we could but not and then procure a dish of bad greens for our own table and never but in the place where the ship was careend met with a sufficient quantity to supply the ship ... Palm cabbage and what is calld in the West Indies Indian Kale were in tolerable plenty, as was also a sort of Purslane. The other plants we eat were a kind of Beans, very bad, a kind of Parsley and a plant something resembling spinage, which two last grew only to the Southward. I shall give their botanical names as I beleive some of them never eat [sic] by Europeans before: first Indian kale *(Arum esculentum)* [*Colocasia esculenta*], Red flowerd purslane *(Sesuvium portulacastrum)*, Beans *(Glycine speciosa)* [*Canavalia maritima*], Parsley *(Apium)* [*Apium prostratum*], Spinage *(Tetragonia cornuta)* [*Tetragonia tetragonioides*]. Fruits we had still fewer; to the South was one something resembling a heart cherry only the stone was soft *(Eugenia)* [*Eugenia banksii*] which had nothing but a light acid to recommend it; to the Northward again a

Banks and Solander botanised for many days in the Endeavour River area. When they left, Banks wrote a summary of the flora of the country in his journal. Many of the plants he mentioned, such as this *Sesuvium portulacastrum* would be engraved from Parkinson's sketches. These engravings have recently been published as *Banks' Florilegium*.

kind of Figs growing from the stalk of a tree, very indifferent *(Ficus caudiciflora)* [*Ficus glomerata*], a fruit we calld Plumbs like them in Colour but flat like a little cheese [Burdekin plum, *Pleiogynium cerasiferum*], and another much like a damson both in appearance and taste; both these last however were so full of a large stone that eating them was but an unprofitable business. Wild Plantanes we had also but so full of seeds that they had little or no pulp ... Other usefull plants we saw none, except perhaps two might be found so which yeild resin in abundance ...

Although Banks was unimpressed by the usefulness of the plants he found, he did admit that 'of Plants in general the countrey afforded a far larger variety than its barren appearance seemd to promise', and also that the Aboriginal people they came across ' ... had a knowledge of plants as we plainly could percieve by their having names for them'.

By early August the *Endeavour* was at sea again, in-between the reef and the mainland. With the pinnace out ahead sounding, and Cook himself at the masthead, the little ship made its way through a maze of hazards. It was about ten days later that it was noticed that the mainland — which Cook named Cape York after the King's second son, the late Duke — had become so narrow that water could be seen beyond it. At last, a little further ahead, land which Cook had thought to be part of the mainland was shown to be an island — one of the dozens in Torres Strait between New Guinea and Australia. After dining in the Great Cabin on 22 August 1770, Cook landed on this island. It is a bleak, windswept little outcrop of rock dotted with stunted scrubby bushes. The only sounds were the screeching of birds and the waves lapping on white sandy beaches and oyster-encrusted rocks. A tall flagpole was rowed ashore.

When the *Endeavour* left England in August 1768, among Cook's secret orders were instructions that if the Great Unknown Southland was found 'You are also with the consent of the natives to take possession of convenient situations ... in the name of the King of Great Britain'. Although Cook knew that New Holland was not *Terra Australis Incognita*, surely similar rules for taking possession applied? But the sole contact of the *Endeavour* crew ashore had been with the Guugu Yimidhirr tribe, and they certainly did not consent to being taken over by anyone, let alone the unknown George III. In the unlikely event that they had, the agreement would only have covered their tribal land as the continent was divided between the 500 to 600 tribes. As there were no long rivers that spanned the continent — none comparable to the Danube, the Nile or the Mississippi — let alone indigenous animals which could be used for transport, the continent was never organised hierarchically as a whole, either by the blacks or the whites, until steamships, horses, trains, the telegraph, radio and the telephone brought the outposts closer.

At six o'clock on August 22, four months after landing at Botany Bay, Cook held a hasty flag-raising ceremony on the windy little island, attended by Banks, Solander and selected members of the crew. With the usual royal salute the east coast of Australia was claimed for Britain. The whiff of that gunpowder was to stay in Banks' nostrils over a decade later — with a little help from his fellow *Endeavour* crew member James Mario Matra — Banks was to recommend that the coast should be settled by the British, and that it was convenient to do so because it was *terra nullius*.

Ironically, the fancy Possession Ceremony with its musket shots and salutes was just 240 kilometres from the Murray Islands. The inhabitants of these neighbouring islands in Torres Strait, with stirring advances by Eddie Mabo, won the High Court battle rejecting the principle of *terra nullius* on 3 June 1992 — 222 years after the erection of the flagpole. This battle, that convinced the courts that the bedrock of Australia's land title system was fiction, started almost within earshot of that cannon. The debate over Aboriginal land title still rumbles on in the closing years of the twentieth century.

On that late afternoon in August 1770, the anxiety to get away was so great that neither Cook nor Banks — nobody in fact — saw that they were standing on a goldmine. A quartz reef near where they all so solemnly saluted the absent king, contained visible gold. Over a century later a shaft was sunk exactly where the flagstaff had been planted.

No European returned to the eastern coast of the mainland for eighteen years. When they did, it was on the recommendation of Banks, by then a respected scientific figure in Britain and Europe. The 'gentleman amateur' botanist was to become a powerful figure on the strength of his voyage to Australia, and was to use this influence to mould its future.

The *Endeavour's* trials on the Great Barrier Reef, and her makeshift repairs on the Endeavour River, had left her vulnerable and Cook was anxious to get her more seaworthy before he attempted the Cape of Good Hope. He headed for the Dutch colony of Batavia, where he could make better repairs, arriving on October 10. It was to prove a fatal decision for the *Endeavour's* crew. Malaria-carrying mosquitoes were rife, and deadly diseases, particularly dysentery, lurked in the colony's open drains. Among those who fell victim were the ever-faithful Tupaia and his servant, Tayeto. Others died after the ship sailed and were buried at sea, including Green, Spöring and the talented and amiable Parkinson. In all, thirty-eight men perished during the voyage, nearly all of them succumbing to disease in the unsavoury climate of Batavia. Banks and Solander were taken seriously ill but recovered and still managed to make collections of Javanese plants.

Cook left Java as soon as he could. Sailing via the Cape of Good Hope, St Helena and Ascension Island, he arrived in England on 12 July 1771. In exactly a year Cook would set sail yet again for the Pacific, but this time without Banks. The cabins which Banks had assigned for himself and his party would be occupied by another self-styled botanist — a German, Johann Reinhold Forster, and his son Georg — who, like Banks, would also employ an ex-student of Linnaeus to describe the plants discovered on the voyage.

Named after James Lee of the Vineyard nursery, Hammersmith, this *Leea rubra* commemorates the great contribution he and his partner, Lewis Kennedy, made in cultivating Australian plants from seeds brought back by plant collectors. (*Banks' Florilegium.*)

11
Cook Returns to the South Seas

The *Endeavour*, and particularly its surviving scientists, arrived home to rapturous acclaim. Within three weeks Banks was presented to the King — an event which marked the beginning of a lifelong friendship. The Admiralty immediately began planning a follow-up voyage and newspapers were soon announcing that in the spring of the following year, 1772, under royal patronage, Banks and Solander would set out on a second voyage and Mr Banks would found a colony in the South Seas. Meanwhile Cook's achievement was recognised with a promotion to commander and, in the middle of August, he too was presented to the King by Lord Sandwich.

The purpose of the second Pacific voyage was, explicitly, to find *Terra Australis Incognita* and to 'perfect the Discoveries that had been begun on the last voyage'. After the close call on the Great Barrier Reef, Cook insisted on having two ships — the *Resolution* and the *Adventure* — to sail in convoy. Banks was again invited by Lord Sandwich to accompany Cook, his entourage originally came to 'thirteen persons besides myself', plus the dogs. Most eminent among the party was the German-born painter John Zoffany (1733 – 1810), a founder member of the Royal Academy, who was engaged for a fee of one thousand pounds. Banks also had 'five others to accompany me, who were to delineate such Objects as I might think worthy to be presented to my friends at home ... [and] Six domestick servants also to collect and preserve'. These included two French horn players! Nothing was said about the fourteenth member of Banks' staff, a 'Mr Burnett', who had gone ahead and was to join the ship in Madeira.

Banks ensured the voyage would be exceptionally well equipped. He had musical instruments, scientific apparatus, screwdrivers, axes, harpoons, artists' paints, drawing-tables, rat traps, wire catchers for insects and birds, magnifying glasses, microscopes, table delicacies, tents for shelter, arms for protection and beads, combs, mirrors, feathers and fish-hooks for trade with the natives.

This bulky paraphernalia, the increased number in his suite, and the fact that larger ships were not chosen for the expedition, made Banks demand that the Great Cabin be handed completely over to him. An additional upper deck was therefore built, with a raised poop or 'round house' for the captain. However, the ship with this dreadful new superstructure had not sailed more than a few miles on its test voyage, before the pilot refused to venture any further. One of the officers on board, his friend Charles Clerke, wrote to Banks: 'By God, I'll go to sea in a grog-tub, if required, or in the *Resolution* as soon as you please; but I must say I think her by far the most unsafe ship I ever saw or heard of'. Cook ordered the top-heavy ship to make for Sheerness where the additions were removed. Banks ordered all his stores off the ship and withdrew. A Navy Board official wrote scathingly about the debacle:

> Mr Banks seems throughout to consider the Ships as fitted out wholly for his use ... [Banks thought] the whole undertaking to depend on him and his People; and himself as the Director and Conductor of the whole; for which he is not qualified, and if granted to him, would have been the greatest disgrace that could be put on His Majesty's Naval officers.

Banks hoped that his threat to withdraw would force the Admiralty to provide what he had originally wanted — larger ships — but the

Although James Cook was not the first European discoverer of Australia, his discovery and surveying of the east coast finally provided a more attractive image of the continent. After his and Banks' account of the eastern side of Australia became known, it was only a matter of time before it was colonised. (Linnean Society collections.)

The large, fleshy fruits of the breadfruit tree were first described and named by William Dampier on his visit to Guam on the *Cygnet* in 1688, when he noted its admirable qualities as a food staple. (Linnean Society collections.)

Top left: James Edward Smith, purchaser of the Linnaean collections and Founder-President of the Linnean Society of London. Smith borrowed money from his father to buy Linnaeus's herbarium, library and other natural history collections in 1788. (Linnean Society collections.)

Top right: Sir Joseph Banks provided Lady Hume with the seeds of the elegant flower *Humea elegans*, the rose-coloured humea, which she succeeded in cultivating in her garden. Smith studied these living plants, giving a detailed description of their habit and growth and honoured Lady Hume in the plant's name. Smith praised this 'accomplished Lady to whom we are obliged for its introduction ... as well as the number of new plants she has introduced into England, and which she is always in the most liberal manner disposed to communicate'. (Linnean Society collections.)

Bottom left: Smith was anxious to dispel the prevailing view that New Holland plants were 'deficient in beauty'. He cited the example of the brightly coloured *Styphelia tubiflora* to prove otherwise. He hoped that it would be introduced into British gardens and remain 'a perpetual assertor of the botanical honour of its country'. (Linnean Society collections.)

Bottom right: This *Pultenaea stipularis*, scaly Pultenaea, figured in *A Specimen of the Flora of New Holland*, was sent to Smith by Alexander Murray, gardener to Benjamin Robertson, from his garden in Stockwell, London. The plants had been raised from seeds brought back from New South Wales in 1792, flowering two years later. As with many Australian plants, Smith found *Pultenaea's* classification difficult, finally putting it into a new genus, named after the 'amiable and deserving English botanist, Dr Richard Pulteney.' (Linnean Society collections.)

Naval authorities stood firm. 'The Dispute between Mr Banks & the Captain' reached the newspapers but the misunderstanding does not appear to have adversely affected their good relationship in the long term. In the end Banks and his staff, instead of sailing to warm tropical islands and down beyond the Antarctic circle, went north in a hired ship to see the volcanoes and the relatively unexplored terrain of Iceland. Mr Zoffany went to Italy. Landscape painter William Hodges, aged 28, went in his stead on the *Resolution*.

Johann Reinhold Forster, a Prussian of Yorkshire ancestry, who had just completed a translation of Bougainville's voyage into English, was hurriedly appointed as naturalist in Banks' place. A former Lutheran minister and a failed schoolmaster, he had many contacts in London scientific circles. He received a Royal Society testimonial recommending him as a 'proper person for going on the expedition', and managed to get his son, Georg, accepted as his assistant and natural history artist.

Another botanist on board also owed his presence to Banks, but in his case Banks had organised for him to go on the expedition as a passenger. Francis Masson (1741 – 1805), a Scot, trained at Kew under its head gardener William Aiton, was to disembark at the Cape of Good Hope. This was to be the base of his plant-collecting activities for the next three years. He was the first of the many botanical collectors to be sent out from Kew under the aegis of Banks.

After Banks' edifices were removed from the *Resolution* the expedition was late in sailing. There were brief stops at Madeira and the island of St Jago in the Cape Verde islands to take on wine, fresh vegetables and water. From Madeira Cook, in a private letter, wrote about a person called Burnett who had planned to join Banks on the *Resolution*. He had caught a ship back to England after realising Banks was no longer on the expedition. Cook wrote: 'Every part of Mr Burnett's behaviour and every action tended to prove that he was a Woman'. Banks, it seems, was imitating the French naturalist Philibert Commerson, whose valet on the Bougainville voyage, turned out to be his mistress dressed as a man.

At the Cape of Good Hope, Forster engaged the able botanist Anders Sparrmann (1748 – 1820), a former pupil of Linnaeus, at £50 a year to join the scientific party. A passionate collector, Sparrmann was also an adventurer. After he left Sweden he had sailed to China as a ship's surgeon and then spent nearly a year collecting in the florally rich Cape. Cook noted in his journal:

> Mr Forster ... met with a Swedish gentleman, one Mr Sparman [sic], who understood something of these Sciences [natural history and botany] having studied under [Linnaeus] and being willing to embarque with us, Mr Forster strongly importuned me to take him on board, thinking that he would be of great assistance to him in the course of the Voyage, I at last consented, and he embarked with us accordingly as an assistant to Mr Forster; who bore his expenses on board, and allowed him a Yearly stipend besides.

Sparrmann remained with the expedition until the *Resolution* returned to the Cape on 21 March 1775, when he left the ship to resume his scientific work in Africa.

Cook did not visit mainland Australia on this second voyage. Indeed, the voyage would not have formed part of the history of Australia, let alone part of the story of the discovery of the flora, if it were not for three points. Firstly, although Cook avoided Australia, Tobias Furneaux, the captain of the accompanying ship, the *Adventure*, stopped briefly in Tasmania, en route from the Cape to New Zealand. Among the plants collected there was Australia's best-known tree, the eucalypt. Secondly, the Forsters and Sparrmann collected the flax plant in Norfolk Island which was the reason for eventual settlement there. Finally, in the books written by Forster after the voyage some Australian plant genera were published for the first time. Among these was the genus *Leptospermum*, found in Australia, New Zealand and Malaysia.

In February 1773 the *Resolution* and the *Adventure* inadvertently lost sight of each other in fog and squally weather. Cook went directly to Dusky Bay, New Zealand. Furneaux took the *Adventure* to Tasmania and named the bay they anchored in after his ship. Although this was the first British landing on the island it was well

After Banks withdrew from Cook's second voyage, a replacement naturalist had to be found quickly. The post went to Johann Reinhold Forster, who also recruited his son Georg as natural history painter. Forster and Cook would clash so badly on the voyage that Cook would refuse to take an official naturalist on board again. (Linnean Society collections.)

known from the Dutch voyage the previous century. Furneaux did not know that Marion Dufresne — who rescued Bonnie Prince Charlie from Scotland in 1746 — had claimed the island for France a year earlier. This famous French seaman, after exploring Tasmania, then sailed on to New Zealand — only to be slaughtered by Maoris.

Furneaux's journal is disappointing. He found no safe anchorage at what he called Adventure Bay; no inhabitants — just traces of their existence such as heaps of shells and ashes from their fires. During five days ashore to collect wood and water, some plant specimens and seeds were gathered. It was high summer. The country would have been dry but with many flowers in bloom or in seed. Alas, the naturalists — the Forsters and Sparrmann — were on Cook's ship, so there are no journal descriptions of the flora collected. It is certain, however, that seeds of *Eucalyptus obliqua* were gathered by Furneaux. These seeds survived the voyage back to England to be grown at Kew, in the Earl of Coventry's garden and other English gardens.

It is seemly that *Eucalyptus obliqua*, the first-named of Australia's most significant genus, was also the first of all Australian plants sold to English gardeners around 1774. Some herbarium specimens at the Natural History Museum in London came from a tree sold by William

Malcolm, a nurseryman of Kensington, to the Earl of Coventry in Worcestershire. Another introduction from Furneaux grown at Kew, and in Banks' own garden, was the white-flowered *Leptospermum lanigerum*.

On this second voyage, over three years long, Captain Cook visited New Zealand three times and Tahiti twice. He never returned to Australia. Why did he avoid a place where so much was unknown? Was it because he was short of rations and Australia offered few palatable fruits and greens? Was it again the story of the old 'scurvy coast' that stopped so many Dutch captains from ever returning?

The closest Cook and the naturalists got to mainland Australia was Norfolk Island, en route from New Caledonia to New Zealand, in October 1774. The Forsters, father and son, found much to collect — succulent cabbage-tree palms, the pine trees that might be masts of ships and the flax plant for which there were high hopes of an economic application.

Johann Forster published *Characteres Generum Plantarum* in 1776 with descriptions of ninety-four plant species collected on the voyage, including some Australian examples. Both Forsters went on to publish a fuller account of the scientific results of this voyage in 1786, under the title *Florulae Insularum Australium* with a long and flattering dedication to the most excellent and celebrated Sparrmann. The unscrupulous elder Forster used some of Solander's unpublished descriptions and names — seen when Banks had generously allowed Forster access to his herbarium — in the full knowledge that Banks and Solander intended to publish these themselves in a major work on the botany of Cook's first voyage.

If there was any bad feeling between Cook and Banks over the second voyage, it had dissipated by the time of Cook's return. One of the first sentiments Cook expressed were his regrets that Banks hadn't been on the voyage. He also sought Banks' approval of the botanical sections of his official account of the voyage.

Almost as soon as Cook had finished writing up his second voyage he was preparing to depart on his third, fatal expedition to the Pacific. A few months before his departure an act of parliament was amended so that a reward of £20 000 awaited any man who found a sea passage between the Atlantic and the Pacific Oceans across the top of Canada — the fabled North-West Passage. Cook was dispatched to try to find out if such a route existed in the frozen wastes of the Canadian Arctic. This objective, however, was to be kept a secret from other maritime powers so the official reason for the voyage was to return the Tahitian O'mai, brought back by Furneaux on the second voyage, to his homeland. King George III and his government took care to furnish O'mai with every item that could be of use in Tahiti and to convey an idea of British power and greatness by material means to the inhabitants of the South Seas. As well as a menagerie of sheep, goats, geese, ducks, a cow, a horse and a peacock, O'mai had handkerchiefs with the words 'Great Britain' printed on them, firearms, port wine and a trousseau any bride would covet. It was because of O'mai's livestock that another collection of plants was made in Australia. Tasmania was visited en route to Tahiti so that grass and other greenstuff for the animals could be gathered.

Cook had not got on well with the Forsters, exclaiming at one point, 'curse the scientists and all science into the bargain!' so on his third and last Pacific voyage no official naturalists were carried on either the *Resolution* or the *Discovery*. This time the work of natural history observation and collection was entrusted to the ship's surgeon, William Anderson. A veteran of the second voyage, Anderson had proved himself a competent naturalist and ethnologist, encouraged by the Forsters and Sparrmann.

Banks wanted to make sure enough collections were made for Kew and not finding anyone suitable there, asked James Lee if he knew of anyone suitable. Ten weeks before the *Resolution* was due to sail, Lee sent a young gardener, David Nelson, with a letter to Soho Square.

> Honoured Sir, I have sent you the bearer, David Nelson, as a proper person for the purpose you told me of; he knows the general runn of our collections and plants about London, understands something of botany, but does not pretend to have much knowledge in it. I have inquired personally into his character and find him

exactly suited for the purpose of a collector. I have injoined him to secrecy whither you make a bargain with him or not. One thing he desires me to mention, which is he will want a little advance money to rigg him out. I am dear Sir with the greatest regard your obedient, humble servant, James Lee.

Nelson was employed and put on the Kew payroll. He spent the weeks before departure studying in the gardens. He was mustered supernumerary crew on board *Discovery* sister ship to Cook's *Resolution*, under Captain Clerke. The sailing master on the *Resolution* was one William Bligh.

Nelson, like Sydney Parkinson, another botanical voyager introduced to Banks by James Lee, was destined to be infected with tropical fever in Batavia and die. However, that was thirteen years away, and Nelson still had his contribution to the Australian Flower Chain to make.

Nelson was apparently a likeable, retiring young man. When the two ships arrived in Cape Town in November 1776, Francis Masson — who had been there since being dropped off by Cook on his second voyage four years earlier — took Nelson and Anderson upcountry on a plant collecting expedition. Clerke wrote to Banks that Nelson 'is one of the quietest fellows in Nature; he seems very attentive and I hope will answer your purpose very well'.

En route from the Cape of Good Hope to New Zealand, Cook finally visited Tasmania, landing there with the *Resolution* still 'so stocked with animals that she resembled Noah's Ark', on 26 January 1777. Cook's journal reflects little curiosity about the place, just a need to collect water and fodder for livestock.

After one day getting 'a little Wood and some grass for our Cattle, both of which we were in great want of', everyone, including Nelson, repaired on board so that 'we might be ready to sail whenever the wind served'. Insufficient breezes forced Cook to wait for three days.

Nelson spent his time ashore busily collecting. Among the plants he found were *Oxylobium ellipticum*, a shrub with leaves in clusters along the stem and bright yellow flowers in dense racemes, as well as specimens of eucalypts and wattles. One of these, *Acacia verticillata* — which Nelson named *Mimosa* — became a conservatory and greenhouse favourite, with its dark prickly foliage and fluffy balls of lemon flowers. Twenty-three lots of seeds were received by Banks and Solander from the voyage, but unfortunately, most of these were unidentified.

Nelson is also credited with collecting the type specimen for *Eucalyptus obliqua*. Charles-Louis L'Héritier de Brutelle, a French botanist working in London, used Nelson's specimen and probably a living tree grown from seed, gathered four years earlier at Adventure Bay by Tobias Furneaux, to make his description. It was this description that established the genus *Eucalyptus*. With its abundant clumps of small creamy white flowers and leaves that are glossy dark green on both sides *Eucalyptus obliqua* is magnificent, a suitably impressive representative of the genus.

L'Héritier enjoyed the hospitality of Banks during a fifteen-month sojourn in England between 1786 and 1787. He made a point of classifying plants from actual living trees which he found growing in England, but also consulted dried specimens, particularly in Banks' herbarium. His classification of *E. obliqua*, published in *Sertum Anglicum* (1788), was illustrated by Pierre-Joseph Redouté. Known as the 'Raphael of flowers', Redouté is now considered to be one of the greatest botanical illustrators ever lived. He drew the eucalyptus specimen brought back by David Nelson at Banks' home in Soho Square.

It had taken almost twelve years from the time it was first collected for Australia's most characteristic tree to be named and described.

Although wood and water were plentiful, Cook was concerned that the 'grass, which we most wanted, was scarce and not good; necessity however obliged us to take such as we could get'. At this time Cook was only ten days' sailing time away from Botany Bay, but the possibility of another visit never entered his head. As he had already sailed thousands of kilometres on that Pacific voyage, what would another 800 kilometres have meant? Though in a position to determine once and for all the question of Tasmania's insularity, Cook did not grasp the opportunity.

This illustration of the type specimen for the genus *Eucalyptus*, *E. obliqua*, was engraved from a painting by Redoute for L'Heritier's work *Sertum Anglicum*. The type specimen was collected by Nelson and L'Heritier was given access to it in Banks' herbarium. (Linnean Society collections.)

The Flower Chain

Cook was always keen to leave animals where they would multiply and be useful either to visiting British ships or future settlers. At Tonga he left a young English bull and cow, a Cape ram and two ewes, a stallion and a mare. In New Zealand, for years, Maoris called wild pig 'kuki' in honour of the man who donated their progenitors. Australia, however, was never so favoured. Cook left no animals in mainland Australia and left only a sow and pig in Tasmania even though his cargo of livestock had been a 'filthy nuisance' from the start. Why did he not take the opportunity to leave more animals in Australia? Why did he shun Australia on his second and third voyages? He had thought to leave sheep, goats and cows in Tasmania, but in his own words, 'soon altered my intention, from a pursuasion [sic] that the natives, incapable of entering into my views of improving their country, would destroy them'. If his view of Tasmanian people extended to mainland Aboriginal people too, he would see no point in making the diversion to Australia. Perhaps he also avoided it, like the Dutch navigators who went before him, simply because the country did not appeal to European eyes — and stomachs — preferring the more fertile and luxuriantly vegetated small islands of the Pacific.

Cook would never get another chance to return to Australia. A final visit to Hawaii in the latter part of the voyage ended in his murder by the native people of the island. However, his name would be evermore associated with Australia, for discovering and charting the east coast — the coast that would eventually be colonised.

12
A Forgotten Florilegium

Dr Johnson remarked to Boswell when pointing to large volumes of John Hawkesworth's account of the *Endeavour* and other voyages, 'These Voyages ... who will read them through? ... There can be little entertainment in such books; one set of Savages is like another'.

In the seventy years since the publication of Dampier's *A Voyage to New Holland* there had been numerous books on the South Seas. However, Hawkesworth's account of Cook's voyage was sold out in three days at four-and-a-half guineas apiece. Purchasers offered ten guineas to get a copy and second and third editions followed quickly.

This amalgam of the journals of Banks and Cook, with a good deal of embellishment by Hawkesworth, was all anyone would ever officially see in print about Banks' efforts in Australia during his lifetime. His own journal remained just a handwritten manuscript. It was not until the mid-twentieth century that it was pulled out of the archives and published. Most of the plant names and descriptions bestowed by Banks and Solander are just archival material.

From the moment Banks returned to England from the *Endeavour* voyage there was a triumphant air to his activities, a confidence which came with fame. Most of the publicity was about the haul of unusual plants from Botany Bay or about Tahiti, where romance was the main preoccupation. The emphasis was on the exploits of Mr Banks and Dr Solander. These 'ingenious gentlemen', who had sailed round the world had touched at 'near forty other undiscovered Islands, not known to other Europeans'. They had gathered 'above a thousand different Species of Plants, none of which were ever known in Europe before', enthused the popular press.

One of the thousands of specimens collected by Banks and Solander in Australia, this *Grevillea pteridifolia*, was sent from the British Museum (Natural History), with some 500 other duplicates of Banks' Australian material, to the New South Wales National Herbarium. Fittingly, Banks' plants now form the core collections of both British and Australian national herbaria.
(P. Olde & N. Marriott, *The Grevillea Book,* Volume I, Kangaroo Press, 1994.)

In August 1771, the newspapers announced that Mr Banks had been introduced to King George III at St James' and 'received very graciously'. Soon afterwards, accompanied by Solander, Banks again met the King, this time at Richmond. 'Mr Banks' and Dr Solander's

THE FLOWER CHAIN

Fame had its price for Banks and Solander. When they returned from the *Endeavour* voyage they were feted by society but they were also lampooned as 'macaronis', foppish young men, for their perceived effeminate activities collecting natural history specimens. (Linnean Society collections.)

curiosities', ran another article, had been seen by most of the nobility, and 'the most extraordinary Phenomena' were soon to be inspected at the Queen's Palace. The newspapers became positively reverential about Mr Banks and Dr Solander — or sometimes Dr Solander and Mr Banks. It was Mr Banks', not Cook's voyage. The nobility were calling at Mr Banks' house to see his curiosities and there was excitement over Tahitian seeds germinating in Mr Lee's nursery in Hammersmith.

Banks and Solander reaped both social glory and scientific acclaim; they received honorary doctorates from Oxford and invitations to the greatest houses in the land. Yet the material that had provided them with their fame — the leaves of the dried plants, the seeds, the blooms from Australia — all languished, waiting to be published, to be known. Banks had returned with grand plans for their publication and, once he got back from Iceland, turned his attention to the major task of getting Parkinson's exquisite drawings completed and engraved. Parkinson's work comprised twenty-one volumes, containing 280 finished drawings and 679 pencil sketches, of which 330 were sketches of Australian plants. Solander was to prepare the botanical descriptions to accompany the plates.

Banks also had his huge collections to organise. Although the *Endeavour* voyage had been an official Admiralty expedition, Banks was the sponsor of the natural history side and the specimens were effectively his. At that time neither Kew nor the infant British Museum were the great repositories of such material that they are today, and there was no precedent for the collections to go anywhere other than into Banks' private collection. They were to stay in Banks' houses, first in New Burlington Street, and thence in Soho Square, for over fifty years. On his death Banks left them first to his librarian, Robert Brown, and then to the British Museum. Brown actually organised for their transfer to the Museum well before his own death in 1858 and today they form one of the core collections of the Natural History Museum's Department of Botany.

Botanical specimens from many voyages were to follow the same route from ship to Banks' personal herbarium, even when a collector had been paid by the Admiralty — as in the cases of Archibald Menzies and Robert Brown. This has been to the advantage of posterity, as they were expertly curated under Banks' care and made available to all comers. They also entered the public domain as an entire collection. If they had gone to the Admiralty, they might well have been lost, neglected or dispersed.

Once Banks returned from his voyaging he became effectively a patron of science. His money paid for innumerable scientific projects, publications and salaries. As such, the results of the endeavours he paid for often became his property and as a consequence he has been accused of appropriating the skilled work and glory of the men he hired. This sometimes caused frustration to the people he employed. One of the artists he took to Iceland, John Frederick Miller, entered a bitter dispute with Banks over an exhibition Miller had held of his work without Banks' permission. In May 1776, Miller wrote: 'You, Sir, was also pleased to say ... that if I did dare publish, draw, or sell any of them, you would prosecute me to the utmost of the law'. Miller went on to explain that he had exhibited in the Royal Academy 'because I did see you withheld the name of those who made the drawings for you'.

When Banks had Parkinson's work engraved, the copper plates were made up for printing without Parkinson's name — they would always be distinguished by the name of their owner, Joseph Banks, not the artist. Banks also entered into an unpleasant dispute with Parkinson's brother, Stanfield, when the latter published Sydney's journal before the official version of the voyage came out, using some of Parkinson's drawings without Banks' permission.

This sort of publicity Banks did not want, but his fame did not come without a price. One consequence of being in the public gaze, even in the eighteenth century, was to become the subject of public ridicule. On the return of the *Endeavour,* rumours and salacious satires surrounded Banks, particularly his dallying with the tattooed ladies of 'Otaheite' [Tahiti]. He became the central figure in an outpouring of outrageous lampoons and cartoons where he was variously portrayed as a fop, a social climber and a dallying and unfaithful lover. Banks had discarded the girl who had regarded herself as his fiancée before his departure, one Harriet Blosset. In the end, Banks quietly paid her off.

While cartoonists drew caricatures of the youthful savant, the scientific community of Europe waited, fascinated to know what would happen to the *Endeavour* plants. An excited Linnaeus referred to it as a 'matchless and truly astonishing collection such as has never been seen before, nor may ever be seen again'. Linnaeus was proud that Solander, his favourite pupil, had followed in the steps of his other 'apostles' by travelling the earth to bring back new plants. It must have been a bitter disappointment to Linnaeus, the recognised authority, that unlike his other protégés and other botanists of note, Solander did not send him any new plants for classification. Although Solander was well known as an appalling correspondent, it cannot be disregarded that Solander was in the employ of Banks, and Banks was planning to publish, in fourteen volumes, a sumptuous and erudite illustrated flora of the areas visited on the *Endeavour.* There were many letters from Linnaeus to both Banks and to Solander, pleading for specimens, but initially none was sent. Eventually duplicates were dispatched, some of which the younger Linnaeus described and named, most notably the genus *Banksia.*

Instead, Linnaeus — and the rest of the scientific world — waited for Banks and Solander's magnum opus. Banks' enthusiasm for the project cannot be doubted. His dream was to produce the ultimate botanical publication of his discoveries, with illustrations of the highest quality. To this end he went to extraordinary lengths and expense to find the best engravers. He concentrated on the supervision of the string of artists that finished Parkinson's drawings, and of the engravers who turned them into copper plates for printing, while Solander worked on the manuscript descriptions.

As time went on, Banks began to realise that the task was far greater than he had anticipated. Several years into the project he wrote to the younger Linnaeus, 'I have not yet advanced above half my intended progress'. His engravers, Gerhard Sibelius, Daniel MacKenzie, Gabriel Smith and others worked incessantly, producing 742 finished copper plates, but at a great financial cost to Banks. Estimates vary, but it seems Banks paid in the region of £10 000 for their preparation, the same as it cost him to go on the voyage in the first place. He had wanted to produce two thousand plates, but eventually realised that this would be impossible, both practically and financially.

Although the project was progressing slowly, and as time went on Banks became increasingly involved in other matters, he still anticipated its completion when, in 1782 he received a dreadful blow. Solander, his great friend, companion and collaborator, died suddenly of a cerebral haemorrhage. Banks was devastated and wrote to Johan Alstroëmer, a Swedish correspondent:

> The botanical work with which I am presently involved is nearing its completion. Because everything was produced by our common effort, Solander's name will appear on the title page next to mine ... Since all the descriptions were made when the plants were fresh, nothing remains to be done, except to fully work out the drawings still not finished and to record the synonyms from books which we did not have with us or which have come out since. All that is left is so little that it can be completed in two months; if only the engravers can put the finishing touches on it.

But Banks was either mistaken or over-optimistic. Solander had died before he had completed the Australian descriptions and classifications; there was far more still to be done than add in finishing touches to the elaborate plates.

Ten years later, the work still hadn't appeared. Banks wrote to Martijn von Marum that it had been 'retarded' by his increasing involvement in public affairs. It was becoming obvious that it never would be published, at least not in Banks' lifetime. If it had, it would have been the most impressive — and expensive — botanical publication of the eighteenth century. In the end, all that appeared were some sets of magnificent proof prints in black and white, sent to selected botanical luminaries in Europe.

Speculation about the non-publication of these volumes has been going on for nearly two centuries. Among the possible reasons put forward are that Banks lost interest; that he was not a professional scientist and could not prepare the work left by Solander; that the final cost of the books would have been too much, even for the wealthy Banks; even that he became too famous in the end to bother.

It is likely to have been a combination of these factors. Certainly, as Banks became more eminent, as President of the Royal Society, unofficial director of Kew, and de facto scientific adviser to the government, he became increasingly involved in other, more pressing matters. The preparation of the Flora slipped down his list of priorities. The Australian collections still had to be systematically arranged and prepared for publication and to have published would have cost Banks thousands more, on top of the thousands he had already spent, at a time when his income was significantly reduced as a result of various wars.

In the twenty years following Banks and Solander's return with their botanical haul the colony at Port Jackson had been established. A stream of Australian botanical material was finding its way back to Europe and was being described and named. Even within his own collection, Banks happily allowed other workers access. His herbarium became a popular drawcard for international botanists who were invited to examine the specimens at their leisure. As time went on, many of the plants in Banks' herbarium were gradually renamed by others. Thus Banks and Solander's *Metrosideros* became *Eucalyptus* and, courtesy of the younger Linnaeus, the *Leucadendron* from Botany Bay commemorated its discoverer by becoming *Banksia*. With others superseding him in describing either plants from his own collection, or specimens of their own that duplicated his, the urgency to publish lessened. Eventually the need for publication of the entire collection was called into question.

There is another reason, that has never really been explored, which may also have contributed to Banks' final reluctance to publish. When they were describing plants during the course of voyage, Banks and Solander relied heavily on Linnaeus' published classifications of plants from the region he called 'Indica', that is India, China and Malaya. Consequently they were to put many of the new plants into Linnaeus' existing groups, when, in fact, they required completely new genera and even in some instances, new families.

In the 1753 edition of *Species Plantarum*, Linnaeus gave his estimate of the total number of plants in the world as 'hardly 10 000' (it is now thought there are over 400 000). This implication, that there were few new genera awaiting discovery, perhaps accounts for why Solander and Banks put many of their Australian plants into already existing genera. When Solander couldn't fit a plant into any genus then known, it became a matter of urgency to create a new one, and he made a provisional designation with a token word, obviously intending to rename it properly when he had more time. He created these new genus names by adding the suffix *-oides* (Greek for likeness) to the name of a known genus which the plant resembled.

In the case of the Australian collection, the redesignation of these *-oides* genera was never done, either by Solander or Banks. Out of the 486 Australian plants listed in the catalogue of natural history drawings commissioned by Banks, 181 end with *-oides*. To have published these without doing the additional work Solander had intended, would have earned a shower of criticism instead of the adulation Banks so enjoyed. Banks was too busy to attempt the work himself, and apart from occasional visitors to his herbarium, it was not until he employed Robert Brown that someone began to study the descriptions again. By this time it was simply too late for the whole work to go to press, even if it had been completed.

Not all of Solander's unpublished classifications would be superseded. The plants he put into Linnaean genera such as *Tribulus*, *Cynometra* and *Drosera* still stand. Examples include the little buttercup-like flowered evergreen *Tribulus cistoides,* which was used by Aboriginal people to cure toothache. Collected on Palm Island by Banks and Solander it was named *Tribulus australis*. The evergreen tree with yellow flowers collected by Solander at Endeavour River fitted into the genera *Cynometra;* the carnivorous sundew, from the same region, Solander immediately placed with its relations in the rest of the world as *Drosera indica;* the unattractive Endeavour River bladderwort correctly classified with its European cousins in the genus *Utricularia.* Solander also recognised the little shrub with whitish flowers found in the Bay of Inlets in Queensland as the same *Vitex erifolia* as described by Linnaeus. At the same time, Solander and Banks failed to recognise some of the other plants which also belonged to genera defined by Linnaeus. These include *Diplocyclos, Centrella, Ammania, Bruguiera, Crotalaria* and *Hybanthus.*

Solander's classification may sometimes have been faulty and incomplete, but many of these descriptions were still of the highest order. Finally, in the early years of the twentieth century, the British Museum (Natural History) published a black-and-white edition of the Australian plant engravings along with Solander's original descriptions. It is sad that the work of one of the eighteenth century's finest botanists had to wait 130 years to be published. As Professor W. T. Stearn commented:

> ... if Banks' ambition for the grandeur of the work had been less and Solander had had more ambition to see his manuscripts printed, then Cook's first voyage of discovery would have shone as botanically the most successful then made.

The story of *Banks' Florilegium* does eventually have a happy ending. During the 1960s a limited edition of a selection of thirty black-and-white images was proposed, and finally published in 1974 amid great publicity, as *Captain Cook's Florilegium*. But this still fell far short of Banks' original vision and in the 1980s an even more ambitious undertaking was successfully

The Flower Chain

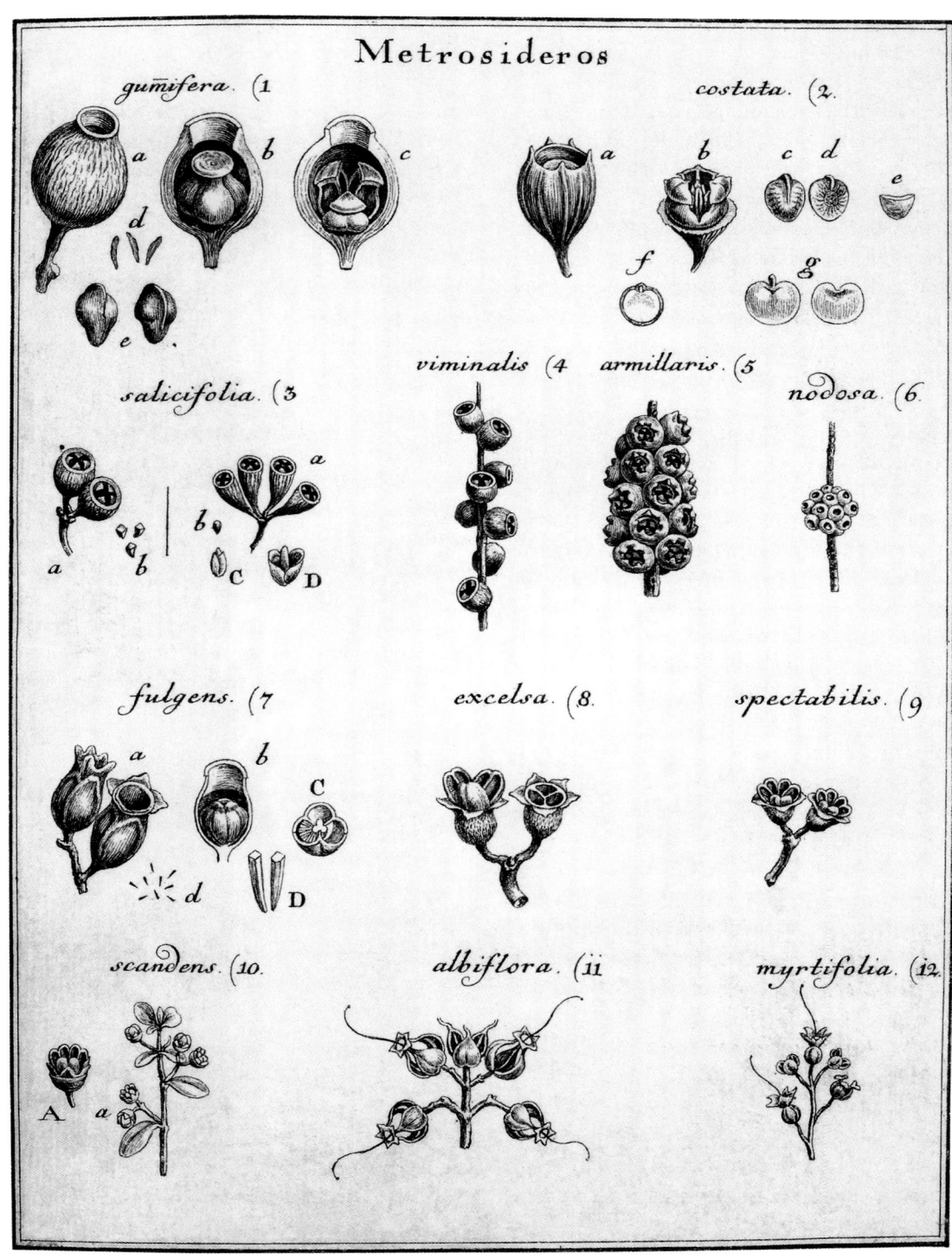

The German botanist Joseph Gaertner was allowed access to Banks' herbarium when he was compiling his great work on fruits, *De Fructibus et Seminibus Plantarum*. In it he illustrated fruits of the genus *Metrosideros*, finally designated as *Eucalyptus*, among others from Banks' Australian collections. (Linnean Society collections.)

completed by Editions Alecto, in cooperation with the Natural History Museum. Using the *à la poupée* technique, where colour is applied to the engraved copper plates by hand, Alecto printed all the 738 surviving plates, in full colour, as *Banks' Florilegium*, grouping the plants under their modern classifications. The reproductions are stunning, and a fitting tribute, 200 years on, to all those people, from Sydney Parkinson onwards, who worked on the project but never saw the fruits of their labour in print.

Banks and Solander did not just bring dried herbarium specimens back to England, they also collected seeds. They were restricted in their collecting by what was in seed at the time, so this collection was nowhere near as large as the dried plants. It is not clear how many seeds arrived back in Europe or how many they tried to germinate and grow. However, we do know that some were given by Banks to the German botanist Joseph Gaertner when he visited England in 1787. Several are figured in his epic monograph *De Fructibus et Seminibus Plantarum*, classified as *Melaleuca* and *Metrosideros*. They include *Eucalyptus crebra* which Gaertner named *Metrosideros salicifolia* before L'Héritier's designation of *Eucalyptus*, being worked on at the same time, was publicised.

Banks' seed collection included two casuarinas, a blue flax lily and the splendid *Eucalyptus gummifera*, one of the eucalypts with such a resinous output that they were given the vernacular name 'gum-trees'.

The obvious place to attempt growing Australian seeds was the King's gardens at Kew where, at the request of the King, Banks became the gardens' unofficial director and supervised its development into a premier scientific institution. William Aiton, Kew's head gardener, published a catalogue, *Hortus Kewensis,* of all the plants grown at Kew in 1789. Of the 5600 plants listed, only eight are Australian and only two, *Casuarina torulosa* and *Pouteria sericea,* came from the *Endeavour* voyage. Whether there were more that simply did not germinate, or whether that was the sum total of the seeds given to Kew, is not recorded.

Banks would be indirectly responsible for a much greater number of introductions of foreign, including Australian, plants to Kew in the years after his return by sending out plant collectors across the globe whenever possible. He built up Kew's reputation for the cultivation of introduced plants and guarded it jealously — a trait not always appreciated by his horticultural contemporaries. The Reverend William Herbert, son of the first Earl of Caernarvon and later Dean of Manchester, launched a fierce attack on Banks in his book *Amaryllidaceae*, commenting on the multitude of rare plants which flourished at Kew 'and perished there unobserved'. He went on:

> The illiberal system established at Kew Gardens by Sir Joseph Banks, whereby the rare plants collected there were hoarded with the most niggard jealousy, and kept as much as possible out of the sight of any inquirer, led, in the first instance, to a feeling of satisfaction whenever it was known that the garden had been plundered, and some of its hidden treasures brought into circulation ... It was the narrow-minded doctrine of Sir J. Banks that he could only render the King's collection superior to others by monopolising its contents and by doing so he rendered it hateful and contemptible: whereas, if he had freely given and freely received, and made its contents easily accessible to those who were interested in them, it would have been a pleasure and a pride to the nation.

It is difficult to sum up Banks' contribution to the study and understanding of Australian flora. If he had completed what he had set out to do, it would certainly have been immeasurable. However, his failure to publish had a detrimental effect not only on the academic study of Australia's plant life, but also on the development of the tiny convict colony at Port Jackson. The First Fleet sailed to Botany Bay with no published account of the plant life they could expect to find there, apart from information gleaned from Hawkesworth's florid account. The opportunity to describe and name the first large collection of Australian plants was missed and there wouldn't be a systematic Flora attempted until the next century; and then it would be by a Frenchman.

And yet he made collections of Australian flora that would remain unsurpassed for decades

The Flower Chain

and his collections of drawings and engravings remain a unique legacy. He also maintained an active interest in Australia's flora later sending out collectors to send plants back to England. Banks' collections, built up over fifty years, slipped into obscurity on the death of Robert Brown. Incredibly, George Bentham did not consult them fully when preparing his massive *Flora Australiensis*. Today, though, they have regained their important status, and form an invaluable part of the collections at the Natural History Museum in London, where they continue to be consulted by experts from all over the world.

13

Sir Joseph and the Settlement of Australia

After the departure of the *Endeavour* in May 1770, the flora of Botany Bay remained undisturbed for eighteen years. From the moment it had been christened, Botany Bay was both a contradiction to its name and a place of little appeal. Cook chose never to return. No British ship came for almost two decades after his brief visit on the *Endeavour*.

Meanwhile, in 1778, seven years after his return from the Pacific, Banks, the enthusiastic amateur, was unanimously elected President of the Royal Society. Some Fellows grumbled that a scholar of mathematics or the physical sciences should be president of Britain's most learned society, not a man whose prestige and authority came from wealth, friendship with the King, and fame from his voyage. Banks was lampooned for his lack of publications, his overbearing nature and his chairmanship of meetings — he would sometimes keep fellows awake with loud strokes of his official hammer. His rural upbringing was also the subject of ridicule — he swore, and was described as all in all 'too common, too ignorant and too vain for the chair of Newton'. But Banks' election gave him a position of authority and influence; that authority would be called upon when the government was seeking advice about the siting of a new penal colony.

In 1779, the year after his election as President of the Royal Society, the year Cook was killed in Hawaii, the year Bank, was married to a rich heiress, he suggested Botany Bay's suitability as such a site to the House of Commons' Bunbury Committee on Transportation. As the sole eminent survivor of the *Endeavour* voyage, Banks' descriptions of Australia were vital and would became the perceptions — and hopes — of all concerned.

Apart from Hawkesworth's unsatisfactory published account of the *Endeavour* circumnavigation there was no other source the authorities could turn to in order to find out about New South Wales. There was not even a sketch or drawing of Botany Bay. The only depiction of the continent was Parkinson's drawing of the *Endeavour* careened in a river over 1600 kilometres to the north. It was on Banks' account therefore that the government was forced to rely. He reported:

> ... that the place which appeared to him best adapted for such a Purpose, was Botany Bay ... that he apprehended there would be little Probability of any opposition from the Natives, as during his stay there ... he saw very few, and did not think there were above Fifty in all the Neighbourhood, and had Reason to believe the Country was very thinly peopled; those he saw were naked, treacherous ... but extremely cowardly.

From Banks' accounts, both at this time and later, the authorities inferred that Australia was *terra nullius*, belonging to no person, no community. This was the basis on which all the land of Australia could be designated Crown land, the basis for the commencement of a 'settler' system of tenure. Banks' statement effectively dismissed the Aboriginal people as being without rights or civilisation; it also dismissed their use of the land. But Banks was a man of his time. It is debatable whether many in his position would have interpreted what he saw any differently.

Despite Banks' favourable report, it took seven years and much discussion before the government decided to colonise Botany Bay. For three years the project hung in abeyance. Then,

By the time New South Wales was being considered as a likely site for a penal colony, Joseph Banks had become an important and influential figure in Georgian England. He was President of the Royal Society, he had been made a baronet and had the ear of both King and Government. When he reported that Botany Bay was suitable for settlement, no one doubted his word. (Linnean Society collections.)

in 1783, James Mario Matra, an American, who had been a midshipman on the *Endeavour*, addressed the British government with a 38-page pamphlet entitled, *A Proposal for Establishing a Settlement in New South Wales*. The pamphlet followed close on the heels of his correspondence on the subject with Banks. Matra's scheme had nothing to do with convicts, his aim was to 'atone for the loss of our American colonies'. Male American loyalists like himself, dispossessed of their land in America, would be settlers, along with two companies of marines with 'artificers, potters and gardeners' and 'women from Tahiti or New Caledonia, as pioneers' wives'. The colony would be a centre for trade with eastern Asia and, in war, a base for ships attacking Dutch colonies. Matra was the only other person with first-hand knowledge of Australia to report on the matter, but even he deferred to Banks, adding weight to his account by indicating that Banks favoured his proposal. It seems likely that Matra would never have put forward his plan without Banks' assistance.

The idea of a new colony for American loyalists never caught the authorities' imagination, even after a change of government in 1784, but there were more pressing consequences of the loss of America. The War of Independence had ended America's use as a depot for English criminals, the numbers of which were swelling every week. Prisons overflowed into decommissioned boats anchored on the Thames, supposed only to be staging posts for convicts awaiting transportation. But with the cessation of transportation to America, these overcrowded vermin-infested hulks had become stop-gap prisons. They became a sore on the social conscience of Britain. An alternative had to be found.

A youthful Joseph Banks, painted by Benjamin West, surrounded by trophies from the *Endeavour* voyage. The Maori cloak he is wearing was woven from native New Zealand flax, *Phormium tenax,* one the few antipodean plants regarded as having economic potential by the early colonists. (Usher Gallery, Lincoln.)

Daniel Solander, pupil of Linnaeus, was to become a lifelong friend of Banks. Solander was an amiable and much-liked addition to the London scene when he arrived in 1760. He never returned to his native Sweden. (Linnean Society collections.)

In April 1785 two Orders-in-Council provided for transportation of convicts to Africa. So great though was the outraged opposition to this suggestion that another Commons Committee was set up to investigate other options. Lord Beauchamp examined how to effect the *Transportation Act* of 1784 — which had replaced the *Penitentiary Act* of 1779 — and which revived the old system of transportation, without specifying a site.

It was as if Banks remembered the whiff of gunpowder from the flag-raising ceremony at Possession Island when he again gave evidence, and again advocated Botany Bay. 'The Eastern coast of New South Wales between the latitudes of 30° and 40° is sufficiently fertile to support a considerable number of Europeans who would cultivate it in the ordinary modes used in England,' he said, stressing that there were very few inhabitants. Asked if they were peaceful or hostile, he replied, 'though they seemed inclined to Hostilities they did not appear at all to be feared. We never saw more than 30 or 40 together.' The gigantic mounds of midden shells, the empty huts, the fires noted in his journal all along the coast during the 2000 mile journey north, were forgotten. When asked whether the natives were armed, and in what manner, Banks said dismissively that, 'they were armed with spears headed with fish bones but none of them we saw in Botany Bay appeared at all formidable'.

The question on which the legality of any future occupation hinged was asked. 'Do you apprehend, in Case it was resolved to send Convicts there, any District of the Country might be obtained by Cession or purchase?' Banks replied that 'there was no probability while we were there of obtaining anything either by Cession or purchase as there was nothing we could offer that they would take except provisions and those we wanted ourselves'. He also commented that 'from the experience I have had of the Natives of another part of the coast [Endeavour River] I am inclined to believe that they would speedily abandon the country to the newcomers'. The die was cast. The Committee accepted the wisdom of the very grand President of the Royal Society, now Sir Joseph, having had a baronetcy conferred upon him in 1781. New South Wales was effectively *terra nullius*, and would wait for the whites.

Banks also assumed that the interior of the continent was uninhabited, although he had no direct evidence for this. In his journal he had noted that:

> ... the wild produce of the Land alone seems scarce able to support them at all seasons, at least I do not remember to have read of any inland nation who did not cultivate the ground more or less, even the North Americans who were so well versd in hunting sowd their Maize. But should a people live inland who supported themselves by cultivation these inhabitants of the sea coast must certainly have learn'd to imitate them in some degree at least, otherwise their reason must be suppos'd to hold a rank little superior to that of monkies.

Despite the stepping stones thrown towards it — a place portrayed as empty and fertile — the Commons Committee's report was not immediately acted upon. Meanwhile, the Committee opposed the government's River Gambia site in Africa, denounced the hulks as a public nuisance and praised the advantages of transportation, which it said was cheap, dispersed criminals, routed gangs and reformed wrongdoers through advantageous work. Further consideration was given to Botany Bay, but it was again put aside on the grounds of distance and unsuitability for trade. Other sites pondered included India, Madagascar, Tristan da Cunha and Algiers.

Early in 1786 there was another strong petition against the hulks. In June the government was considering the West Indies, Canada and Africa. Das Voltas Bay, at the mouth of the Orange River, on the west coast of Africa, was the favoured site — until a ship sent to reconnoitre gave a damning report. The African scheme was rejected on 18 August 1786 and the next day the Cabinet finally approved an outline plan to colonise the east coast of New South Wales — convicts were to be sent, after all, to Sir Joseph's Botany Bay. The decision may have been helped by Lord Hawkesbury, at the same time, licensing the firm of whalers, Enderby & Sons, to expand British whaling in the southern hemisphere by whittling down the monopoly of the East India

THE FLOWER CHAIN

Company. Whalers and sealers were soon to join the convicts on the route to Botany Bay.

Within months of the decision, Captain Arthur Phillip was commissioned as the founding Governor of New South Wales. He was to lead the First Fleet, composed solely of sailors, officials and convicts, to this unknown land. His territory was defined as extending from Cape York in the north to South Cape in the south, and westwards as far as the 135th degree of longitude. It included all the islands in the Pacific from latitude 10° 37' S to 43° 39' S. New South Wales was to be a gaol of some four million square kilometres.

The philosopher Denis Diderot (1713 – 84), like Jonathan Swift, wrote disdainfully about the arrogance of taking possession of countries by unilateral declaration. Could one discoverer lay claim to a land already occupied, however

Banks maintained that the local Aborigines were essentially cowardly and would pose no threat to the new settlers. This engraving from a drawing by Parkinson of two Aboriginal warriors gives quite a different impression.
(G. Badger, *Explorers of the Pacific*, Kangaroo Press, 1996.)

primitive the inhabitants? Was possession of an unoccupied country always to be recognised? How could Cook take possession of part of a continent already claimed, named and mapped by the Dutch? Or did their claim not cover any part which they had not sighted, forgetting that when he claimed possession, Cook was on the western side of Cape York, one of the first places reached by the Dutch? Anyway, if the 'sighting' principle was applied then what right had the British to claim the rest of the continent? As it turned out no other European power bothered to dispute the British claim to New South Wales. No-one else really wanted the place.

Was this general lack of interest, and the implication of *terra nullius*, the reason why much of the flora of Australia was overlooked and supplanted? Certainly there was no suggestion that the white colonists should survive on the natural productions of the new land and there was no time, no resources and no inclination to find out more about it. Banks had likened the climate of Botany Bay to that of Toulouse in the south of France, and deduced it should therefore support a similar range of food crops. Thus, the First Fleet, under Banks' supervision, was stocked with a wide range of European plants and seeds to be grown for food. Space on board was made for sacks of seeds, for cereal crops and for cows to provide butter and beef. Despite the fact that, 'the Proportion of rich soile was small in proportion to the barren', it would, judged Banks, 'support a very large Number of People'. He anticipated that the colony would be self-sufficient within two years. Although the people of the First Fleet were going to the southern hemisphere, their diet of beef, beer, bread and butter would be the same as in Britain. It was their grain culture which would supplant the indigenous flora. It seemed Botany Bay would be an extension of Europe in every way. Even the Seal of the colony — designed in England before departure — depicted Industry sitting on a bale of goods with distaff, beehive, pickaxe and spade, with oxen ploughing, habitations rising, and a church and a fort standing in the background. Although Banks had risen to fame because of his botanical collection from Botany Bay — which was still unpublished — there was no local plant, bird or mammal, and certainly no native Australian person, on the Seal. The Seal had nothing to do with Australia, but it was an imprint of what it would become.

As well as the Seal for the new country, provisions, equipment and convicts, the ships carried men with false assumptions. They sailed to that huge continent believing that there were only a few tribes on the coast, who would run without a fight, surrender or die out. The land was there, waiting to grow cereal crops, waiting to be fenced, waiting to be given by the Governor as a prize to good convicts, waiting to be sold. The Home Secretary was anxious that criminals transported to Botany Bay should never return to Britain after completing their sentences. They were therefore to be given land. Here they would be landowners; in Britain they were trespassers. It was on Banks' evidence alone that according to British law, millions of square kilometres were now designated Crown land. Title deeds and surveying instruments came on the ships. The Aboriginal people were now British subjects, their resistance would be dealt with not as warriors defending their country, but as criminals who had transgressed the authority of the Crown. Looking back on the settlement of New South Wales, Jeremy Bentham wrote, 'the savages of New South Wales, whose way of living is so well known to us [had] no habit of obedience, and thence no government, and thence no laws — no laws, and thence no such things as rights, no security, no property'. What chance did they have?

The First Fleet set sail for the other side of the world in May 1787 under the command of Captain Arthur Phillip. By the time the government had made a decision for the site of the new colony it was too late to send an advance reconnaissance ship as the pressure to do something about the prison hulks was too great. The men and women of the First Fleet knew virtually nothing about the land they were going to. Their perceptions of Botany Bay were gleaned from Joseph Banks' recollection of his six-day stay there seventeen years previously, and from the sole book available, Hawkesworth's glorified and inaccurate amalgam of the journals of Cook and Banks, published in 1773. James Mario Matra, perhaps the only man available who had

THE FLOWER CHAIN

actually been to Botany Bay, and had shown a desire to be involved in its colonisation, was not chosen to go with the First Fleet. Not one person who had ever been to Australia travelled with those first ships to the promised land. No-one really knew where they were going. They went equipped with all manner of alien seeds and plants. Additional plants from the Cape of Good Hope and Rio de Janeiro supplemented their supplies with such exotics as citrus fruits, coffee and maize. They went equipped with eighteenth century European values and skills as well as foodstuffs. Their arrival was to change Australia forever.

14
Mutiny

While Banks was involved in the organisation of the First Fleet, another scheme began to form in his mind. When in Tahiti he had been fascinated by the beautiful breadfruit trees that grew there in abundance and produced several crops a year of large starchy fruits.

The breadfruit tree, *Artocarpus sp.*, is related to figs and mulberries in the family Moraceae. When it first came to Banks' attention, its many varieties were widespread in hot, moist areas in the eastern tropics, and had been grown in the Malay archipelago since remote antiquity. A highly valued and important element of the diet of all Pacific islanders, breadfruit became a curiosity in Europe after William Dampier wrote about it in *A New Voyage Round the World* and coined the sometimes misinterpreted name 'breadfruit'. He meant that the fruit provided the staple for the islanders (of Guam — where he encountered it) and, when cooked, tasted somewhat like bread — not as some people first thought, that the tree produced unbaked loaves! Breadfruit can be eaten raw, but the islanders usually baked or steamed it. To provide for times of want, they also perfected a method of preserving the fruit by pulping and fermenting the flesh in large pits. In this form, it could be stored for several months.

Banks observed the many advantages of breadfruit over other tropical crops. It cropped copiously virtually throughout the year, the trees were sturdy and able to withstand high winds, they grew quickly and needed little or no attention. He wrote of its cultivation and use in Tahiti:

> In the article of food these happy people may almost be said to be exempt from the curse of our forefather; scarcely can it be said that they earn their bread with the sweat of their brow when their cheifest sustenance Bread fruit is procurd with no more trouble than that of climbing a tree and pulling it down. Not that the trees grow here spontaneously but if a man should in the course of his life time plant 10 such trees, which if well done might take the labour of an hour or thereabouts, he would as compleatly fulfill his duty to his own as well as future generations.

Cook also commented on the fruit, saying that its flavour was 'insipid with a slight sweetness resembling that of the crumb of wheaten bread'. After his and Banks' return interest grew in the prospect of transporting breadfruit trees across the oceans to the West Indies, where they could provide food for the growing slave population. At this time the slaves were reliant on plantains and bananas which were susceptible to storm damage and which required the slaves to be given time off work to tend them.

In 1772 Valentine Morris, Governor of St Vincent, wrote to Banks requesting information about the possibility of breadfruit's introduction into the Caribbean. Banks and Morris were old school friends from Eton. The idea surfaced and resurfaced over the following fifteen years but no practical measures to facilitate the scheme were taken. However, news that the French were also planning to translocate breadfruit in the mid-1780s, coupled with food supply problems in the Caribbean, finally stimulated a revival of the idea in 1786. Local hurricanes had devastated plantain and banana crops and shipping of food had been severely disrupted due to the American War of Independence.

It was these circumstances that inspired in Banks a colossal scheme. Why shouldn't one or two of the ships of the First Fleet, being at that

The Flower Chain

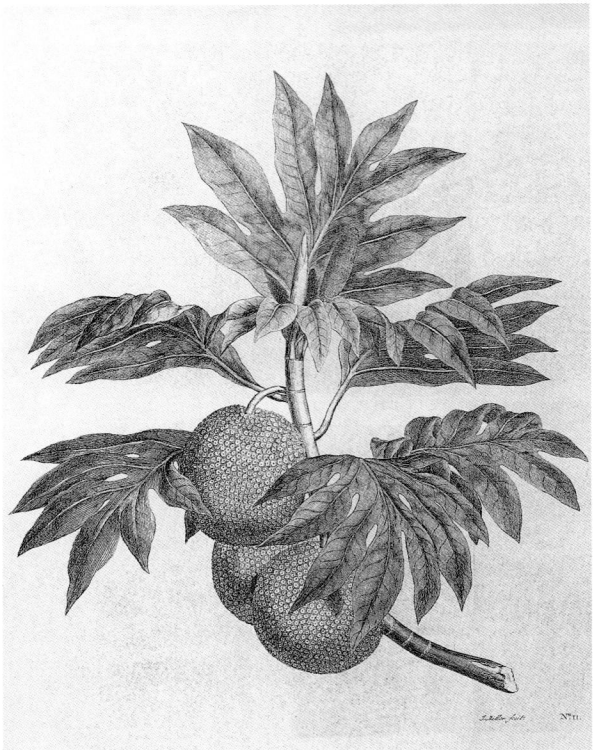

Nature's bounty, the prolific breadfruit. The fruit crop from a single tree could sustain a family for an entire year. Both Banks, and Dampier before him, recognised the value of this fruit in the diet of the Pacific islanders. (Linnean Society collections.)

moment fitted out for their momentous journey, sail to Tahiti to collect breadfruit saplings after dropping off convicts at Botany Bay? The ships could then take their leafy cargo on to the Caribbean. A gardener would be employed to supervise the operation and to care for the plants on their long journey. In a few short years breadfruit would hang off the fast-growing, hurricane-resistant trees' branches — cheap food for Negro slaves.

Moving breadfruit from Tahiti to the West Indies became another facet of the Botany Bay plan. Banks organised for two gardeners to be part of the complement. If the scheme had succeeded, these same gardeners might have had a chance to assess the situation at Botany Bay before they sailed on to Tahiti, and the First Fleet would not have been so badly off for botanical knowledge after all. Then, only nine weeks before the departure of the First Fleet, Banks suddenly recommended to the Admiralty that the two projects be separated. In a letter to his old friend Lord Sandwich at the Admiralty, Banks wrote:

> The plan of sending out a vessel from England for the sole purpose of bringing the bread fruit to the West Indies is much more likely to be successful than that of despatching transports from Botany Bay and I am inclined to believe it will be at least as economical.

Banks proposed David Nelson as the chief gardener and William Brown as his assistant. Nelson had already 'sailed with Captain Cook on his third voyage round the world in my service for the purpose of collecting plants and seeds and was eminently successful in the object of his mission,' wrote Banks. Nelson had originally been recommended to Banks by James Lee of the Hammersmith 'Vineyard' nursery. On his voyage with Cook Nelson had 'made acquaintance with the inhabitants of the South Sea Islands and their language which will in all probability facilitate his obtaining the number of plants', concluded Sir Joseph. Indeed, Nelson's experience would prove invaluable, but in a quite different context from that envisaged by Banks at the outset of the expedition.

A ship named the *Bethia* was purchased for £1950 and renamed the *Bounty*. Refitting began in Deptford shipyards in June 1787, the month after the departure of the First Fleet from Portsmouth. In August, 33-year-old William Bligh, the sailing master on Cook's last voyage, who knew the botanist Nelson, was chosen as commander. He was not, however, promoted from lieutenant to captain, and could therefore not have a complement of marines on board. The lack of an armed cadre of men loyal to Bligh was to have major repercussions. Among the forty-four strong crew was 23-year-old Fletcher Christian.

When Nelson arrived at Deptford early in September the ship had been transformed. The Great Cabin, traditionally sacrosanct to the captain, had become the centre of a plant nursery with a false floor with hundreds of holes to take pots laid across it. There was even an irrigation system. The ship would be a floating garden. It took months before both ship and crew were ready but finally the *Bounty* departed, two days before Christmas 1787, seven months after the departure of the First Fleet.

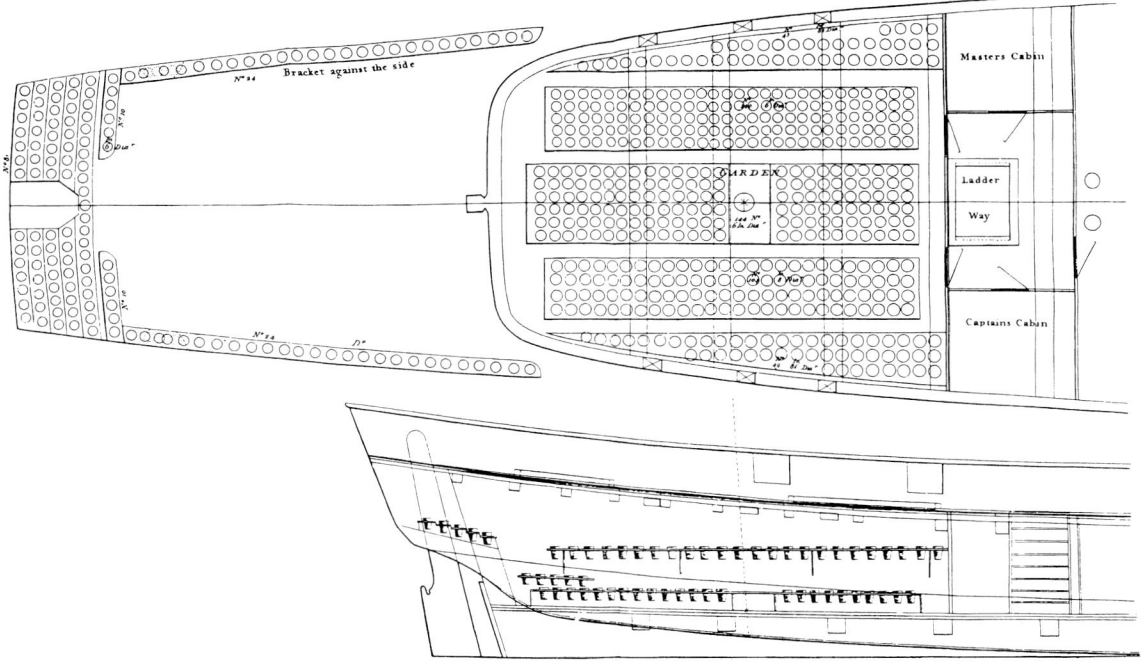

The *Bounty* was transformed into a floating greenhouse with the addition of a complex irrigation system and supports for thousands of pots to hold the breadfruit saplings. Unfortunately, the adaptations also made the living conditions on board far more cramped. (G. Badger, *Explorers of the Pacific,* Kangaroo Press, 1996.)

After a long stay at the Cape of Good Hope, Bligh headed eastwards across the Indian Ocean and finally anchored at Adventure Bay, Tasmania, on 21 August 1788. Both Bligh and Nelson knew the area from their visit with Cook eleven years earlier. It was here that Nelson had collected the specimen of *Eucalyptus obliqua* that was to be described by L'Héritier and eventually become the 'type' of the entire genus. During the *Bounty's* short stay in Adventure Bay, Nelson, in the tradition of travellers, planted a garden of fruits and vegetables.

The *Bounty* enjoyed an uneventful voyage on to Tahiti and anchored at Matavai Bay at the end of October. A camp was established ashore, and another British garden was dug. Bligh wrote in his journal, '... and as I had collected a large assortment of Seeds at the Cape of Good Hope, a quantity of each kind was sown'. He told the chief that 'All these good things [were] sent by King George to his friends at Matavai', and suggested that in return they might send the King some breadfruit as a present.

Nelson and Brown began the task of digging up the shoots that sprouted from the roots of breadfruit trees, planting them in pots with soil, then waiting to see which failed or survived. Those that did not establish were replaced until just over a thousand were growing in pots. Nelson reported that two fine shaddock trees that he had planted there in 1777, were 'full of fruit'. During the five months of this gardening activity, most of the men lived an indulgent life ashore with island women. But the idyll had to end.

Literally stacked to the gunwales with plants, the *Bounty* sailed at sunset on 4 April 1789. On board there were 1015 healthy breadfruit plants. Seven hundred other plants had also been collected and potted for Kew by Nelson and Brown, most of them representing the lush tropical vegetative cover of the island. Bligh reported that 'all these I was particularly recommended to collect by my worthy friend Sir Joseph Banks'.

Twenty-three days into the voyage there was a dispute over coconuts. Bligh said that someone had stolen coconuts from his personal pile stacked between the guns on the quarter deck. He ordered every coconut on board to be brought on deck, and subjected each man to a mortifying cross-examination. Bligh called Christian a thief and other abusive names, humiliating him publicly. He then confiscated the officers' coconuts to replace those stolen, announcing they were to have their grog quotas stopped and their yam rations reduced. To protect their private yam stores, the seamen hid as many as possible. The atmosphere on board the ship was terrible. Christian feared he was next to be flogged.

The incident sparked tensions that had been building ever since they left Tahiti. The next night, the mutiny on the *Bounty*, the most famous mutiny in history, took place. Although the rebellion was bloodless, Bligh and eighteen men, including Nelson, were cast adrift in the ocean in an open launch not twenty-five feet long; death would come later.

'Christian was now in command and among the men left on board was gardener William Brown. It is often claimed that the mutineers threw all the breadfruit trees overboard, but this was not so. They may have disposed of some of the plants crowding the ship, but not all. The *Bounty* was remembered by islanders as a floating garden. The mutineers knew that in order to avoid the hangman's noose they had a life ahead as fugitives, and that these trees might well be their future source of food.

The six-foot-nine-inch-wide launch crowded with the nineteen souls of Bligh and his loyal men was dangerously low in the water as they rowed away from the *Bounty*. It sat a little higher, however, after their visit to Tofua to forage for food, as one of their number, John Norton, was stoned to death by the islanders. Bligh decided that his best course of action was to make for the Dutch colony of Timor — about 3600 nautical miles away.

It was naturally thought that Bligh would head for Botany Bay — half the distance of the voyage to Timor. But Bligh did not know if the colony had endured so did not risk the detour. He had a compass, a quadrant, a sextant, four cutlasses, a few pounds of salt pork and bread, 28 gallons of water, 6 quarts of rum, 6 bottles of wine, some coconuts and a couple of squashed breadfruit. High winds, high seas, lashing rain and hunger pursued them across the Pacific. Bligh weighed out each man's daily ration on makeshift scales of two coconut shells, using musket balls as weights: 21 grams of bread, 140 millilitres of water, sometimes 14 grams of pork — although it was quickly deteriorating. Now and then there was a teaspoon of rum, occasionally a boobie bird caught by hand. Entrails, blood and flesh were distributed and eaten raw. 'Our situation was miserable', wrote Bligh of their 41 day voyage, 'always wet, and suffering extreme cold in the night'.

After thirty-two days, the perilous breakers of the Great Barrier Reef were seen and eventually a passage was found through them. On 29 May the exhausted, bedraggled men, pulled the open boat ashore about 300 kilometres north of where Cook had repaired the *Endeavour*. Bligh called the rocky outcrop Restoration Island, for as well as refreshing the men it was the anniversary of Charles II's restoration to the English throne. They scavenged along the Queensland coast, trying to find supplies to take with them. There is no record of how successful Nelson was in finding palatable greens here, but Bligh recalled how the sailors constantly teased Nelson about identifying the plants. Bligh wrote in his journal:

> Cut down Palm Tree Tops [possibly *Livistona australis*] & found the part next the Tree good eating & did well to mix with our dinner & Stew. Tryed Fern Roots but found them indifferent [*Blechnum orientale* or *Acrostichum aureum*].

On 30 May they left the island just as a large group of Aboriginal men armed with spears and throwing-sticks arrived. Nervous of attack, Bligh found another refuge on a nearby island but refused to stay for more than a night. The tensions of the *Bounty* exploded again. The search for food was interrupted by the carpenter angrily challenging Bligh's command. Nelson remained loyal to his commander but, alas, was already weakening. The next day he was seen returning to the boat 'in so weak a condition that he was obliged to be supported by two men'.

Suffering from sunstroke and battered by wild weather, the exhausted band made the final leg of their journey north of Australia and miraculously arrived at the Dutch settlement of

Koupang on Sunday 14 June. The men, wrote Bligh, were so weak and ill, that some were 'scarce able to walk'.

Despite surviving to Koupang, Nelson died on 20 July 1789 of a fever caused by the privation and hardship he had suffered. Bligh repaid his debt to his loyal supporter by providing a grand funeral. His journal relates:

> The corpse was carried by 12 soldiers dressed in black, preceded by the minister; next followed by myself and the second governor; then ten gentlemen of the town and the officers of the ships in the harbour; and after them my own officers and people. After reading our burial service the body was interred behind the chapel, in the burying-ground appropriated to the Europeans of the town. I was sorry I could get no tombstone to place over his remains.

The genus *Nelsonia* was named to honour this man who had died while collecting plants for the edification of the botanists and gardeners of the world. Of the remaining seventeen men, three others died at Batavia, one disappeared on his passage home, and one died on the voyage back to England. Eleven of the eighteen men set adrift with Bligh survived.

The fatalities among the mutineers themselves were much higher. Within five years of casting Bligh adrift, at least half of them were dead. Although they had reportedly shouted 'Huzzah for Otaheite!' as they set Bligh adrift, Christian knew that British search parties would soon be sent for them, and if they returned to Tahiti they would be found and arrested there. The Society Islands were never even a possible destination for Christian. The *Bounty* sailed back and forth between the islands of Toobouai and Tahiti, collecting provisions — including orange trees which must have been from John Gore's original garden — 312 hogs and nearly a hundred hens. Eighteen mutineers elected to stay in Tahiti. The nine who remained on the *Bounty* were augmented by six Tahitian men and twelve women who agreed, or were tricked into, going with them. One woman had a small child. Christian and his fellow fugitives set sail in search

The beautiful genus *Nelsonia* was named by Robert Brown after the plant collector David Nelson, veteran of Cook's last voyage and the ill-fated *Bounty* voyage. Nelson remained loyal to Bligh and survived the open-boat journey to Timor only to die there a few days later. Bligh gave him a splendid funeral. (*Banks' Florilegium.*)

of an island where they could live for the rest of their lives without being discovered. They criss-crossed the Pacific three times, visiting the Society, Austral, Tonga, Fiji and Cook groups.

The ship was remembered as 'a floating island' upon which grew 'two large plantations' and which contained 'two rivers of water' — the pumps watering the trees. Full advantage had been taken by the mutineers of the structural refinements made to the *Bounty* to transplant trees. Although the original object of the voyage — bringing breadfruit to the West Indies — was not achieved, other plants were scattered by the mutineers across the Pacific.

Christian's visit to Rarotonga, which became the seat of government for the Cook Islands, is well remembered. The *Bounty* was the first European ship to visit the islands, so the mutineers were its European discoverers. Brown planted some of the orange trees ashore, unwittingly starting an industry. After the missionaries came, orange juice joined the pearl shells and copra as important exports from the island. The prosperity of the Cook Islands started with the trees from the *Bounty*.

Eventually, in early 1790, Christian located uninhabited Pitcairn Island, whose location had been marked incorrectly by the navigator Carteret on the charts. Landing was difficult as there is no sheltered bay, no corner of calm water. The sea perpetually pounds all around it. Even the livestock had to swim ashore through the surf and be hauled up the steep cliffs.

The fear of the mutineers of being found is shown by their ruthless killing of their dogs and by the burning of the boat — their only means of ever leaving their island of exile. Discovery by a passing ship investigating the sound of barking dogs or seeing the silhouette of the stolen ship would have meant arrest, imprisonment or even the noose for the mutineers. Their fears were very real. On hearing Bligh's version of events the Admiralty wasted no time in dispatching the armed frigate *Pandora*, under the command of Captain Edward Edwards, to Tahiti to pick up the mutineers. Two of Bligh's loyal men also went on the voyage. The *Pandora* found fourteen of the mutineers who had stayed on Tahiti (two had since died) and imprisoned them aboard. While searching for Christian and his companions the *Pandora* was wrecked on the Great Barrier Reef. Edwards did not release the imprisoned men and four of them consequently drowned. The others made a miraculous escape and, with eighty-nine crew members and the ship's cat, followed in Bligh's footsteps by making the hazardous journey to Koupang in an open boat. Back in England, the ten surviving mutineers were court-martialled. Three were hanged, four were acquitted and three pardoned.

Meanwhile, Christian and his companions were busily establishing their tiny community on Pitcairn. The work of Brown, the gardener, is described in John Williams' *Narrative of Missionary Enterprise in the South Sea Islands*. It shows how Brown laid the foundations of Pitcairn Island's self-sufficiency, in stark contrast to the struggle the colonists were having across the ocean in New South Wales.

Four years after the landing of the small band on Pitcairn only eight of the original complement of nine white and six Polynesian men were still alive. This was soon reduced to four. Most of the deaths were murders committed in a flurry of violence as smouldering racial tension and a protracted dispute over the women finally erupted. Among the first victims were both Christian and Brown, murdered by the Tahitians. On the tenth anniversary of the mutiny, just two of the men, both mutineers, survived: John Adams (alias Alexander Smith) and Edward Young, along with eleven women and twenty children — descendants of the deceased mutineers.

Young eventually died from asthma and John Adams, with the help of the Bible, was left to organise the inhabitants into the pious community finally discovered by chance by an American ship fifteen years after settlement. Captain Mayhew Folger, having delivered a cargo of rum to Tasmania, anchored the sealer *Topaz* at Pitcairn and found, to his complete surprise, the descendants of the mutineers living in neat houses surrounded by gardens.

Although Folger sent a copy of his log about this discovery to the Admiralty in London 1809, it was ignored — the *Bounty* was old news and no ship was sent to arrest the last mutineer.

William Bligh, a brilliant navigator and survivor of three mutinies against him. He was absolved of blame for the *Bounty* mutiny and went on to successfully introduce breadfruit to the Caribbean and to become Governor of New South Wales. (G. Badger, *Explorers of the Pacific*, Kangaroo Press, 1996.)

Eventually two British frigates the *Briton* and the *Targus* went to Pitcairn in 1814 and the islanders became celebrities. Even Queen Victoria later sent the grand-daughters of the mutineers a piano.

One wonders if the little community of mutineers and Polynesians on Pitcairn Island would have survived if one of its trailblazers in 1789 had not been the gardener William Brown. He had the practical skill to plant and tend the crops, trees and vegetables. On windswept, rocky Pitcairn he established the horticulture that enabled them to become rapidly self-sufficient. Once peace had been established, the expanding community survived without boats bringing supplies for over fifty years.

Bligh was unable to give evidence at the court martial in London of the recovered mutineers because, with true British fortitude, he was leading another breadfruit expedition at the time. With another ship, the *Providence*, another crew, and another two gardeners he returned to Tahiti, again via Adventure Bay in Tasmania, to collect more trees. Also on board was the young Matthew Flinders who would have his own role to play in the discovery of the Australian flora in the opening years of the nineteenth century. The *Providence* voyage gave Flinders an unparalleled introduction to the problems of plant transportation. Bligh put the health of the breadfruit plants before the health of his crew. Men with parched tongues licked droplets of water from the leaves of plants when the ship ran short of drinking water. But Bligh's determination paid off — five years after the original plan was proposed, breadfruit trees from Tahiti were growing in Jamaica. It was a triumph in British eyes.

Bligh went on to have a long career, and to endure two more mutinies against him, on the *Nore* and during his governorship of New South Wales. Throughout it all, he never lost the friendship and support of Joseph Banks. If Banks had not changed his plans and separated the breadfruit voyage from the First Fleet, a member of the botanical team would have helped lay the foundations of Botany Bay, instead of Pitcairn Island — and what was to become regarded as the most notorious mutiny in maritime history might never have taken place.

15

The British and the French in Botany Bay

On 2 January 1788, three European expeditions were on the high seas bound for the Pacific: Captain Arthur Phillip and the First Fleet were fast approaching Botany Bay; Lieutenant Bligh on the *Bounty*, was heading for Tahiti with two gardeners to collect breadfruit for the Caribbean; and finally Jean-François de Galaup Comte de La Pérouse, commanding two ships and with two botanists on board, was heading for Botany Bay to witness the British arrival. By coincidence, it was exactly a hundred years since Captain Read, at the helm of the pirate-crewed *Cygnet*, had first sighted Australian land.

1783 saw the signing of the Treaty of Versailles, peace in Europe looked set to last. In France, the scientific community was anxious to catch up with British geographical and scientific discoveries gained from their voyages of discovery, particularly in the Pacific. They urged the King, Louis XVI, to add his support to a proposed French expedition around the world. This Louis did with enthusiasm, and the leading scientific societies in France devised detailed programmes for astronomical, geographical, zoological and, of course, botanical observations.

Although there were strategic and political reasons for a French presence in the Pacific, the scientific aims of this voyage were paramount. The instructions to the chosen leader of the expedition, La Pérouse, came directly from the King, and two ships, the *Boussole* and the *Astrolabe* were made ready. La Pérouse himself chose his crew and the scientific complement, including the botanists — Joseph de Lamartinière and Jean-Nicolas Collignon. The services of three artists, Duché de Vancy and the Prevosts, uncle and nephew, were secured. La Pérouse sought the interest and support of

Jean-François de Galaup Comte de La Pérouse, commander of the *Boussole* and the *Astrolabe*. His French expedition around the world was instructed by Louis XVI to divert to Botany Bay to investigate what the British were doing there. They arrived just a few days after the First Fleet and the French botanists on board were the first and only plant experts to investigate the area in the first days of the colony. (Linnean Society collections.)

scientists worldwide — Joseph Banks sent a flattering letter praising La Pérouse's abilities and arranged for the Royal Society to present the expedition with two dipping needles that had been used by Cook.

The elaborately equipped *Boussole* and *Astrolabe* departed from Brest on 1 August 1785, bidden farewell by the King and Marie-Antoinette. In the following three years they visited Madeira, Tenerife, Brazil, Chile, Easter Island, Hawaii, North America, Kamchatka, the Philippines, Samoa, and Tonga, as well as numerous other Pacific islands, gathering a wealth of scientific information. While charting the Kamchatka Peninsula, the farthest outpost of the Russian Empire, the itinerary was changed. At the end of the bleak Siberian summer La Pérouse received new instructions, rushed from the King by courier from Paris. He was to divert to Botany Bay.

Although at this time France and Britain were not at war, they still had potentially conflicting interests in the Pacific, and Louis XVI wanted to know what the British were doing on the other side of the world. Arriving six days after the First Fleet in January 1788, La Pérouse saw them depart almost immediately for Port Jackson, fifteen miles to the north. Despite the ever-present Anglo–French rivalry, in the weeks that the French ships spent in the area, contact between them and the British at Port Jackson was cordial.

The *Sirius*, the first ship of the First Fleet, had arrived on 18 January 1788 — the height of summer. Within days, a thousand convicts and their keepers in eleven ships from England congregated in the bay of Banks' botanical triumph. At a single glance Phillip and his officers saw that Banks' choice had been wrong, that Botany Bay was unsuitable for settlement. The land was perversely either swampy or arid and the supply of fresh water was poor, even when deep holes were sunk in the ground. Mosquitoes were an additional source of discomfort.

Despite orders that he was not to waste time searching for anywhere better than Botany Bay, Phillip sent one ship up the coast where it immediately found Port Jackson — Sydney Harbour — 'the finest harbour in the world'. Less than a week after the *Sirius* had dropped anchor, Phillip gave orders for the transfer of the settlement to Sydney. Although Port Jackson proved a splendid and sheltered anchorage, it did not have soil rich enough to grow sufficient vegetables or crops without manure, which was scarce as farm animals were few. Even so, Australia Day is celebrated on the anniversary of the day of arrival in Sydney Harbour, 26 January, not 18 January, the date men from the First Fleet first set foot on Australian soil at Joseph Banks' Botany Bay.

The excitement of the French encounter over, the British set about the uphill struggle of establishing a settlement. When the starving, scorbutic officers and convicts sat down to dinner in the new colony, they gnawed into a piece of putrid salt beef and bread made from weevilly flour, washed down with beer — rations drawn from England, the Cape, Batavia and later China. By contrast, the Aboriginal people, squatted around a fire to enjoy a varied, but to the colonists alien, diet of local leaves, grasses, fruits, roots and berries to supplement freshly caught meat and fish.

Ignorance prevented the colonists from enjoying the same food. The settlers foraged for what they could in the bush, but lack of knowledge meant that they found little to tempt their appetites. When the First Fleet set off from England for its strange destination, it did not have a botanist, horticulturist, competent farmer or gardener — either convict or free — to evaluate the land or find edible, nutritious plants. Omitting to dispatch a botanist was curious, as it was relatively commonplace by this time for ships to carry such experts.

For early settlers in this land so far from England there were vital reasons for examining and assessing the vegetation. No advance party had analysed the soil, identified the edible plants or ascertained whether European crops would prosper. Food had to be grown, and native plants might prove a useful resource. Timber was needed to build houses and some unique species, perhaps a medicinal plant or wood, might provide valuable exports if only they were known about. It seems incredible that Banks, always so keen to send gardeners, botanists and plant collectors to far-flung places across the globe, did not acknowledge this. Given his important involvement in the fitting out of the First Fleet it is out of character that he did not use his influence to get a botanist of some description on board, even if only to collect plants for his own herbarium and the King's gardens at Kew. Did he perhaps feel that with David Nelson and William Brown about to be dispatched on the *Bounty*, there were no other suitable men available?

Arriving in the scorching heat of January, the convicts were hindered by the weather and uncompromising soils. They had little agricultural expertise among them and were bewildered as to how to grow vegetables in this unfamiliar earth. The tough hardwood trees felled for timber blunted saws and axes. For over a decade the colony suffered from threats of short rations, famine and starvation — all in an area which had supported Aboriginal people well.

Ironically, the only botanical assessment made in these first days was by La Pérouse's two botanists, who made some quick excursions around the area. They reported to Phillip that they had been unable to find the flax plant that Cook had described and that the British authorities had high hopes might prove commercial. But La Pérouse and his botanists were soon gone, leaving the colonists to struggle alone to establish their crops in this unpromising land.

When La Pérouse left, bound for the Friendly Islands, his final act, his last contact with the European world before he navigated to the Solomon Islands and shipwreck, was to deliver into the care of the British, a box containing journals and dispatches for France — drawings, paintings and maps about his voyage around the Pacific. Fifteen months later the box arrived in

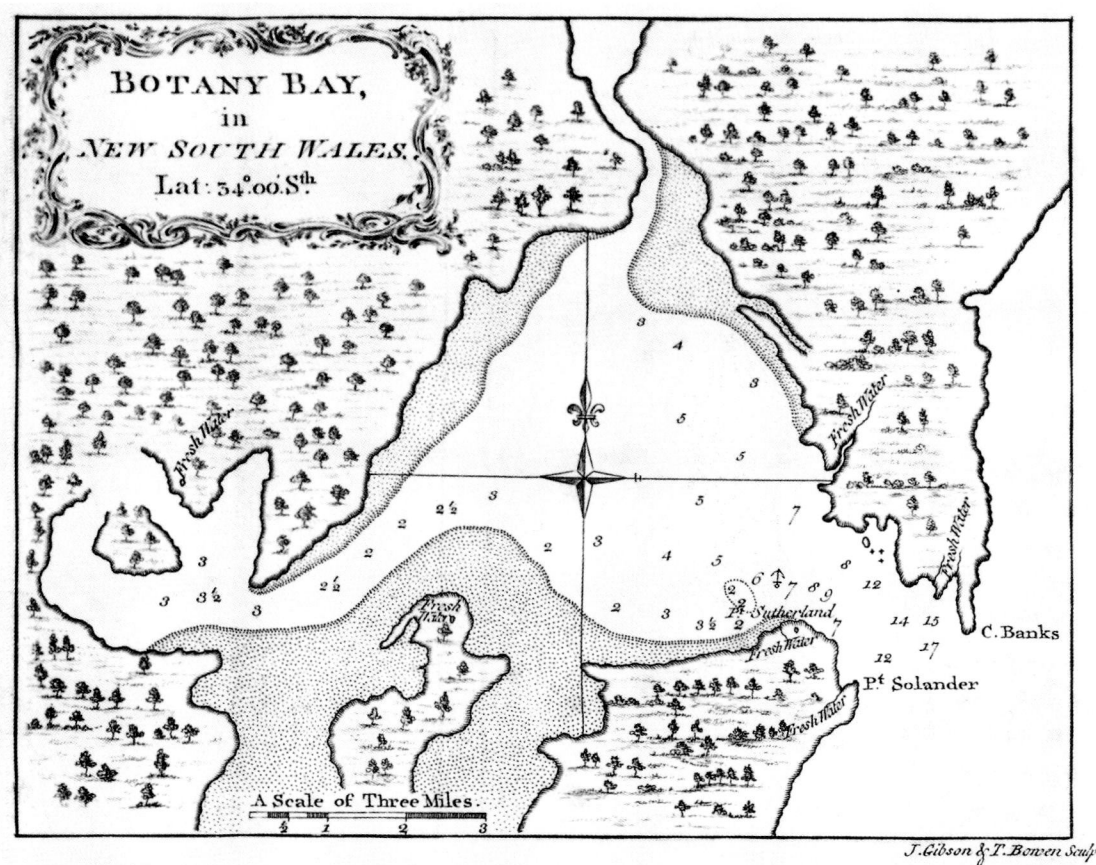

Botany Bay as charted by Cook. Although it presented a promising aspect, the land around it proved completely unsuitable for settlement. Contrary to his instructions, Phillip immediately sent a ship to investigate northwards and found spectacular Port Jackson, the future site of Sydney.
(Illustration from collections in the London Library.)

THE FLOWER CHAIN

This drawing of the landscape of New Holland, from Baudin's expedition in the early nineteenth century, gives some idea of the terrain the first settlers would have seen. Note the Aboriginal shelter in the foreground. (Linnean Society collections.)

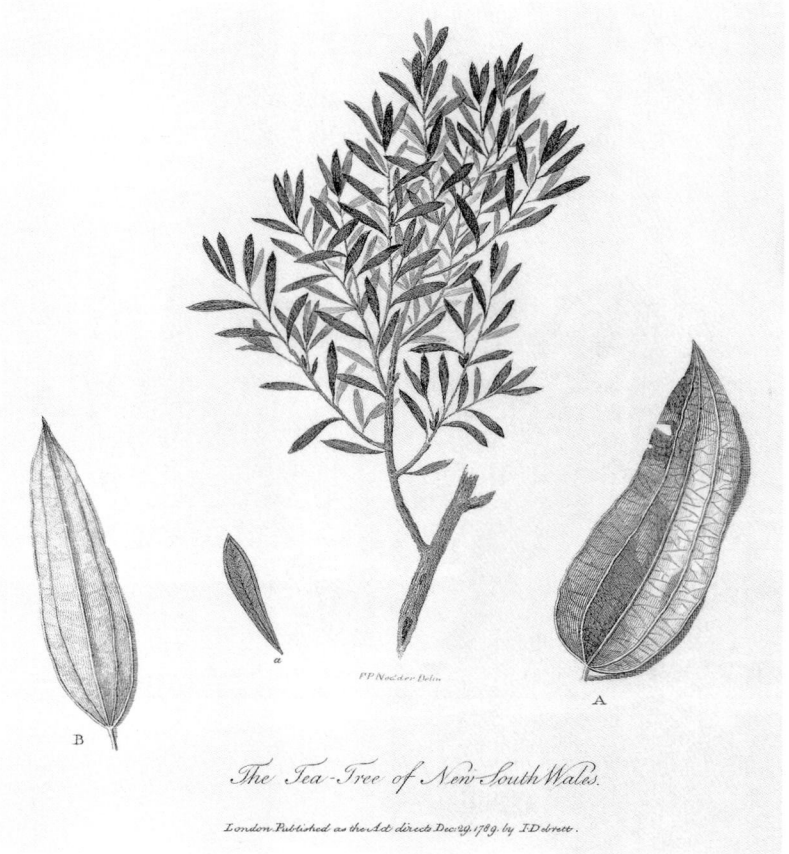

The local flora was generally cleared by the settlers without regard for its appearance or potential use. Surgeon John White was one of the few who attempted to describe and find out more about the natural history of New South Wales. This illustration of the sweet tea tree *(Smilax glyciphylla)*, a source of sarsaparilla, appeared in his published journal describing the first few months of the colony. (Illustration from collections in the London Library.)

A species of *Oxylobium* was found by Nelson in Tasmania on Cook's last voyage. This example was collected by Banks and Solander and is figured in *Banks's Florilegium*.

Three exotic plants grown by Empress Josephine in her garden at Malmaison and featured in *Jardin de la Malmaison*.

ABOVE LEFT: Josephine was growing Australian plants, such as this *Leptospermum triloculare,* in her garden even before the arrival of Felix Delahaye as gardener.

TOP RIGHT: The botanical results of Baudin's voyage were disappointing. The most tangible outcome was the delivery of Australian seeds to the Empress Josephine by Captain Hamelin, who was sent home with the collections and documents of the voyage. Josephine successfully grew many of these seeds, including this spectacular *Hibiscus heterophyllus.*

LEFT: *Kennedya rubicunda* named after a pioneer of Australian plant cultivation, Lewis Kennedy of London.

Paris, a few weeks before Bastille Day on 14 July 1789. The expedition would never be heard of again.

Before long famine hung like a black shadow over the infant settlement. Hunger even drove the miserable guards to banditry: the first execution in the history of the colony was that of a sixteen-year-old boy who was hanged for the theft of food. Then six marines were executed in one dreadful batch and others were flogged — because, by force or stealth, they took food. In 1790 the food supply threatened to disappear completely. As everyone was fed from the public stores — which came from half-way around the world — week by week the rations were cut down till they were near vanishing point. At one point the daily allowance was so insufficient that work was almost halted.

When describing the long hunger, one Captain Hill wrote that he was 'little better than a leper, obliged to live on a scanty pittance of salt provisions, without a vegetable except when a good neighbour robs his own stomach in compassion for me'. If the plate of the second captain in the regiment was so bare, the convicts were even worse off.

Their haggard faces sallow and drawn, their eyes lustreless and encircled by dark rings, 'sullen Convicts [dragging] the clanking chain', became victims of scurvy. Yet, the British government was spending £35 per year on every convict, far more than the cost of keeping them in the hulks. According to an estimate published in England in 1791, the 2029 convicts shipped to that date had cost Great Britain £300 per man. With such a huge amount invested in the colony, why omit the simple measure of sending a botanist to discover local resources, or a horticulturist to help grow vegetables, or a few genuine farmers to till the soil and instruct others in what should be done to make the most of local conditions?

Governor Phillip excused the convicts from work on Saturday afternoons so that they could tend their own vegetable gardens and, whenever possible, they were sent out fishing or into the bush to hunt kangaroos. John White, the Surgeon-General to the First Fleet describes in his book *A Journal of a Voyage to New South Wales*, the danger to the men in foraging parties of being attacked by Aborigines. He wrote about debility due to scurvy preventing convicts from undergoing the entirety of their five hundred lashes, and about men becoming 'so hardened in weakness and depravity ... that they seem insensible to the fear of corporal punishment, or even death itself'.

Captain Watkin Tench, commander of a detachment of marines, also gave a graphic account of the colony's first days. He stated how he cannot but regret that 'an experienced botanist was not sent out'. He was echoing the sentiments of Arthur Phillip. The far-sighted future governor had argued strongly that an advance party should be sent to New South Wales to build huts and cultivate vegetables so that the new settlers would have some protection against starvation and the ravages of scurvy when they first arrived. Such measures, however, would have delayed the departure of the fleet to an unacceptable extent, and the request was refused. The authorities were desperate both to empty the hulks of their prisoners and get the convicts disembarked in New South Wales in time for the fleet to sail on to China and pick up the tea crop destined for Europe.

Phillip had to make do with what he was given, but his reports back to the government are full of problems that could have been avoided if the equipping of the fleet had been more thorough. As early as May 1788 he wrote to Lord Sydney:

> It is not ... in my power to give more than a very superficial account of the produce of this country, which has such a variety of plants that I cannot, with all my ignorance, help being convinced that it merits the attention of the naturalist and the botanist.

He pointedly commented that, 'being myself without the smallest knowledge of botany I am without one botanist, or even an intelligent gardener, in the colony'. He made reference to the relatively unsuccessful attempts of the untrained convicts to find local plants they could live on and begged that few new convicts be sent out unless they be 'farmers who can support themselves and assist in supporting others'. He went on to add that 'if 50 farmers were sent out with their families they would do more in one year in rendering this colony independent of the mother country, *as to provisions* than 1000 convicts'.

The bitter complaints of Phillip and others filtered back to Britain and Banks organised for two plant collectors to be sent to New South Wales on the supply ship *Guardian* in 1789. Their detailed instructions from Banks were concerned with the care of the plants being sent to the colony, and the care and collection of plants to be sent back to Banks. There was no mention of assessing the vegetation for the benefit of the settlers. However, George Austin and James Smith had no chance to fulfil either task, for they were drowned when the *Guardian* was wrecked at the Cape of Good Hope on her outward journey. In September 1791 the *Gorgon*, sent as a replacement for the *Guardian*, disembarked gardener David Burton at Port Jackson. Burton's official post was as Supervisor of Convicts but he was at Phillip's disposal to undertake a botanical and agricultural survey of the colony. Burton, related to James Lee the Hammersmith nurseryman, was also under instructions from Banks to make and send collections to London. Although Burton did manage to report some of his findings to Banks, his contribution to the knowledge of Australia's flora was cruelly cut short when he died in April 1792 as a result of a freak shooting accident. After these abortive attempts Banks did not send other collectors to the colony until the next century when Robert Brown travelled with Matthew Flinders on the *Investigator*, and George Caley was sent to New South Wales.

It was not only Australia's botanical productions that were ignored in the early years. By the time the First Fleet disgorged its convicts into their harsh new prison camp, other British colonies were already providing wealth. Australia would have to produce something special to make the long sea transport to Europe worthwhile, yet no experts were sent to assess Australia's natural resources. Tench remarked:

> Previous to leaving England I remember to have frequently heard it asserted that the discovery of mines was one of the secondary objects of the expedition. Perhaps there are mines, but ... no person competent to form a decision is to be found among us.

The colonists found little of commercial use — even Australia's splendid timber was undervalued. John White reported that there were only three types and that it was generally so dense that it blunted their tools. Five years after settlement, a book appeared in London lamenting that in New South Wales no plants had been discovered with 'a proportionable degree of usefulness to mankind'. Australia would have to produce commercial commodities from imported plants and animals. The only way to make New South Wales self-sufficient was to cultivate tried and tested food plants from Europe, South Africa and South America. There was no time for investigating the native flora.

It was the aim of the first three governors to attain self-sufficiency in food but it was not until 1805 that the colony was independent of imported supplies in basic foodstuffs, and 1808 — twenty years after the arrival of the First Fleet — before the first government purchases of locally produced beef and mutton were made.

The British Empire, built with war treaties, words and guns, not discoveries, was mainly a collection of appropriated countries, discovered by other powers. The east coast of Australia was different. Its colonisation, which spread from Botany Bay, is a rare example of British development of an area they actually discovered and then occupied themselves.

For fifteen years, despite the horrendous problems and near starvation faced by the colonists, a tenuous foothold was maintained. Apart from the forty-odd square kilometres of rocky Norfolk Island, 1700 kilometres north-east of Sydney, settlement was confined to the plains and rivers around Port Jackson. The Blue Mountains enclosed the colony to the west, the Pacific bounded it on the east. British tenure was the equivalent of occupying Gibraltar or Malta and laying claim to the whole of Europe. This fragile claim led to a defensive attitude towards the French, the only European power which displayed any interest in Australia. No other country disputed British possession. The Dutch, discoverers of the northern and western coasts, never planned any colonies. Although, the French sent five expeditions between Cook's voyages and the Battle of Waterloo, they never seriously challenged Britain's supremacy in Australia.

Britain set out to turn their new land into a nation of small farms owned by former convicts. But Australia's nutrient-poor soils had never been subjected to European-style agriculture and the species the colonists attempted to grow were inappropriate. Without the time or the wherewithal to investigate the suitability either of the ground to grow European species, or the local vegetation to feed themselves and their animals, the colonists had an uphill struggle.

There were devastating ecological ramifications of this poor understanding of local vegetation. Settlers treated most native trees and foliage as an enemy, seeing nature as something to be conquered so they could farm. They gave orders to 'chop the bloody things down' before identifying what was being destroyed. The bush was regarded as 'wild and uncivilised', the prevailing maxim being 'if it stands still, cut it down'.

Seeds of European weeds were unwittingly imported along with those of intended food plants, and gradually these began to invade. As areas were cleared, and new plant species encroached, some native plants became locally if not completely extinct. Imported wheat, cows, sheep and a host of other alien species overcame endemic species at the urging of the colonists.

Far from commemorating the glories of nature, Botany Bay soon became a by-word for penal servitude and unthinkable physical hardship. Although Port Jackson was eventually chosen for settlement, it was Botany Bay's name that lingered on in British folklore as a horrific place of deportation; it echoed through ballads and prisons, evoking dread and fear instead of innocent delight in the foliage and flowers that inspired its original naming. Ironically, it was also the name Botany Bay that would represent the irreparable alteration and destruction of much of Australia's native flora.

16

The Surgeon, the Convict and the Gentlemen

In the first months of the colony, the vital task of describing, classifying and studying the uses of the indigenous plants of New South Wales was carried out by an unlikely trio: a naval surgeon, a London gentleman and a rich botanist, aided by an unhappy convict artist. The efforts of John White, Thomas Wilson, James Edward Smith and the reluctant Thomas Watling, all contributed to getting a small selection of Australia's flora and fauna described, illustrated, into print, and available to an interested public back in Britain. Their work appeared in various publications, including the first book exclusively devoted to Australian plants. This is something more than Sir Joseph Banks ever directly achieved.

The very year that Australia was settled James Edward Smith founded the Linnean Society with the collections of the influential Swedish naturalist Carl Linnaeus. It was Linnaeus' work on these collections that established a standard system of classification and the basis of modern taxonomy. Small though this learned society was, along with the Royal Society and the Royal Gardens at Kew, it formed strong links with the new colony. These three scientific societies had one man in common: Joseph Banks — the unofficial director of Kew and the President of the Royal Society.

Linnaeus had been dead ten years when Australia was settled, but his influence still spread across the oceans. His followers scoured the globe for flora and fauna, fossils and minerals, and attempted to fit them into coherent systems of classification. The building up of herbaria — collections of dried and pressed plants against which other species could be compared — was essential for the classification, naming and study of plants. Linnaeus' type specimens — annotated by him or his students — were then the most significant botanical collection in the world. Linnaeus also extended his work to the animal kingdom and his collections reflected the jigsaw puzzle of relationships between families, genera and species which would inspire Darwin and others to formulate their theories of evolution. Linnaeus left his collections of 9000 plants, 828 shells, 2100 insects and 477 fish, from all over the world, to his son, also a talented naturalist. However, the younger Linnaeus' early death left the collections in jeopardy. The family was in need of funds and the authorities in Sweden seemed little inclined to purchase the plants, fish, shells and insects for the nation.

When a letter from Linnaeus' widow arrived at Banks' Spring Grove home, just before Christmas in 1783, 24-year-old James Edward Smith happened to be breakfasting there. The letter was a request, following the untimely death of Linnaeus the younger, for Banks to buy the collections and Linnaeus' library for the hefty sum of 1000 guineas. Banks, for reasons of his own, decided not to make the purchase. Instead he threw the letter down and turning to Smith, suggested that if he wished to make a name for himself, he could do a lot worse than acquire the Linnaean collections.

Smith was then studying medicine, but his over-riding interest was in botany. The next day he wrote enthusiastically to his father, a wealthy Norwich wool merchant, requesting a loan to make this auspicious purchase. 'I hope you will look on this scheme in as favourable a light as my friends here do,' he enjoined. 'There is no time to be lost, for the affair is now talked of in all companies, and a number of people wish to be purchasers.' His father baulked at the scheme,

The Banksia serrata in Flower
London Published as the Act directs Dec. 29, 1789, by I. Debrett.

Frederick Polydore Nodder's detailed drawings of Surgeon John White's specimens, such as this *Banksia serrata*, were faithfully engraved for publication in White's *Journal of a Voyage to New South Wales.* These were some of the first images of Australian plants to be published in Britain. (Illustration from collections in the London Library.)

pointing out that apart from the expense of the purchase itself, Smith would need a small house in which to 'place so capital a collection'. He also doubted that the Swedes would, in the event, let it out of the country. Eventually, after seeing various negotiations with other interested parties fail, and realising the immense value of the collection, Smith senior relented.

In October 1784, twenty-six cases containing the priceless acquisition arrived in the Port of London on the brig *Appearance*. One version of the story of the transfer of this fragile cargo to England is that the King of Sweden, on hearing that Linnaeus' collections were to actually leave Swedish soil, sent an armed convoy after the *Appearance* to retrieve them, but to no avail. Smith hired rooms in Paradise Row, overlooking Chelsea Physic Garden, to house them. Here he began to arrange the books, plants, fish, insects and shells, aided by Banks and his librarian, the appropriately Swedish, Jonas Dryander.

Basking in the glory of his acquisition, Smith eschewed his medical studies and, employing a housekeeper to look after the collections,

THE FLOWER CHAIN

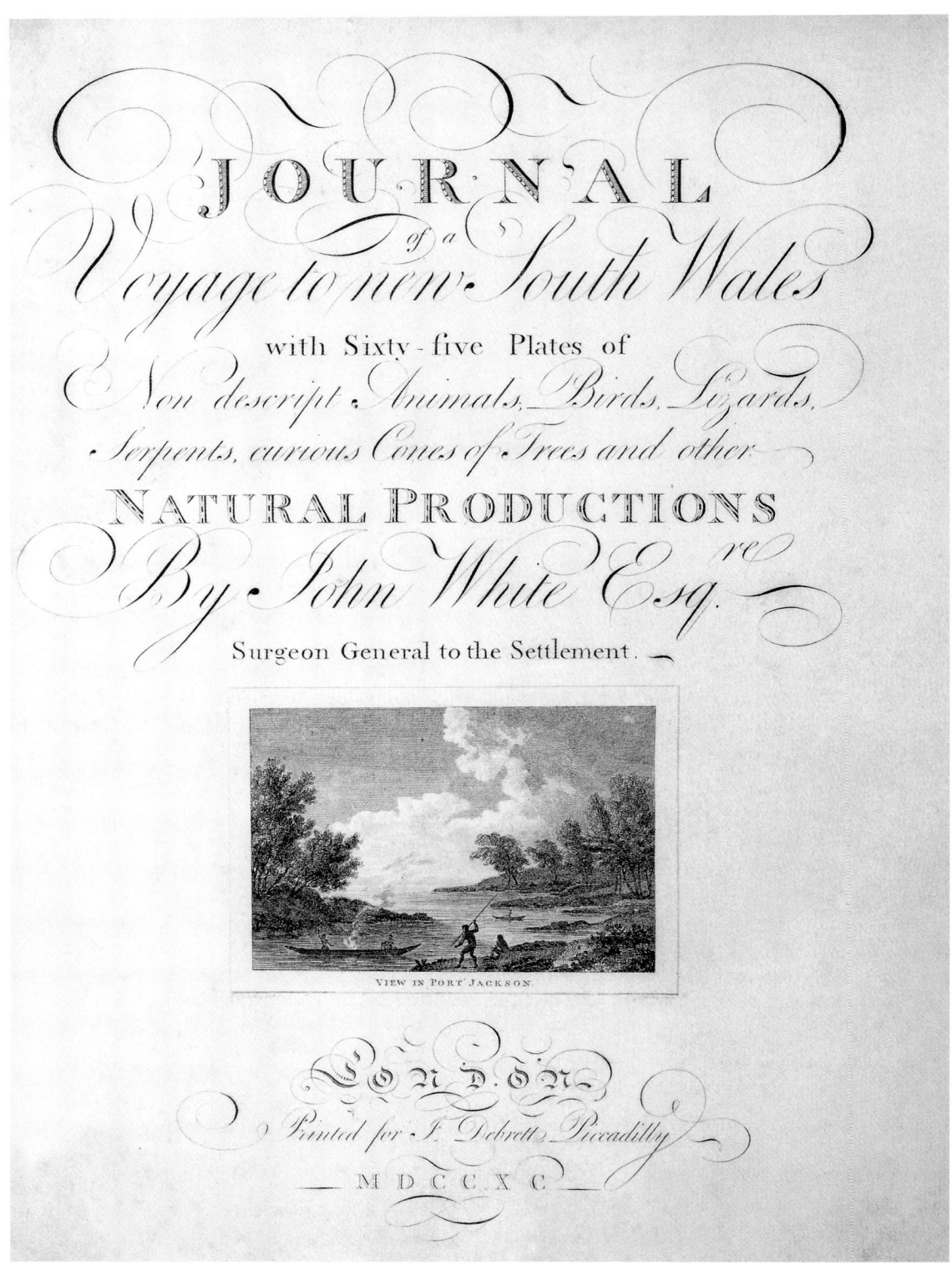

Thomas Wilson saw through the publication of John White's journal extremely swiftly. Unfortunately, the editing suffered as a consequence and there were many errors in the text that had to be corrected in subsequent editions. Nonetheless, the work was extremely popular and was soon translated into French, Swedish and German.
(Illustration from collections in the London Library.)

finished his education with a Grand Tour of Europe. While he was away he began collecting the further 18 000 specimens that he was to add to the herbarium over the next four decades. On his return to London, Smith turned his attention once more to the treasures in his Chelsea rooms. His dream was to found a natural history society based around them. With this goal in mind he moved to better accommodation in Great Marlborough Street. Plans for the new society finally crystallised on 26 February 1788, at a meeting which included Smith, Banks and Dryander at the Marlborough Coffee House. The first public meeting of the Linnaean [sic] Society of London was held at Smith's new rooms on 8 April 1788. Smith was elected President and he grandly declared that he held the Linnean treasures in trust for the sole purpose of making them useful to the world, to natural history in general and the Society in particular — aims that the Society continues to fulfil to this day. It is now the oldest society devoted to natural history in the world.

Initially, the new society competed in interest with the increasingly moribund Society for the Promotion of Natural History, also based in London. There was talk of merging the two but this did not happen until the next century. As the Linnean Society gained popularity the `leading natural historians of the day boasted membership of both organisations. One such, Thomas Wilson of Gower Street, was to have a marked influence on the promotion of Australian botany in England.

Due to the lack of any experts resident in Botany Bay, interested parties in England with a curiosity about the plants and animals of the new colony had to rely on information from amateurs and laymen. The best known of these amateurs, who sent both information and specimens, was the colony's surgeon-general, John White. His exact birthdate is unknown but White was reportedly 75 years old on his death in Sussex in February 1832. He was born in Drumaran, County Fermanagh in Ireland and after graduating in medicine from the University of St Andrews in Scotland he went to sea and became a naval surgeon's mate. Several appointments on different vessels followed, including three years in the West Indies. Described as 'a young man of much credit in his profession', and recommended as able, adventurous and well suited to take charge of the medical arrangements in a new colonial venture, White found himself, at the age of thirty, bound for Botany Bay. Between joining the Fleet at Plymouth in March 1787 and its departure on 12 May, he busied himself arranging medical supplies and trying to improve the sanitary conditions of the ships.

After his appointment, and before he joined the ships, White was in contact with Thomas Wilson of Gower Street, London. It seems likely that White already had an interest in natural history, and perhaps even approached the Society for the Promotion of Natural History, of which Wilson was an active member, with an offer to provide information about Botany Bay. White was elected to membership of the Society in 1789, during his absence in New South Wales, and Wilson asked him to write a journal of the nine-month voyage to Botany Bay and the first few months of the colony. Wilson also encouraged him to make observations and collections of the natural history. White duly kept the journal and in a letter he sent to Wilson along with the manuscript he wrote:

> As the following Journal was undertaken at your Request, and its principal Object to afford you some Amusement during your Hours of Relaxation, I shall esteem myself happy if it answers that Purpose.

With descriptions of convicts and kangaroos, hunger and hardship, floggings and punishments, the Aboriginal people and the myriad difficulties that the settlers faced, White's journal gives a vivid account of the voyage and the first months of the colony up to October 1788. Published in London in 1790, with 65 black-and-white plates illustrating the natural history of the new land, it was so popular that French, German and Swedish editions soon followed. More importantly, it included the first published accounts and illustrations of Australian flora. James Edward Smith, proud new President of the Linnean Society, wrote about four species of banksia, three eucalypts and the sweet tea plant, *Smilax glyciphylla*. For this we have Wilson to thank. In London he passed the Australian plants (with lay descriptions in English), seeds, animal and bird skins, shells and drawings sent to him by White, to experts, including Smith, for their opinions.

On the other side of the world White had employed artists in Port Jackson to draw the flowers and fruits of the pressed plants which were dispatched to England. Wilson arranged for further paintings to be made of the specimens for publication. He engaged five different artists, including the expert natural history illustrator, Frederick Polydore Nodder, who had worked on Banks' as yet unpublished Australian flora collection some ten years previously. The finished drawings were then engraved under the supervision of Thomas Milton.

Wilson, though, was a less than competent editor and the *Journal*'s appendix, with Smith's and others' descriptions of the natural history, like the text of the *Journal* itself was poorly organised. But Wilson worked quickly. He advertised the work in August 1789 and the first copies were available just twelve months later when a review appeared in *The Gentleman's Magazine*. As the voyage to Botany Bay from England could take up to a year — it could take two years to get a reply to a letter — it was an amazing feat to bring out an illustrated account within three years and three months of the departure of the First Fleet. Despite a substantial price tag of £1.16s.0d for a copy in boards, it sold very well indeed and the list of original subscribers included Sir Joseph Banks and Samuel Goodenough, the Bishop of Carlyle.

The President of the newly formed Linnean Society, just three years after the appearance of the Journal, published a much more comprehensive work on the botany of Australia using more of White's collections. *A Specimen of the Botany of New Holland* was the first work devoted entirely to Australia's plants. Smith dedicated the *Specimen* with the words, 'To Thomas Wilson, ESQ., F.L.S. at whose persuasion this work was undertaken and on whose friendly communications it is founded, the following pages are inscribed'.

None of the 'friendly communications' survive among Smith's correspondence at the Linnean Society in London, but one can assume that the President was in frequent personal contact with Wilson. No doubt it was through Wilson that Smith acquired the additional plants collected by White on which he based the bulk of the descriptions. He also had access to sixteen on-the-spot drawings, again provided by White. These were used as reference by James Sowerby, the artist employed by White to illustrate the *Specimen*. Sowerby, a founder associate member of the Linnean Society, was a distinguished flower painter and regarded as an expert on the depiction of Australian plants. Like Nodder, he had also worked on the completion of Parkinson's drawings for Banks.

Some of the plants sent by White are still extant at the Linnean Society — as are the watercolours he sent from the colony on which Sowerby based his illustrations.

In 1793 Thomas Watling, a young Scot, came to New South Wales as a convict under sentence of transportation for fourteen years. He was the first professional artist to arrive in the colony since its inception nearly five years earlier. Watling's paintings left vivid and accurate visual impressions of the colony and its people.

In Scotland, the very year that Botany Bay had been settled, Watling had been arrested on charges of forgery — for falsely presenting the Bank of Scotland twelve promissory notes for the sum of a guinea each. The Lord Advocate in Scotland recommended him to the attention of those in command as 'an acquisition to the new colony' because of his artistic skill. When he arrived in New South Wales he was not put to hard labour clearing and cultivating the country, but assigned to White to make drawings of birds, animals and plants (though his preference was to paint landscapes). In the two years he worked for White, Watling made numerous drawings now in the collection of the Natural History Museum in London.

Watling did not enjoy his indenture to White. He wrote to his aunt that his letter was being penned 'in much indigence, sickness and indescribable sorrow', in stolen hours 'by one who has to toil as a slave by day and [is] prohibited from such an attempt under the terror of rigid punishment'. But his pictures provided Smith and Sowerby with important references for the illustration of Smith's books on Australian flora.

Smith records in his preface that the *Specimen* was:

> An attempt to make the Public acquainted with some of the productions of a country of which they have lately heard so much, and in which they are now as a nation so deeply interested — a country too so extremely unlike those best known to Europeans.

He recognised that a complete flora was difficult, if not impossible. 'The present must be considered only as, what it pretends to be, a *Specimen* of the riches of the mine of botanical novelty,' he explained.

His fascination with Australia's flora, and the difficulties faced by those who would classify it, is no better expressed than in the following passage, prefacing his description of a gum tree:

> When a botanist first enters the investigation of so remote a country as New Holland, he finds himself as it were in a new world. He can scarcely meet with any certain fixed points from whence to draw his analogies; even those that appear most promising are frequently in danger of misleading, instead of informing him. Whole tribes of plants, which at first sight seem familiar to his acquaintance, as occupying links in Nature's chain, on which he has been accustomed to depend, prove, on a nearer examination, total strangers ...

Smith's work, however, reflected more than just an academic curiosity about the productions of New South Wales, it also had a more practical side. Once the colony had been established in 1788 a steady, and gradually increasing stream of seeds and live plants found its way back to England. Smith hoped that his work would 'inform the cultivators of plants concerning what they have already obtained from New Holland, as well as point out some other things worthy of their acquisition in future.'

Smith, concerned that his *Specimen* should be of use to his 'countrymen and countrywomen', wrote it in English rather than the customary Latin used for botanical descriptions. He acknowledged the interest in botany and horticulture shown by women. Such pursuits were regarded as especially appropriate for ladies. In thumbnail sketches of each plant Smith included useful details: preferred soil type; whether the plant needed to be grown in a greenhouse; and the rough form and dimensions of the fully grown plant.

Not all the plants described were in cultivation at the time of writing, but if they were Smith often recorded the name of the garden where they were grown. These descriptions give invaluable insight into the distribution of Australian flora in British gardens in the years immediately following the establishment of the Port Jackson colony.

Smith received, for instance, a living specimen of scaly pultenaea *(Pultenaea stipularis)* from Alexander Murray, gardener to Benjamin Robertson, from his garden in Stockwell. The flax-leaved pimelea *(Pimelea linifolia)* had flowered in the greenhouse of Lord Viscount Lewisham and at Sion House, the Dowager Lady Clifford had the only living specimen in Europe of the spectacular waratah *(Telopea speciosissima)*, now the floral emblem of New South Wales, in her garden at Nyn Hall near Barnet. At this point Lady Clifford's waratah, received as a living plant from 'Sidney Cove', had not flowered.

It was not just private individuals who cultivated Australian plants at the time — commercial nurseries also had some success. Smith reported that the cut-leaved embothrium *(Grevillea filifolium)* had flowered at Messrs Grimwood's, a well-known nursery in Kensington, in 1793. Smith made no mention of any living specimens from Kew or from Joseph Banks' own garden, but did acknowledge access to Banks' Australian herbarium in his research for the *Specimen*.

Although general interest in Australian flora was increased among gardeners and horticulturists in England, there was still a feeling that it was not getting the attention that its uniqueness deserved. Smith suggested why this might have been the case. Firstly he almost apologised for the fact that Australia offered few edible plants, stating that among the great variety of Australian plants 'there has not yet been discovered a proportionable degree of usefulness to mankind, at least with respect to food'. His description of the beautiful crimson styphelia (*Styphelia tubiflora*) suggested a further reason:

> It has lately been a complaint among cultivators of plants, that the vegetable productions of New Holland, however novel and singular, are deficient in beauty. We do not think the censure by any means just in general; and if it were so, the shrub here delineated might atone for a multitude of unattractive ones, by its own transcendent elegance ...

Smith did not stop in his attempts to publicise Australian flora to a wider audience. In 1804 he published his *Exotic Botany*, another beautifully illustrated work, describing 'New, Beautiful or Rare Plants as are worthy of cultivation in the Gardens of Britain'. He included many examples of Australian plants and again, with the cultivator in mind, made 'remarks on their qualities, history and requisite modes of treatment'. Sowerby was again employed to make the drawings, from both live and herbarium specimens, including those sent by White up to fifteen years earlier. His acute observations when making drawings were of use to the taxonomists. Smith recorded that it was Sowerby who first noted the presence of minute glandular structures on the stalk of *Dillwynia ericifolia* that were absent from dried specimens.

Smith indicated that a number of Australian plants were in cultivation in Britain by the beginning of the nineteenth century, just twelve years after the establishment of New South Wales. He mentioned several growers by name and referred to Australian plants being 'raised by many cultivators about London'. But despite the interest of some growers, the impression that Australian plants were generally not enthusiastically received persisted in *Exotic Botany*. Displaying the fervour of an evangelist, Smith attempted to convert British gardeners to the delights of Australia's 'fine species' — plants being entitled 'to a place in our conservatories' or 'desirable acquisitions to the gardens' because of their beauty or uniqueness. He bemoaned the fact that some worthy plants were not getting the recognition they deserved. *Viminaria denudata*, the leafless rush-broom, introduced to the gardens of Europe soon after the settlement of Port Jackson and successfully cultivated, 'is not now' reported Smith, 'common in greenhouses'. He put this down to the plant being 'more singular than ornamental'. Few Australian plants would become as popular, or as familiar a sight in English gardens, as exotics from other parts of the world such as the rhododendron, the camellia, the fuchsia or the marigold.

In *Exotic Botany* there is further insight into Banks' role in the distribution of plants to English gardens. Contemporary criticism that he kept all new plants for himself, or more specifically, for the King's garden at Kew, resisting requests to distribute them more widely was levelled against Banks. It certainly seems Banks was anxious to maintain the pre-eminence of Kew, but occasionally distributed seeds and plants to a select wider audience. Smith recorded, for instance, that Lady Hume had several plants of the eponymous *Humea elegans* flower in her garden — grown from seeds provided by Banks.

Mr Robinson's garden in Stockwell was an important source of live specimens, but in *Exotic Botany*, Smith also referred to gardens further afield such as the cultivation of several melaleucas in Cambridge. The eminent French botanist, Ventenat, received a *Melaleuca*, from an unspecified nursery in England, possibly for the Empress Josephine's garden at Malmaison.

About this time there was a new source of plants from Australia, some of which would end up in the Linnean Society. Banks employed George Caley, whom he had trained at Chelsea Physic Garden and Kew, as his personal collector, describing him as 'young, full of health, and abounding with zeal'. Caley reached Sydney in 1800 and went directly to Parramatta where he started cultivating a garden, commenced botanising, and began to antagonise his superiors. Conflict arose because his salary was paid by Banks personally, but his house and rations were supplied by the government. Considering himself only answerable to Banks, he often did not co-operate with the Governor, holding back specimens of flora and fauna either for himself, or to send back to Banks in England.

A former stable boy with only a smattering of Latin and Greek, Caley's contribution to knowledge of Australian flora was practical, not academic. Perhaps because of his lack of botanical Latin, Caley recorded Aboriginal names on his specimen sheets, thus providing the first real data for the future study of Australian ethnobotany.

Caley, fearless in his explorations, covered much new ground, especially around the Blue Mountains and stayed for ten years. When he returned to England — with his adored pet parrot and the Aboriginal tracker who had helped him on his tedious collecting journeys in the bush — he profited from the specimens he had guarded so assiduously by selling his collection of quadruped, bird and reptile skins to the Linnean Society. On his death in 1829 he left money for the care of his parrot, and his executors presented the Linnean Society with his superb selection of Australian timber specimens to join White's collections and Watling's drawings. These, though, were sold in 1863 when the Society decided to restrict its collections to those of Linnaeus and Smith, but in the sale, some of Caley's specimens found their way back to Australia.

With Thomas Wilson and James Edward Smith disseminated knowledge about Australia's plants, the Linnean Society provided a focal point for the study of Australian flora in England in the early years of the colony. Above all, the Society promoted Linnaeus' classification and taxonomic methods which his followers were applying to the increasing number of Australian plants that found their way to Europe.

17
The French Discovery of Australian Flora

During his short stay in Botany Bay La Pérouse sent two letters — his last — to Paris via the returning convict transports. These letters told of his plans to head for the Solomon Islands and the New Hebrides. 'I will go to the Friendly Islands', he wrote, before he sailed into the tropics during the cyclone season. From there he would go to the Isle-de-France (Mauritius) where he was expected in 1789. He never arrived. The ships were so long overdue that there was deep concern for their safety, especially by the Société d'Histoire Naturelle for La Pérouse's scientific staff of thirteen. Nothing had been heard of the ships since they left Botany Bay in early March, 1788.

In Paris, the Revolution had occupied public attention to the exclusion of all else, but now the Société petitioned the National Assembly to send a search party which would continue La Pérouse's scientific research in the south-west Pacific. A pitiful picture was painted of the possible survivors, stranded on an alien shore, 'their gaze wandering over the immensity of the seas'. The Société pointed out that if Britain could find the resources to send the *Pandora* after the *Bounty* mutineers, surely France could send out a search party for the worthy La Pérouse.

The National Assembly voted a million francs to send two ships, the *Recherche* and the *Espérance*, under the overall command of Admiral Antoine-Raymond-Joseph de Bruni d'Entrecasteaux. Huon de Kermadec had command of the *Espérance*. When they left on 28 September 1791 the plan was to explore the southern coast of Australia, then to sail for Fiji, following La Pérouse's probable route after his departure from Botany Bay. When the ship left Paris it was just two months after the King's flight to Varennes and the tense atmosphere of the Revolution was bought to Australia on the decks of d'Entrecasteaux's ships. The captains and officers were ardent royalists, while the crews and scientists were, in general, ardent revolutionaries. The scientists, as sons of the Enlightenment, were opposers of the *ancien régime* — especially the botanist Jacques-Julien Houtou de Labillardière, (1755 – 1834) — usually known simply as Jacques-Julien Labillardière. Felix Delahaye, the gardener-botanist, avoided being categorised as a supporter of either party. The invidious distinction regarding status and promotion rankled; there was plenty of scope for tension.

Antoine-Raymond-Joseph de Bruni d'Entrecasteaux, commander of the first expedition sent out in search of La Pérouse. Although it would not succeed in finding any evidence of the missing French ships, the scientific results of the voyage would be substantial.
(G. Badger, *Explorers of the Pacific*, Kangaroo Press, 1996.)

Labillardière, the chief botanist, was born in Normandy in 1755. Having studied medicine at Montpellier, and botany under Antoine Gouan, he collected plants in the Swiss and French Alps then studied in England for two years. Here he visited Joseph Banks' herbarium at Soho Square and even met Banks himself, an association that later proved invaluable to him. A collecting trip to Syria and Lebanon resulted in the publication of *Icones Plantarum Syriae Rariores*. Labillardière 'seized with avidity' the opportunity to join the Pacific expedition and ensured that he was as well equipped as possible, taking 30 000 small pins for mounting specimens, 15 litres of sulphuric acid, 11 000 sheets of drying paper and a vast library.

Felix Delahaye (1767 – 1820) came to Paris when aged twenty as an apprentice at Paris' Jardin du Roi, eventually becoming director of the city's Ecole Botanique. On the Pacific expedition his assignment was to effect plant exchange on a spectacular scale, introducing various European plants around the islands they visited, and to bring back seeds, shoots and young plants for introduction into France or her colonies. Delahaye was eventually to work at la Malmaison for the Empress Josephine, whose passion was growing exotic plants.

The expedition left Brest in September 1791 and the voyage to the Cape of Good Hope took a lengthy three months. When they arrived in Table Bay, a rumour was heard — although quickly denied — that Captain John Hunter (later Governor of New South Wales) had seen canoes manned by Admiralty Island natives wearing French uniforms. Although the information was suspect, d'Entrecasteaux felt obliged to follow it up, so a route was charted to the Admiralty Islands via the Moluccas (Maluka). But once at sea his slow progress forced d'Entrecasteaux to modify plans again. Supplies were rotting and so maggot-ridden he decided to follow a route similar to that of Bligh on the *Bounty* — across the Indian Ocean on the Roaring Forties — so that he could refresh quickly in Tasmania, and then enter the Pacific via the Tasman Sea.

Instead of arriving in Tasmania at Adventure Bay as they had expected, they found themselves in the ruggedly beautiful region near where Hobart now stands. One bay d'Entrecasteaux called after his ship, *Recherche*, naming another channel and island after himself. They continued on to Adventure Bay, establishing that it was in fact part of a small island, not the main island of Tasmania at all. They also made more detailed maps of the area than those drawn during the voyages of Cook and Bligh.

Labillardière was delighted with the flora and fauna of this untouched environment and collected *Eucalyptus globulus* (Tasmanian blue gum) as well as hundreds of other plants, including the old favourite of seamen, sea parsley, which had never been named before. He called it *Apium prostratum*, named so 'because of the position of the stem which creeps along the ground ... We carried a large quantity on board with us.' He also collected many seeds.

The expedition left Tasmania on 28 May 1792. Soon after they left Bligh would stop once again at Adventure Bay on his second breadfruit voyage. Two pomegranates, a quince tree, three fig trees, an apple tree (which died) and a few acorns were planted near a tree inscribed by Cook to commemorate his only visit there in 1777. Bligh too, had an inscription carved onto the tree trunk to mark his visit and to draw attention to the fruit trees. At the end were the words: 'Messrs. S. and W. botanists', referring to Christopher Smith and James Wiles who had been chosen by Banks to care for the breadfruit plants, and to select and bring back other plants for Kew.

Meanwhile the French sailed north-east to New Caledonia, passing and stopping at island after island in the search for La Pérouse, of whom they found not a trace. At the Admiralty Islands they had dealings with the natives, but found no evidence for the French uniform story of Hunter. They stopped at Amboina for provisioning, where they were received cordially enough by the Dutch, despite the deterioration in French relations with the rest of Europe as the Revolution progressed. In October they headed for the west coast of Australia, reaching Cape Leeuwin, the south-western corner of the continent, in December 1792. They anchored at the entrance to King George Sound but rough sea prevented them entering so they carried on, finally anchoring at Esperance Bay — named after their ship. Here they stayed for a week, going ashore several times. On one occasion Riche, one of the naturalists, went missing, and it was only on Labillardière's insistence that the expedition waited for him to be found, nearly three days later. Labillardière made exciting collections here, finding what was to become known as kangaroo paw, the beautiful *Anigozanthos*, one species of which, *A. menglesii*, is now the floral emblem of Western Australia. He also found two new species of banksia (one is now designated as *Dryandra nivea*) and a bush bearing edible fruit later named by Robert Brown *Billardiera* in his honour.

Labillardière's professional approach is reflected in the fact that he often recorded detailed descriptions of the plants he found directly into his journal. He had the following to say, for instance, about his discovery of the kangaroo paw:

> In those arid wastes, grows a fine plant which nearly resembles the iris and which naturally classes itself with the genera dilatris and argolafia. It forms, however, a new and very distinct genus, principally by its irregular corolla. I have delineated it under the name of *Anigozanthos*. Its flowers have no calix.
> The corolla has the form of a tube, the edges of which are divided into six unequal parts recurvated inwards. It is covered with reddish pili. The stamina, which are six in number, are inserted under the divisions of the corolla, which is placed upon the ovarium.
> The style is simple, as well as the stigma.
> The capsule is nearly spherical, and of the same colour with the flower by which it is surmounted. It has three cells filled with a great number of angular seeds.
> The top of the stalk is covered with reddish pili, like the flowers.
> I had denominated this species *Anigozanthos rufa*. [*A. rufus*.]

The expedition then returned to Tasmania, arriving at Recherche Bay on 21 January, 1793. The same day, thousands of miles away in Paris, Louis XVI went to his death, still anxious to know the fate of the man d'Entrecasteaux was searching for; he reportedly enquired on the steps of the guillotine 'At least, is there any news of Monsieur La Pérouse?' Oblivious of the turn of events in France, Labillardière found Bligh's trees doing well — apart from the dead apple tree — but the ardent revolutionary was indignant at the inscription; he objected to the botanists having to display deference to Bligh by putting only their initials and giving the captain his full name.

The expedition stayed in Tasmania for a month, getting on well with the local Aborigines. They left on 27 February and headed straight for New Zealand but did not make a landfall, hurrying on to Tongatapu where they took fruit and other fresh provisions on board, including 300 breadfruit tree saplings. They continued to New Caledonia where they were horrified at the evidence of cannibalism that they found. Here Huon de Kermadec died of an illness from which he had been suffering since they left Tasmania.

As the search ships carried on towards New Guinea, they sighted an island near Santa Cruz that they named after the *Recherche*. Never has a naming been more ironic. If only they had gone ashore the French would have found that it was on this island, now known as Vanikoro, that five years earlier, La Pérouse's ships had met their end, smashed against the rocks during a storm. At that point they might even have found some survivors. By a cruel turn of fate, the ships of the search party sailed within sixty-five kilometres of where copper plates, timber decorated with the fleur-de-lys, guns, bells and a silver sword sheath were discovered almost forty years later. Unaware of their near miss, d'Entrecasteaux searched the Solomons and the Louisades in vain during May and June, finally giving up and turning the ships, with their exhausted, scorbutic crew, towards Java on 9 July.

The two search ships, like the lost ones they were seeking, never returned to France. D'Entrecasteaux died of scurvy and dysentery on the slow voyage to Java where the expedition ended in chaos. In the span of four years after the departure from Brest nearly half the crew perished. Unbeknown to the weary survivors, Dutch relations with France had worsened dramatically in that four years. The ships reached Java on 19 October 1793 to hear the devastating news that France was at war; her King and Queen

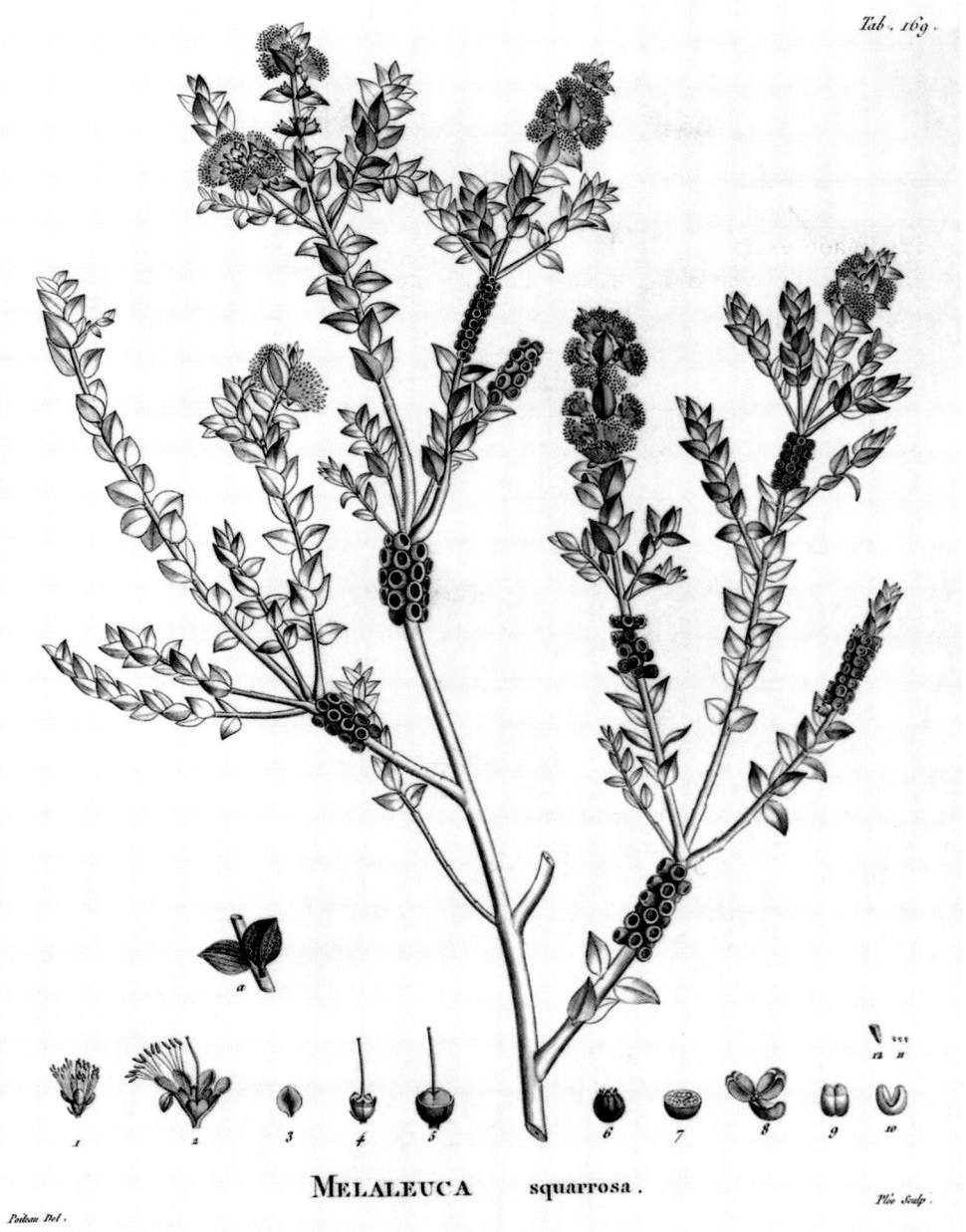

Melaleuca squarrosa, the scented paper bark, described and figured by Labillardière in his major work on the flora of Australia. (Linnean Society collections.)

had been guillotined; the National Assembly had been replaced by the Commune. The Terror had begun — some 16 600 aristocrats, artisans, peasants and priests would share the fate of French royal family before it would end.

Reflecting the violence in France, fighting broke out on board ship as the expedition dissolved into two factions, the republicans, led by Labillardière — who were desperate to get to the already revolutionised Isle-de-France — and the royalists. Anxious to gain support from the Dutch, the new captain, d'Auribeau, hoisted the white banner of the Bourbons with its golden fleur-de-lys, and had Labillardière's collections confiscated. The Dutch confused matters by not letting any of the Frenchmen leave. Seven republicans, including Labillardière, were arrested and marched for fifteen days to Samarang, over

300 kilometres away, where they were kept under house arrest.

It was from here, in April 1794, that Labillardière wrote to Sir Joseph Banks in London, thanking him for his advice in the preparation of the voyage but informing him of the sad news that his work of the last three years — his collections — had been seized by d'Auribeau. He enclosed a similar letter for L'Héritier. The letters took two years to reach 32 Soho Square and Paris. Britain was then at war with both Holland and France.

D'Auribeau died in August 1784 and his successor, Rossel, took over the Labillardière collections. He and other French officers, were finally given permission to leave on the *Hooghly* in a Dutch convoy of ships. It departed Batavia in January 1795, fourteen months after the French had arrived, carrying the precious collections of plants from Australia. Six months later, after many near mishaps, the *Hooghly* was captured by the British as it was leaving St Helena on the homeward leg of its voyage.

The captain of the British ship *Sceptre* seized Labillardière's collections, papers and documents from the *Hooghly*, much to the anger of the two French officers guarding them. Two weeks later, west of the Azores, a cutter came from the *Sceptre* to transfer the two French officers and their baggage to yet another ship. They were given no explanation for their transfer. The *Hooghly*, which had started leaking badly, was abandoned and set on fire. It was only because of luck and war that the Australian collection was not on board.

Finally, after this bizarre journey from the other side of the world, the collections were unloaded in England in November 1795. At this point Labillardière's original letter to Banks from Java still had not arrived. The French king-in-exile, Louis XVIII, expressed a desire that the collections should be given to Queen Charlotte, wife of George III, who like her former mother-in-law, Princess Augusta, spent much time at Kew. In March the thirty-six trunks were taken from the Customs House to the London residence of the royal French ambassador, the duc d'Harcourt, for safekeeping. The Queen commanded Joseph Banks to examine them and advise whether she should accept the gift. Banks quickly inspected the large collection as best he could without looking at the specimens in any detail. He had recently finally received Labillardière's letter from Java, written two years earlier, but had yet to receive a direct request from Labillardière, just safely arrived back in Paris, for the return of the collection. Banks wrote to the Queen's Vice-Chamberlain, Major Price:

> The collection of plants bears testimony of an industry all but indefatigable in the Botanists who were employed, the chief of whom [Labillardière] I am sorry to say was the principal fomenter of the Mutiny, which took place in the ships, built on the strongest Jacobin Principles.

He recommended that the Queen accept the collection and offered to select one specimen of each species for her, a task that given the size of the collection (he estimated about ten thousand specimens), would take him about a year. He did not suggest what might be done with the thousands of duplicates.

At the same time as Banks was assessing the collection, the Directoire appealed to the British government for its return. Banks then also received a personal letter from Labillardière requesting his help in getting his specimens back. Labillardière also wrote to James Edward Smith at the Linnean Society 'Please make, my friend, all possible efforts. You know how much could be lost for science if collections of this nature were not returned to those who made them.'

The battle over the collections' destination raged. One side believed that they belonged to the French Crown and should be given to Queen Charlotte as Louis XVIII wanted, meanwhile the French authorities and savants at the Jardin des Plantes, pleaded for them to be sent across the Channel to France. This row illustrates how plant exploration, botany and gardens, were a matter of state, and that ministers were no strangers to the botanical sciences.

A second approach was made by the Directoire to the British in May. They also appealed directly to Banks. Having appeared committed to acquiring the collection for his Queen, Banks then completely changed stance and began to work behind the scenes to get the collection returned. On 9 June he wrote to Labillardière that

The seeds of this plant were brought back to France by Captain Hamelin from Baudin's circumnavigation of Australia. Her botanist Ventenat named the plant *Josephinia imperatricis* in honour of his Empress. (Linnean Society collections.)

Charles Alexandre Lesueur, natural history artist on Baudin's voyage, produced some beautiful representations of Australia's fuana. Although not always accurate, they now provide pictorial evidence of species now extinct, such as these King Island emus. (Badger G. *Explorers of the Pacific*. Kangaroo Press, 1996.)

The beautiful Bougainvillaea, here illustrated in *Bank's Florilegium*, was named after Captain Antoine de Bougainville by Philibert Commerson, naturalist on his circumnavigation in the 1760's.

The French botanist Labillardière was commemorated by Robert Brown in the naming of the genus *Billardiera*. He was also recognised in the species name *Trachymene biliardieri*. (Linnean Society collections.)

members of the Cabinet were sympathetic to his arguments, and later that month got a verbal agreement from the Foreign Secretary, Lord Grenville, that they might be restored. When nothing had happened a month later Banks wrote to the authorities again requesting a 'speedy answer to this interesting subject, and to deprecate a refusal'. In early August an agreement was finally reached: the collections would be returned and Banks had the unpleasant task of telling the Queen that she wouldn't be receiving any plants from them after all. Banks wrote to his friend de Jussieu in France the same month:

> I confess I wish much to learn from his specimens some of those discoveries in the natural order of plants which he must have made, but it seemed to my feelings dishonourable to avail myself even of the opportunity I had of examining them ... all will be returned to him. I shall not retain a leaf, a flower, or a Botanical idea of his collection, for I have not possessed myself of anything at all of his, that fortune committed to my custody.

The capitulation by the British may have been an olive branch to the Directoire, as it was thought they might be weakening and about to reinstate the monarchy; but, it is doubtful that the incident would have been concluded so fairly without the intervention of Banks. It is also noteworthy that this correspondence was conducted, and a satisfactory conclusion achieved, despite the fact that Britain and France were at war.

At the height of the dispute, Labillardière had written a letter stating:

> I believe that to persuade the English to return them to the Republic it is essential to treat them as personal property, the war between us would be a powerful reason for the retention of anything belonging to the nation.

It is debatable whether the collections actually were the personal property of Labillardière, but his subsequent classifications and publication of the flora of Australia and New Caledonia, justified his actions.

The expedition in search of La Pérouse, like that of La Pérouse himself, had ended in chaos. Yet out of this extraordinary attempt at reconnaissance, in which so many lives were lost, came a remarkable haul of plants — the first large collection of flora from Australia, since that of Banks and Solander, to return to Europe. Thanks to Labillardière's unstinting work, it would also lead to the first major published work on Australian flora.

18

Spain and Britain in the Pacific

Despite suffering frequent near famine, a settlement at Port Jackson had been created from nothing, but the day was still distant when the colony would not have to rely on food from ships coming half-way around the globe. The port was becoming busy; whalers, traders and cargo ships found their way into Sydney Harbour including the *Atrevida* and the *Descubierta*, ships of the first major Spanish voyage of exploration to the Pacific for many years. Led by Alessandro Malaspina, a highborn Italian, the expedition was to provide the first opportunity for assessment of the colony by professional botanists. Malaspina anchored for a month in the autumn of 1793 and during that time, he and his crew were able to see and judge the new settlement at close quarters.

The Spaniards had been the first Europeans in the Pacific. For more than two centuries their slow-moving galleons, heavy with cargoes, crept across from Panama, via Guam, to Manila in the Philippines along one uniform course, thirteen degrees south of the equator. These galleons, unless diverted by weather or pirates — such as Read and Dampier — seldom strayed from their plotted route. The Spanish controlled settlements on the eastern and western shores of the Pacific, but they had not been near Australia since the time Torres, in 1606, had sailed through the strait named after him.

Malaspina's grand expedition, which sailed from Cadiz in July 1789, was one of the rare occasions when the Spanish officially deviated from the Manila–Panama route. With two graceful and splendid frigates, superbly equipped and staffed with scientists and artists, it ranks along with the La Pérouse voyage as one of the most organised and expensive-eighteenth century European ventures into the South Pacific. It was noteworthy in having one of the best health records of any of the early Pacific voyages: out of a crew and staff of well over 200, there were only ten deaths (from the usual murder, accident, fevers or disease) during its five-year duration. Malaspina was particularly successful in conquering scurvy, which usually plagued such voyages.

Malaspina was the perfect choice to lead this prestigious Spanish expedition, with its noble scientific aims: to advance the frontiers of knowledge. He had unrivalled maritime experience, and in the opinion of the Spanish naval minister Valdés, was the foremost officer in the navy for reasons of his 'knowledge, lineage, nobility and elegance of person and manner, proud bearing, firmness of manner and talent for society'.

The ships visited Montevideo, the Falkland Islands, Cape Horn, Central America — where Malaspina suggested a canal might be cut through the isthmus to link the Pacific and Atlantic oceans — and the west coast of the United States and Canada. They then crossed the Pacific stopping at several island groups and New Zealand before heading for New South Wales, where they arrived in March 1793. The expedition spent a month in Australia and then sailed to the Vavau islands of Tonga, claiming them for Spain, before returning to Cadiz in July 1794, via South and Central America.

The five-year voyage — it was not a circum-navigation — sailed from Spain full of promise with a carefully selected scientific staff on two superbly equipped ships. No expense had been spared in fitting out the expedition and the ships' identical crews of sixteen officers and eighty-six sailors. The French government supplied maps as well as details about the missing La Pérouse expedition in the hope that Malaspina might discover something of its fate.

There were two naturalists on the expedition of which the most eminent was Luis Née, a naturalised Spaniard of French descent. He had worked in the Royal Botanical Garden in Madrid during the reign of Charles III. The King's interest in botany is marked on the garden gates with the words 'restorer of the botanic art for the health and delight of his citizens'. He breathed new life into the gardens, and under him Spain was ambitious to become a world leader in plant exploration.

Malaspina wrote to Sir Joseph Banks in January 1789 about the scientific aspects of the expedition. He informed him of the 'two specially built ships which will set sail about the first of July [will have aboard] botanists and artists [to follow in] the trails of the later voyages, especially those that Captain Cook and La Pérouse have blazed for us'. He then requested that Banks 'point out any research — be it of a physical or maritime nature — that you might deem most helpful for this kind of voyage'.

Malaspina did not receive a response and wrote once more, on 17 June. This time he got Banks' reply full of advice and encouragement, and sent Banks a final letter just before he sailed. 'Nothing', he wrote to the veteran of the *Endeavour*, 'can dispute your right [to know] everything which pertains to botany and natural history in general from this kind of voyage'.

Nearly a year into the voyage a third botanist, Thaddeus Haenke, joined Née and his colleague Antonio Pineda at Santiago in Chile. This famous Bohemian intellectual had missed the ships in Cadiz, but was so keen to participate that he sailed to the Atlantic side of South America, then travelled by donkey, horse and foot across the Andes to the Pacific to catch up with the Spanish frigates then en route to Acapulco, Manila, Tonga and countless Pacific islands.

In February 1793, when Malaspina was off New Zealand near Dusky Sound, strong winds forced his ships offshore. He decided to head for Botany Bay. Judge David Collins, who was responsible (under the Governor) for the colony's entire legal establishment, wrote in his journal of the arrival of these graceful frigates, 'they were the two ships of whose expected arrival information had been received from government in the year 1790: and to whom it was recommended that every attention should be paid'. The letters from Malaspina to Joseph Banks four years earlier had paved the way. Collins continued:

> They were well manned, and had, beside the officers customary in king's ships, a botanist and limner on board each vessel ... The arrival of these strangers, together with that of the ship from Bengal, gave a pleasant diversity to the full routine that commonly prevailed in the town of Sydney; everyone striving to make their abode among us as cheerful as possible, and to convince them that though severed from the mother country, and residing in woods and among savages, we had not forgotten the hospitalities due to a stranger ...

The Spaniards were warmly received and there was much exchange of hospitality. The Spanish even killed a cow on board for a dinner for the British officers and their ladies. The colony, a little over five years old, made a favourable impression, especially on a jaunt up-river to see the farms established on the more fertile soils at Parramatta.

Haenke wrote to Banks from Port Jackson in which he referred to the colony as a future new Rome. 'It is difficult to express the longing I felt in approaching and beholding a land, a large part of which you once happened to see ... and which has added such a number of Plants to the treasury as to be judged worthy of being known by the name of the beloved Science of Botany [i.e. Botany Bay]'. He went on to describe the beauty of the banksias and how the number of plants surpassed their expectations.

Louis Née gave a detailed description of his own botanising in the area:

> I went out to herbalise when the rain did not prevent me. I usually started at 9 in the morning because before that hour the dew is so heavy that it is as bad as rain. I explored all the hills surrounding Port Jackson, collecting rare plants. One day I started to Botany Bay at 4 in the morning accompanied by two soldiers. I found

the narrow paths covered with undergrowth and the dew was so heavy that I was wet to the skin. The soil is arid and there existed no water except in a few ditches. Here and there stood a group of trees and some thickets, and for the rest there was hardly any vegetation. I saw a few places suitable for agriculture, among them patches of black earth but no water, and a plain of half a league wide lay between Port Jackson and Botany Bay which I think will yield wheat and barley. Various species of melaleuca, rushes and sedge show there is humidity in the soil, which is covered with vegetable moss ... Some half a league before I reached the bay I found a valley with an abundant stream of water, so abundant that it would suffice to fertilise the soil, a good deal of which is marshy and would be suitable for rice until the water can be drained ... Upon the shore we found three sorts of armulus [Armuelle] of which one was bearing fruit: three kinds of convoluli, one very like soldanella; two ranunculi and among many other plants three geraniums, one resembling coloured grass, and in the standing water some reeds and three new droseras. A little further from the sea there were casuarinae, *el mangle* [mangrove], which is also common in the Philippines, and various banksias with curious cryptogams. Such is the quantity of plants that grows there that, in order to classify and collect them, it would be necessary to live there fore many years. Having satisfied my curiosity and loaded myself with plants I resumed my way to Port Jackson. I reached the river again but could not cross it because of the tide, so I waited for it to go down, employing my time in increasing my collection by eight plants ... At last I crossed the river, collecting nine new plants as I went, and arrived safely at the town, where I dried and pressed my collection, robbing the moments from rest and sleep. He who knows what it is to study flora will be able to judge of the extent of my observations when he learns that in 27 days I collected more than 1000 plants of a new kind and of each plant various species.

Malaspina noted that the colony was obviously still very new but he was impressed by the 'corn, wheat, and barley, [which] though not too abundant, were giving signs of an attractive harvest ... The fruit trees, vegetable patches, and especially the lemon and the grapevine, gave new stimulus to the common activity and aspirations.' He was disappointed that 'because of this season of the year, the botanical collections of Messrs. Haenke and Née were rather sketchy, although both of them had worked very hard'.

Describing this extensive plant collection as 'a little sketchy' was too strong a criticism as it was from this that Antonio José Cavanilles published over forty Australian plants in 1800, including three important new banksias — *B. oblongifolia*, *B. robur* and *B. marginata*. He also named *Melaleuca quinquenervia* (as *Metrosideros quinquenervia*) because of its dark-green, usually five-veined leaves.

About 12 000 of the 16 000 plants that Née brought back to Spain (1500 of which were collected in Australia) are still preserved at the Real Jardin Botanico, Madrid. These were studied by Née himself and by Cavanilles. Both were quite old when they started to sort out the material and Née, who wanted to produce a vast treatise on his findings, died before he could publish.

Haenke's 15 000 specimens fared a little better. Most were acquired by the Prague Museum, and some were distributed to institutions in Europe and the United States. The major botanical results were published in the late 1820s in C. B. Presl's *Reliquiae Haenkeana*. Haenke had disembarked in Peru on the homeward voyage and never returned to Europe. His interest in South America was such that he stayed there until his death nearly thirty years later. The job of classifying the plants therefore fell to other botanists, who often found it difficult deciphering Haenke's illegible notes in half a dozen different languages jammed up on tiny bits of paper.

The notes of the scientists and the drawings of the artists were scattered at the end of the voyage, and it was nearly a century before a report on the expedition was published.

The suppression of the scientific papers was a consequence of the dashing Italian Malaspina's flirtations with the Spanish Queen Maria Luisa. The subtle power and vindictiveness wielded by the meretricious Queen, and her fat but weak husband Charles IV, were immortalised by the court painter Goya in his candid portraits of the two very flawed royal characters. Unfortunately, Malaspina was to fall victim to the pair's machinations.

Malaspina had sailed two weeks after the fall of the Bastille, and returned to Spain at the time of the Terror in France. There was a bloodthirsty reaction in Spain against liberal thought. Malaspina rashly tangled with chief minister Godoy, the Queen's lover, criticising Spanish policy in the government of its colonies, and even worse, competing with him as a rival for the favours of the Queen. She persuaded the handsome Malaspina to put his radical views in writing and to leave them in her care. He was critical of the 'closed shop' of Spanish administrative practice, pointing out the advantages of autonomy and free trade. The Queen betrayed him. Ostracised from royal circles as an insurgent, the seven lavish volumes of reports from his voyage, which would have included an account on the botany of Sydney, were abandoned. Malaspina was imprisoned in the castle of La Coruña for seven years. Forbidden — and unable in his cramped cell — to write up his own journal, or to continue supervision of the scientific results of the voyage, Malaspina fell into a state of melancholy. Banished from Spain forever he died seven years after his release — which had been instigated by Napoleon — at his home in northern Italy. Alexander von Humboldt (1769 – 1859), the great German scholar said, 'this able navigator is more famous for his misfortunes than for his discoveries'.

Malaspina's was not the only expedition in the Pacific during the 1790s, and the botanical results of a simultaneous British voyage, led by George Vancouver, had also had a chequered history. The north-west coast of America, from San Francisco to Alaska, was sketchily known and both Britain and Spain had an interest in the area. In 1789 a British expedition to chart the coast and investigate the North-west Passage was being planned when Spain's aggressive territory-seeking in the area added a political dimension to the voyage. Spain suddenly laid claim to Nootka Sound, a fur trading post on what is now Vancouver Island. They arrested some British ships there, much to the indignation of the British government. Diplomatic negotiations between the two nations over the so-called Nootka Sound Affair rumbled on for months and eventually, Captain George Vancouver, with two ships, the *Discovery* and the *Chatham*, was sent to repossess the trading post for the British. Vancouver was also to chart the coast and to visit Australia during the course of the four-year voyage.

Banks organised for the surgeon-botanist Archibald Menzies to travel with the expedition and in February 1791 sent him a long and detailed letter with instructions on plant natural history observations and on native peoples. He also instructed him to keep a journal. Menzies had experience of the north-west American coast from an earlier voyage which had provided Banks with many specimens. Menzies and Vancouver, though, got off to a bad start, and the lack of clarification of Menzies' status on board meant

Archibald Menzies, here pictured in later life, was already an experienced plant collector when he went on Vancouver's Pacific voyage. He made extensive collections in Australia on this voyage, as well as some perspicacious observations on the relationship between the Aboriginal people and the land.
(Linnean Society collections.)

that their relations were intermittently strained — in fact, so bad in the latter part of the voyage that Menzies spent three months under arrest. During this time his collections of live plants, assiduously collected and cared for, suffered irreparably. Despite his trials and tribulations Menzies managed to retain his dried specimens and manuscripts, duly delivering many of the former to Banks on his return. Among the collections were plants collected in King George Sound Western Australia.

Vancouver set out in April 1791 bound for the Cape of Good Hope via Tenerife. From the Cape they headed for New Holland — as the western half of Australia was still known — and sailed along the coast from Point d'Entrecasteaux to King George Sound, where Albany now stands. The expedition stayed in this florally rich area for just over two weeks during September and October 1791, and Menzies made some perceptive observations of the flora as well as collecting plants, including some new banksias. He made:

> various excursions around the Sound making copious collections of its vegetable productions, particularly the genus *Banksia* which were there very numerous.

He found the land far less barren than he had expected, being 'impressed with a very rich idea of its fertility from the richness and abundance

Menzies did some significant collecting at King George Sound, here pictured during a later French expedition. He also recommended it as a suitable area for colonisation. (G. Badger, *Explorers of the Pacific*, Kangaroo Press, 1996.)

anxious for a relatively civilised landfall. Instead, he carried on to Tasmania, New Zealand and Tahiti. Resuming the voyage again he sailed to Hawaii, finally arriving in the Juan de Fuca Strait in April 1792 after several stops on the American coast. Vancouver successfully negotiated the Nootka Sound handover with the Spanish representative Don Juan Francisco de la Bodega y Quadra, and they agreed to name the disputed area 'Quadra and Vancouver Island'.

Vancouver stayed in the north Pacific area for the next two years, charting much of the north American coast and revisiting Hawaii, while Menzies took every opportunity to botanise. On the way home in January 1795 HMS *Discovery* arrived at St Helena, just as the convoy carrying Labillardière's confiscated collection was departing. By a strange coincidence, these two important collections of western Australian plants, gathered by Menzies and the revolutionary Frenchman, briefly came together.

The expedition finally arrived home in October 1795. The strained relations between Vancouver and Menzies that had existed intermittently throughout the voyage did not persist on land and Menzies was allowed to take his collections. He immediately set about curating his specimens, comparing them with both Banks' and the Linnean Society's collections. He showed them to James Edward Smith, Robert Brown and W. J. Hooker who published descriptions of some of the new species. Although Menzies did not publish anything himself, there is evidence that he was preparing a manuscript on the collections but this has since been lost. Menzies' contribution to the establishment of new species described by others using his specimens still needs to be fully assessed. The annotations on his herbarium sheets indicate that he had his own ideas about the classification of different species. They show, for instance, that he recognised a distinction between the banksias and the hakeas.

A large number of the specimens went to his sponsor Joseph Banks, but these too, like most of Banks' collections, would never be published — yet more Australian plants destined to languish, undescribed in Banks' herbarium. Though some

Menzies collected examples of *Eucalyptus cornuta* at King George Sound, but never published his findings. Labillardière, who also collected in the area, included it, and several other species collected by Menzies, in his two-volume work on Australian flora, from which this illustration comes. (G. Badger, *Explorers of the Pacific,* Kangaroo Press, 1996.)

of its vegetable productions'. Menzies regarded Australia as 'a fine field for Botanizing!', and his enthusiastic reports of the flora of the Albany area would make it a mecca for botanists.

When Menzies found eucalypts showing evidence of having been burnt he speculated that the local Aboriginal people may have had some part in the burning. He also recommended that this part of New Holland would afford an 'eligible situation for a settlement'.

Vancouver elected not to stop at Botany Bay, much to the disappointment of the crew who were both curious about the new colony and

The Flower Chain

of the species Menzies collected were destined to be described instead by others, their own specimens acquired later. *Eucalyptus cornuta*, for example, collected by Menzies in King George Sound, was eventually described by Labillardière from a specimen he collected in the Esperance area in 1792. The same is true of the genus *Adenanthos*, a member of the Proteaceae family, which Menzies also collected.

Despite the huge potential of his collection, few of Menzies' Australian plants were ever described as type specimens. Even today there is no complete listing of his collections. However, Menzies also brought back seeds from the voyage, some of which were successfully germinated. Descriptions of two banksias, *Banksia praemorsa* and *B. grandis*, were made from plants grown from such seeds.

19
Australia at Malmaison

The latter years of the eighteenth century in Europe were characterised by an increasing political tension between Britain and France, culminating in the Napoleonic Wars. By coincidence, much of the Australian botanical work was being done at the same time, not by English but by French academics. Because of contemporary antipathy towards France, or perhaps because of the language barrier, this has often gone unacknowledged both in England and Australia — especially outside the academic botanical community — as has the Empress Josephine's enthusiastic cultivation of new Australian plants at her beloved chateau, Malmaison, near Paris.

As Felix Delahaye, gardener on d'Entrecasteaux's ill-fated voyage, sailed around the Great Australian Bight towards his Tasmanian garden in January 1793, 16 000 kilometres away in Paris, events that were to shape his future were also changing the social order in France. Louis XVI went to the guillotine closely followed by

Josephine spent a fortune on the house and garden of Malmaison, the chateau she bought outside Paris. It was in these gardens that she cultivated exotic plants, including many Australian examples. Although the house survives, Josephine's garden no longer exists in the form that she knew it. (Linnean Society collections.)

his wife Marie-Antoinette. Her garden, La Trianon, despised and neglected after her death, was eventually to fall under Delahaye's care, as was the garden of another French queen — the Empress Josephine's at Malmaison.

Delahaye's adventures in the chaos at the end of the voyage were less traumatic than those of his colleague, Labillardière. He had not been labelled a republican and was allowed to continue botanising in Java. After a pleasant sojourn collecting he was sent, with 280 living specimens — including several healthy breadfruit trees — to the Isle-de-France. The breadfruit trees went to French islands in the Caribbean and Delahaye returned to France. He also had some two and a half thousand herbarium specimens — duplicates of Labillardière's collection which had been taken to England.

Delahaye's return to troubled France took nearly four years, but eventually he arrived on the frigate *Cybele* in the spring of 1797. It was not long before this worthy gardener was appointed Jardinier-Chef at La Trianon in 1798. These adored gardens of Marie-Antoinette (1755 – 93) lie within the gilded iron gates of the palace of Versailles. Originally built as a retreat for Louis XIV in 1670, over the next century La Trianon expanded to include a botanic garden and La Petit Trianon, built for Louis XV's mistress, the Comtesse du Barry (1741 – 93). However, after the King's death in 1774 Madame du Barry was dismissed from court, and La Trianon became a favourite residence of Marie-Antoinette, the wife of the new King.

Marie-Antoinette's name is associated with frivolous extravagances in the closing years of the *ancien régime*; her garden at La Trianon was the setting for a mimic peasant life. She had the garden laid out in the English style, with rustic villas and winding walks, where the grass was covered with violets and daisies. It is this garden, not the grand French parks with their statuary, topiary, straight lines and formal vistas, which is always associated with the ill-fated French queen. For six years Delahaye resurrected it from the neglect and disorder which all Versailles suffered after the Revolution. It is now one of the most visited gardens in Europe. He also started a horticultural establishment in Versailles which

Empress Josephine, here depicted with the flowers she so adored, was a keen horticulturist. Her efforts in the beloved garden at Malmaison ensured the introduction of many Australian plants to France. (Linnean Society collections.)

his wife ran so successfully that it was later carried on by his sons.

While Delahaye was re-establishing his career, his fellow naturalist on d'Entrecasteaux's voyage, Jacques-Julien Labillardière, began his seminal work on their collections of Australian flora. Soon after Labillardière's return to Paris in March 1796, following his horrific three-year journey from the shores of Tasmania, he was off on another excursion. He had hardly had time to write letters to London, pleading for the return of his collections, before his great breadth of learning and knowledge of the fine arts was required by the Directoire. Napoleon, having successfully

The flannel flower, *Actinotus helianthi*, was one of the many new species described by Labillardière in his major work on the flora of New Holland. (Linnean Society collections.)

invaded northern Italy, was planning the transportation to France of an enormous body of Italian paintings by Bellini, Correggio, Vecchio, Perugino, Raphael, Titian and others. Labillardière was recruited to travel to Italy and evaluate these works of art — and to collect plants. When the thirty-six trunks containing the fruits of his labours on the d'Entrecasteaux voyage finally arrived in Paris, Labillardière was absent in Italy. By some strange irony, this same collection would end up in Florence some thirty years after his death.

Undaunted by his Italian distraction and his experiences at the end of the voyage, Labillardière finally settled in Paris and began work on the first major account of Australian flora ever to be published. The two volumes appeared in Paris in 1804 and 1806 as *Novae Hollandiae Plantarum Specimen*. It was not just the publication of these two illustrated tomes which was a notable achievement, it was the fact that Labillardière had personally classified, named and published more of the flora of Australia than anyone else in the world. Robert Brown's *Prodromus*, which came out in 1810, although more comprehensive, was not illustrated. Labillardière also wrote up the flora of New Caledonia, and a book describing the whole expedition, *Voyage in*

THE FLOWER CHAIN

Search of La Pérouse. Always steadfast in his purpose, he secluded himself in Paris on a seventh floor, not because he was a misanthrope, but to ensure that he had few visitors to distract him from his absorbing work. Aloof, honest, with a sharp tongue, an amusing wit, a great sympathy for the Australian Aboriginal people and an appreciation of Australian vegetation, Labillardière's contribution to the history of Australia's flora deserves particular recognition.

While Labillardière was assiduously describing Australian plants, his future empress delighted in growing them. In Josephine's garden beds, orangeries and glasshouses at Malmaison some of the first European-grown *Eucalyptus*, *Angophora*, *Callistemon*, *Leptospermum* and *Acacia* species were thriving.

Probably few houses in modern history are more associated with a personality than Malmaison is with Josephine. Three years after her marriage to Napoleon in 1796, she acquired this small chateau in Rueil, thirteen kilometres west of Paris, across the Seine from Croissy. For Josephine the house and garden of her beloved Malmaison were inseparable and she spent a fortune on both. The daughter of a sugar planter in tropical Martinique in the Caribbean, Josephine had a passion for flowers. When Lord and Lady Holland visited Malmaison in 1802, Josephine told them 'these are my conquests'. Plucking a branch of jasmine introduced from her native Martinique, she added 'the seeds were sown and tended by my own hands — they remind me of my country, my childhood and the ornaments of my adolescence'.

Josephine modelled her garden on the romantic English school of landscape design. On the edge of a small lake, fringed with weeping willows, was an antique temple with eight Ionic columns; winding paths led the visitor to glades and vistas. Much to Napoleon's displeasure, Josephine's chief gardener was also English, a Mr Howatson. Napoleon wanted a more formal garden and it was he who introduced the urns and statuary which marred the park. Josephine just wanted plants and more plants. Fortunately, her despotic husband was there for brief intervals only, so could not taint what was one of the most beautiful gardens in Europe.

Josephine began importing plants for her Malmaison garden around 1800. First she received seeds from her family back in the West Indies, and soon plants and seeds were arriving from Africa, Asia and South America. Notable donors included James Edward Smith and the Lee and Kennedy nursery in England, and the renowned naturalist Alexander von Humboldt in Germany. Sir Joseph Banks personally sent her *Nicotiana undulata*. Bonaparte himself also became involved in this plant exchange. In 1801 he wrote to Josephine saying he had some plants for her received from London, and in 1809, the year of their divorce, he sent her some 800 plants and an unknown number of seeds from Schönbrunn. For the fourteen years before her death, rare plants poured in and were carefully tended, propagated, displayed and distributed.

In March 1804, Josephine wrote to her gardener:

> I want Malmaison to become a source of wealth for all the Departments of France. That is why I have sent them so many trees and shrubs ... I want each of them to possess ... in ten years' time ... a collection of precious plants issued from my nurseries.

Josephine was as generous as she was extravagant. It was this extravagance that finally provided Napoleon with the excuse he wanted to dismiss Howatson, dispensing with him when he received an excessive bill for the transportation of shrubs to Malmaison. Charles-François Brisseau de Mirbel stepped into the vacancy — and into the story of Australian plants in Europe. For with de Mirbel came Felix Delahaye, fresh from his success at La Trianon, Versailles. Delahaye would be the conduit by which many Australian species found their way to Malmaison. First of all he provided Josephine with seeds that he and Labillardière had brought back from their voyage with d'Entrecasteaux. Delahaye worked for Josephine for the rest of her life, and so close was their relationship that he was present at her deathbed.

Josephine's garden at Malmaison has long since gone, but the Australian plants which Delahaye introduced and tended there were distributed all over France. From Josephine's hothouses many different plants, some grown for

Australia at Malmaison

The Raphael of flowers, Pierre-Joseph Redouté, was employed by Marie-Antoinette, Josephine and the restored Bourbons to paint flowers. His exceptional talent as a botanical artist was put to good use by Josephine when she employed him to illustrate *Jardin de la Malmaison*. (Linnean Society collections.)

the first time outside Australia, were distributed to be cultivated in the open air of the Côte D'Azur and then to other countries around the Mediterranean.

Josephine's garden was immortalised in the book *Jardin de la Malmaison*, with its stunning colour engravings by Pierre-Joseph Redouté of the wide range of exotic plants, including many from Australia, that she cultivated there. This beautiful production, with descriptions by the eminent 'Botanist to Her Majesty' Etienne-Pierre Ventenat, cost her 130 000 francs to produce. Many of the 184 exotic species Josephine nurtured at Malmaison, including hibiscus, phlox, camellia, myrtle, geranium, cactus and dahlia, as well as a host of Australian examples, were figured in this two-volume masterpiece of Ventenat and Redouté.

Josephine first met Redouté in 1798 and she commissioned him to paint watercolours for the walls of her bedroom at Malmaison, for which she paid 7200 francs. This highly talented artist, born in present-day Belgium, had been flower painter to Marie-Antoinette before the Revolution and was a close friend of the botanist Charles Louis L'Héritier, accompanying him on his visit to England — and Joseph Banks' herbarium — in 1786 – 87. When L'Heritiér made the first description of the genus *Eucalyptus* in his *Sertum Anglicum*, it was Redouté who drew the type specimen, *Eucalyptus obliqua*, collected in Tasmania by David Nelson back in 1777.

Redouté also knew Etienne-Pierre Ventenat, and when Josephine commissioned Ventenat to write her book on the exotic plants at Malmaison, Redouté was the obvious choice of artist. Josephine employed him at a cost of 18 000 francs per year. He also illustrated Aimé Bonpland's later work on the flowers of Malmaison and Navarre (1812 – 17). Redouté's association with Josephine was to lead to his most famous work *Les Roses*. Although this beautiful volume was not produced until after her death, the first paintings were done while Redouté was in Josephine's employ.

The Flower Chain

Redouté's descriptions of the gardens he had seen in England, particularly Kew, inspired Josephine to imitate some of the ideas in her own greenhouses at Malmaison. The largest of the hothouses was comparable to that at Kew, and in some ways may even be regarded as its superior. It also served as a salon with exquisite furnishings and decorations.

In the quiet surroundings of the garden Napoleon found his greatest peace and inspiration. He even had a tent specially constructed in the grounds to provide an outdoor study, declaring that the fresh air, being conducive to the 'expansion of ideas', helped him to think.

Josephine was more than just interested in plants, she also possessed a good working knowledge of botany gained from her association with men such as Redouté, Delahaye, Ventenat and de Mirbel. Guests to Malmaison were astounded at her recall of the Latin names of all her acquisitions, and one commentator noted that she kept several botanical textbooks at her bedside. Josephine's knowledge was practical too. In a letter to her daughter Hortense in 1811 she describes a plant of the Morus family that Hortense might expect to find in the woods around Fontainbleau, and instructs how she might successfully transplant and cultivate it.

The cult of gardens and beautiful and unusual plants was a tradition of the former kings and queens of France, but Josephine was also a leader of fashion in every sense. Every fabric she wore was reprinted or rewoven by the textile mills in imitated designs; every dress she had was copied by modistes all over France. The same flattery followed through to her garden; what she grew, other people wanted. The gardeners of France followed her lead and nothing pleased Josephine more than having supplied France with a beautiful adornment.

Despite his irritation at her extravagance, Napoleon recognised the joy that Josephine found in her garden. After their divorce he even gave her four thousand livres (a small fortune) to spend on Malmaison, saying it would allow 'you to do as much planting as you like'. It was to Malmaison that Josephine finally retired and she died there in 1814. Napoleon revisited Malmaison with Hortense in 1815 after Waterloo and before his exile to Elba.

Although she created a rich horticultural heritage Josephine is rarely remembered as a gardener. The only work that commemorates and celebrates her passion for gardening is *Jardin de la Malmaison*. Ventenat's dedication sums up Josephine's contribution to exotic botany:

> You have gathered around you the rarest plants growing on French soil. Some, indeed, which have never before left the deserts of Arabia or the burning sands of Egypt have been domesticated though your care. Now, regularly classified, they offer to us as we inspect them in the beautiful gardens of Malmaison, an impressive reminder of the conquests of your illustrious husband and a most pleasant evidence of the studies you have pursued in your leisure hours.

Ventenat went on to name the beautiful *Josephinia imperatricis* after his empress and patron. Fittingly, *Josephinia* — an Australian plant — was first grown in Europe at Malmaison.

20
Australia Circumnavigated

The tenth anniversary of the new settlement at Port Jackson was marked by the initiation of the most ambitious natural history voyage yet seen. In 1798, two years after Labillardière, and a year after Delahaye had returned to France, the botanical explorer and sea captain, Nicolas Baudin, proposed that another expedition be sent to explore Australia. Several stretches of the coast were imperfectly known. There was still debate, for example, as to whether the Gulf of Carpentaria led to a channel that actually divided the continent into two. Baudin gained the support of the Institut National (which became the Institut de France in 1806), and Napoleon agreed to the proposition. An advisory committee, which included such luminaries as Bougainville, de Jussieu, Laplace, Lacépède, Cuvier and Fleurieu, ensured that the expedition would be unsurpassed in its scientific complement and equipment.

It was, perhaps, audacious of the French to plan a survey of the areas so close to a British settlement — especially as the British had not surveyed or mapped all the Australian coast themselves. Since Britain and France had been at war for over six years and the French were therefore obliged to request passports. Britain's humiliating defeat by the American colonists in the 1780s had been followed by a long struggle against Napoleon whose colonial ambitions were well known. Although Napoleon's support of the venture was tinged with national interest, passports were granted as the overriding objectives of the expedition were scientific.

New South Wales was firmly established as a British colony, and was already more than just a place of penal servitude. The gaol-without-bars had expanded to a population of around 6000 souls and some of the colony's natural products — whale and seal oil — were being exploited and exported. Stories of schools of huge whales off the Australian coast abounded; a sperm whale had been seen in Sydney Harbour and another had capsized a small boat. But this was nothing compared to the tales of some captains who reported gigantic schools of whales between Tasmania and Port Jackson. One captain assured Governor Phillip that he had seen more whales on this coast in one voyage than in six years off the coast of Brazil. After landing their convict cargoes some of the transport ships, which were actually owned and run by private contractors, went whaling with zest in the hope of taking home such lucrative products as oil and corset bones. In 1801, one ship alone took 155 tonnes of oil. Sealing in Tasmania was becoming another major industry. Groups of men were landed on islands to ruthlessly club to death seals — male and female, young and old — for their valuable fur.

Back in France, the detailed preparations for the latest venture to the South Seas were complete. Nicolas Baudin (1750 – 1803), Post Captain and Commander-in-Chief of the elegant corvettes *Géographe* and *Naturaliste*, set sail for Australia from Le Havre on 19 October 1800. These two beautiful ships were showcases of the new revolutionary republic. On board were twenty-two naturalists, more than Baudin had originally intended. They included the naturalists Leschenault de la Tour and François Péron — widely regarded as the father of modern anthropology — as well as the artists Charles Alexandre Lesueur and Nicolas Martin Petit, and a plethora of other zoologists, mineralogists, astronomers and gardeners.

Baudin's instructions were to examine in detail

Nicolas Baudin had an exceptional reputation as a captain-explorer, but his great voyage to chart the coastline of Australia ended in tragedy, clashing irrevocably with his large contingent of scientists. He died of tuberculosis before he could complete the voyage. (Linnean Society collections.)

the west and north coasts of Australia. Combining this information with the maps already done by the English on the east coast of New South Wales, and by the French on Tasmania and the south-west coast, would give Napoleon's government a map of the entire continent.

The departure of Baudin's expedition prodded the British to action. They could not stand by and let the French chart, and perhaps claim, parts of the Australian coast. Matthew Flinders, a young midshipman from Boston in Lincolnshire, had written to his countryman Sir Joseph Banks about the possibility of mounting a British expedition to complete the surveying of the coast of New Holland. Flinders, with George Bass, had recently explored the south coast of Australia, at last confirming Tasmania's island status by sailing through Bass Strait. Flinders had written up this work in 1800 and published it in London with a dedication to Banks. Typically, Banks responded enthusiastically to Flinders' idea, and late in 1800 got the support of the Admiralty. In contrast to the detailed and expensive preparations of the French, the British Admiralty hurriedly refitted the rather leaky ex-collier, *Xenophon,* and renamed her *Investigator* for the voyage. There was no committee as in France to choose the scientific party, everything was left to the eminent, now middle-aged, president of the Royal Society. In April 1801 Banks wrote a note to the Admiralty asking, 'Is my proposal for an alteration in the undertaking of the *Investigator* approved?' The reply from the Admiralty gives a glimpse at his role in the affairs in the colony: 'Any proposal you may make will be approved. The whole is left entirely to your decision.'

Although none of his first choices went on the voyage, Banks ended up with a scientific complement of such high quality that the voyage proved to be a triumph for botany, as well as cartography and geography. Robert Brown was the botanist, Peter Good the gardener, Ferdinand Bauer the natural history painter and William

Perhaps no plant illustrates the Flower Chain better than this *Banksia serrata*, one of the finest engravings in *Banks' Florileg* and named after the man whose collections of Australian flora would eventually lead to the European colonisation of a continent. (Badger G. *Explorers of the Pacific.* Kangaroo Press, 1996.)

Jose Cavanilles named this plant collected by Louis Nèe *Melaleuca quinquenervia* for its particularly fine-nerved leaves. The same species had been collected by Banks and Solander and is here figured in *Banks' Florilegium*.

Now spelt *Sparmannia*, this South African genus was named after the talented Swedish botanist, Anders Sparrmann, employed by the Johann Forster at the Cape of Good Hope to assist him with botanical discoveries on Cook's second voyage. (Linnean Society collections.)

Robert Brown's expertise as a botanist was recognised by Joseph Banks, who sent him on Flinders's circumnavigation of Australia. Brown spent three years in Australia collecting plants and on his return became librarian, first to the Linnean Society and then to Banks himself, being the beneficiary of his sponsor's vast library and collections on Banks's death. (Linnean Society collections.)

Most of Bauer's superb drawings, such as this *Grevillea refracta*, were never published. Brown and Bauer's hopes to bring out a comprehensive illustrated flora, following on from Brown's *Prodromus*, never transpired due to lack of finances. (Olde P. Marriott N. *The Grevillea Book*. Kangaroo Press, 1994.)

Westall the landscape painter. Flinders, still only twenty-eight, was appointed as Lieutenant-in-Command and was readied to follow a similar route to Baudin.

There was even a large collapsible greenhouse on board — and one of the most determined and skilled botanists in British history. The journey would establish Robert Brown — discoverer of Brownian motion and the fact that living cells contain a nucleus — as the most distinguished botanist of his time. Born in Montrose, Scotland in 1772, this well-educated son of an Episcopalian minister, had studied medicine at the University of Edinburgh and gone on to be an army surgeon. But his main interest was natural history. When a recruiting campaign for his regiment had taken Brown to London, he had managed to meet the great Sir Joseph Banks. Duly impressed, Banks pulled strings to have Brown made an associate of the newly formed Linnean Society, and allowed him the use of his library and herbarium. When Brown went to Australia, he was familiar with the flora from studying the *Endeavour* specimens. Banks took a major role in Brown's preparation, insisting that he compile a copy herbarium of some thousand Australian plants from Banks' own duplicates, to take with him on the voyage for reference. Brown also assiduously copied out Solander's unpublished descriptions.

Ferdinand Bauer, another Banks protégé, produced exquisite work on this expedition. It has been said that his depictions of Australian flora and fauna have never been surpassed. The youngest of three sons of the court painter to the Prince of Liechtenstein, Bauer was orphaned in 1761, aged just one. A priest encouraged him and his two brothers in botanical drawing. In Vienna Professor John Sibthorp of Oxford — the celebrated son of the professor incumbent during Banks' time at the University — was so impressed by 26-year-old Bauer that he commissioned him to accompany him to the Mediterranean. This resulted in the much celebrated work *Flora Graeca*, which Bauer illustrated, and in 1800, an invitation from Sir Joseph Banks to sail to Australia and record the flora and fauna.

Little did Flinders know when he was made commander of the *Investigator* that it would be over ten years before he would return to England — and his new bride. Born in Donington, Lincolnshire, in 1774, the son and grandson of surgeons, he had gone to sea without the support of his family when only sixteen. Having diligently studied mathematics and navigation Flinders quickly impressed his superiors. Bligh chose him to sail on the second breadfruit voyage to Tahiti on the *Providence*, where he assisted in preparing charts and making scientific observations. His next voyage was to New South Wales on the *Reliance* in 1795, which took the second governor John Hunter, a keen amateur naturalist, to the colony. It was on this trip that he, with ship's surgeon George Bass, explored the coast in dreadfully inadequate little boats, discovering that Australia and Tasmania were separate.

With a French passport setting forth the peaceful mission of his ship, Flinders took the *Investigator* to sea on 18 July 1801. Baudin had a head start of nearly nine months but Flinders was determined to do a good job declaring that 'no person shall have occasion to come after me to make further discoveries'. His ship though, was barely up to the task. He had hardly left the English Channel before the *Investigator* was leaking up to the rate of eight centimetres an hour. In Madeira the ship's carpenters tried to caulk up the leaks, but water poured in so much that in Cape Town they had to stay for eighteen days while they borrowed expert caulkers from a visiting warship to effect repairs. It was to be a tragedy for the men, and for the specimens collected, that the ship was not equal to the navigator, botanist and artists she carried.

On 7 December the *Investigator* entered King George Sound, which had been discovered, named and charted ten years earlier by George Vancouver. The bottle and parchment which Vancouver had buried under a cairn of stones was never found, nor was the garden which Menzies had made of 'vine cuttings, water cress and the seeds of various fruits'. During the *Investigator's* three-week stay, Brown found this florally diverse area as fascinating as Menzies and Labillardière before him and collected around 500 species, many of them new. Just as Labillardière had been plagued on board with rats attacking his drying paper, Brown had a constant problem with mice and damp.

From King George Sound the *Investigator* sailed close to the coast so that accurate charts could be made. They crept around the southern coast making numerous landings for collections and expeditions. Brown's diary reveals the hardships that the naturalists underwent in their quest to collect plants and make observations:

> We slept, or rather lay down ... In a gully without water and without fire ... At daybreak we descended the mountain and about 7 o'clock got to the bottom where we found our servants whom we had been obliged to leave yesterday, scarce half up the mountain, exhausted with fatigue ... the heat of the day and want of water ...

In the four months they had been on the Australian coast there had been no sign of any recent European visitors. Flinders, it seemed, had beaten the French expedition in the charting and naming of the south coast of the continent. But on 8 April 1802 they at last encountered the French who were sailing westwards. Flinders ordered the decks to be cleared and the red ensign hoisted. Baudin, on the *Géographe*, hoisted the French ensign. The atmosphere was tense. If hostilities ensued, the poorly armed *Investigator* would have no chance against the superiority of the French vessel. They did not know that the war between France and Britain was over and that the Treaty of Amiens had been signed on 27 March. But the French declared peaceful intent and showed a British jack, Flinders replied with a white flag and ordered a boat. With Brown as an interpreter he went aboard. All was friendly and courteous, although the French had laid claim to all they had seen, and renamed the south coast 'Terre Napoleon'. Not knowing Flinders had preceded them, they had christened features already delineated by him with names such as 'Golfe Bonaparte' and 'Golfe Josephine'. Next morning there was a second talk between the two commanders, then the ships parted. Flinders named the coastline opposite where they had met Encounter Bay. Today Flinders' names generally survive although some of the French ones have persisted.

Weeks of charting the southern coast with collecting by Brown, and arduous trips inland by foot followed — including an excursion into the heathlands of the Mornington Peninsula. Here Brown collected 96 species, including the native holly *Lomatia ilicifolia*. Flinders was keen to get to Port Jackson before the storms of winter and they arrived on 9 May. 'At one o'clock we gained the heads, a pilot came on board, and soon after three the *Investigator* was anchored in Sydney Cove.' The place had changed little since Flinders had left it more than two years earlier. Flinders, in an account of the voyage to send back to England reported to his sponsor, Banks, full of praise for his companions:

> ... it is fortunate for science that two men of such assiduity & abilities as Mr Brown & Mr Bauer have been selected: their application is beyond what I have been accustomed to see.

Brown wrote that he had collected specimens of 750 species of vascular plants. He also sent a letter to the Hon. C. T. Grenville, which showed that despite Flinders' praise, there was friction between the commander and the botanist:

> Captain Flinders, who does not rate the importance of such collections very high, thought, I suppose, he did enough in affording me opportunities of landing at our different anchorages. The trouble of ordering boxes to be made and the occasional employment of his carpenters in that business, he does not seem to have reckoned on. However, as I would rather attribute his conduct to his inexperience in such matters than to any other causes, I think a few words from Sir Joseph will set him right in his notions of collectors and collections.

A convict ship left for England carrying this letter and the official report by Flinders for the Admiralty, plus 253 packets of seeds for Kew from the gardener Peter Good. Several excursions were made into the interior by Brown, Bauer and Westall, aided by George Caley the plant collector recently sent to the colony by Banks. More and more plants were gathered and hundreds were planted in the Governor's garden to await transport to England in the collapsible greenhouse which was being erected on the deck of the *Investigator*. To protect the dried specimens from the predations of white ants and rats they were stored at the Governor's residence.

On 20 June a ship was seen in difficulty just

Matthew Flinders was another talented navigator whose career was coloured by misfortune. After a nightmare expedition with the leaky *Investigator* to circumnavigate Australia, Flinders was imprisoned by the French on Mauritius under suspicion of being a spy. His health suffered badly but after his release he managed to write up his voyage, dying just as Robert Brown, his botanist, delivered the first copy to him. (Linnean Society collections.)

outside the heads of Sydney Harbour. It was the *Géographe*, her officers and crew so weakened by scurvy that only a reported four, out of the complement of 170, were fit for duty. Governor King offered assistance and once on shore the sick were admitted to hospital. Despite shortages in the colony, food was found for them and most made a rapid recovery. The French expedition had not fared well. A stop at Timor had left several of Baudin's men dead, dying or ill, thanks to dysentery and malaria. Baudin himself had contracted the latter and was also suffering from tuberculosis. Scurvy too, had taken its toll, especially on the *Géographe*. The *Naturaliste* had fared slightly better, reaching Port Jackson in better shape eight days after the *Géographe*. Baudin decided to send the *Naturaliste*, under the command of Emmanuel Hamelin, back to France with the documents, the collections made so far and the crew members he considered too

THE FLOWER CHAIN

Ferdinand Bauer's drawings of Australia's flora and fauna have been described as among the finest ever made. He developed a complex coding system for colours, with which he used to work up his pencil sketches later with an astonishing accuracy. (G. Badger, *Explorers of the Pacific*, Kangaroo Press, 1996.)

sick to continue. He planned to carry on along the coast once his crew had recovered. In Port Jackson he purchased a schooner, christened with the botanical name *Casuarina*, and left the British settlement on 18 November 1802. On this final part of the voyage they collected live animals including kangaroos, wallabies and emus, many of which survived the voyage to France — two of the emus spent a short time in Josephine's garden at Malmaison. They continued along the south coast confirming, as Flinders had told them, that several likely-looking bays did not offer a seaway to the north. Baudin returned to Timor to refresh before a survey of the north coast. As before, Koupang proved a fatal port, and more men died there. Baudin himself was also unwell. He completed some of the survey then headed for the Isle-de-France, reaching the island in August, but a few weeks later Baudin died, probably of tuberculosis. The crew of the *Casuarina* transferred to the larger ship and they headed for France, arriving on 24 March 1804.

The task of writing up the voyage fell initially to Péron, the only senior surviving naturalist. He had made many anthropological and zoological discoveries and his work was illustrated by the paintings of Lesueur. Baudin had adopted a high-handed attitude at times, and during the long voyage had often come into conflict with his large complement of scientists. Like many of his shipmates, Péron had crossed swords with Baudin and his disdain is apparent in his account of the voyage, never referring to his commander by name. Baudin fell into disfavour with the French authorities because of the great number of lives the expedition had lost. Fear of association with this discredited leader of the expedition may also explain why Péron avoided using Baudin's name. Péron died completing only one volume and the job was finished by Louis Freycinet, commander of the *Casuarina*.

The voyage produced an astounding number of specimens and drawings, particularly with relation to zoology and the study of native people. Péron's observations of the Aboriginals were so profound that they are now regarded as marking the beginning of the study of anthropology. But botanical results from the expedition were few, and it has been suggested that some of the specimens collected might have been included by Labillardière in his comprehensive two-volume work on the Australian flora. Some of the specimens were later sent to Robert Brown in London, who used them in his own work on Australian flora — his *Prodromus* — and then returned them to the Museum d'Histoire Naturelle and to obscurity. They were found, still wrapped up, in the basement just a few decades ago. Hamelin, returning with the bulk of the collections on the *Naturaliste* in 1802, did a little more by ensuring that Australian plant seeds were passed on to Josephine, and these she eagerly cultivated. Several entries in her book *Jardin de la Malmaison*, record introductions via this source, such as the spectacular *Hibiscus heterophyllus*.

A few weeks after Baudin reached the Isle-de-France, Flinders also arrived there on the *Cumberland* after a catalogue of disasters. Back in Port Jackson, Flinders had been delighted when Governor King informed him that the 60-tonne brig *Lady Nelson* was at his disposal for exploring. After more than two months in Sydney the *Investigator*, complete with greenhouse, had set sail heading north along the east coast. The original plan of circumnavigating the continent in a clockwise direction was now reversed. Nine convict volunteers were signed on, as were two young Aboriginal men, Boongaree and the adopted child of Surgeon John White, Nanbaree. Stores included 6750 litres of rum purchased from some American ships in the harbour. It was to be a voyage full of misfortune and hardship. Flinders examined the coast up to Percy Isles and from Cape York to Arnhem Bay in what is now the Northern Territory, but was forced by the condition of the ship, lack of fresh food and water, and the monsoon season to sail for Timor. Flinders wrote:

> In addition to the rottenness [sic] of the ship, the state of my own health and that of the ship's company ... and from the want of nourishing food. I was myself disabled by scorbutic sores from going to the mast head, or making any more expeditions in boats; and, as the whole of the surveying department rested on me, our further stay was without one of its principal objects.

After a perilous voyage down the west coast of the continent and again along the south coast they returned to Sydney on June 9, eleven months after they had departed. Four men had died during the voyage and another four, including the gardener, Peter Good, were to die within a few days of landing. Fourteen others were unfit for duty. At the same time that Peter Good died the seeds he had so assiduously collected arrived in England. Banks wrote, 'they are all sown in Kew Gardens & much hopes built on the success of them, which we expect will create a new Epoch'.

The *Investigator* was completely unseaworthy and it was decided that it would be better to leave her in New South Wales, and for Flinders to sail to England quickly with the charts he had compiled and return in another ship. On 10 August the *Porpoise* sailed with Flinders as a passenger and the greenhouse on the quarter deck, crowded with plants for Banks. They headed for Batavia via the Torres Strait. Fortuitously, Brown and Bauer had asked to remain in the colony to continue their botanical work.

A week out from Sydney disaster struck. The ship was wrecked on a reef off the Queensland coast. The specimens and seeds collected by Brown, and the live plants nurtured in the Governor's garden before being loaded into the collapsible greenhouse, were lost. Flinders later recalled:

> The rare plants collected in different parts of the south, the east and north-west coasts, for Her Majesty's botanic garden at Kew, and which were in a flourishing state before the shipwreck, were totally destroyed by the salt water; as were the dried specimens and plants.

Flinders organised a miniature colony for the shipwrecked crew, fitted up the cutter, and sailed back to Sydney in thirteen days. Brown had kept duplicates of the dried specimens. Brown wrote:

> Melancholy intelligence of the loss of HMS Porpoise ... almost everything of consequence has been savd ... except the Garden and specimens so that I must consider myself as the greatest sufferer by this most unfortunate accident.

When Flinders arrived with another ship to rescue the crew stranded on the reef, he was given a rousing welcome. He described his return as 'one of the happiest moments of my life'. In Sydney the despondent Brown went to Tasmania and Norfolk Island to make further collections.

Flinders again tried to return to England, this time on the ten-metre schooner *Cumberland*, put under his command by Governor King. When he reached the Isle-de-France, his passport was questioned as it named the *Investigator*, not the *Cumberland*. On this flimsy pretext, Flinders was held on the island under suspicion of spying for the next four years. For a while, his incarceration was made more bearable by the company of his cat for whom Flinders wrote *A Biographical Tribute to the Memory of Trim*, but for the most part his time under arrest was frustrating and dreary. He did manage, in 1807, to send his journal and various papers to Sir Joseph Banks.

Meanwhile Bauer and Brown returned together on the *Investigator*, which was still leaking and had a condemnation order made in 1805.

When Flinders finally returned to England in October 1810 his papers, were restored to him and from them he wrote *A Voyage to Terra Australis*. The first copy was sent to him the day before he died on 19 July 1814. Flinders had wanted to anglicise the name of the land he had circumnavigated to, 'Australia ... as being more agreeable to the ear', but Banks dissuaded him.

Brown began, but never completed, the first systematic British attempt at a classification of the flora. His *Prodromus Florae Novae Hollandiae et Insulae Van-Diemen* — An Introduction to the Flora of New Holland and Tasmania — published in 1810, was a groundbreaking work, but was ill-received and he was never able financially to follow it up with a further volume, illustrated by Bauer, as he had planned. The *Prodromus* described over 2000 Australian species, over half of which were new to science. He also used a so-called 'natural system' of classification, the principles of which eventually superseded Linnaeus' 'artificial system'. This, in itself, was a huge advance in the study of botany.

The pictorial records of both the French and the British expeditions are remarkable. The paintings by Lesueur — mostly of fish, reptiles and mammals — are now displayed in a special museum in Le Havre and the publication in 1814 of Flinders' *A Voyage to Terra Australis* contained nine plates of William Westall's superb landscapes. But it is Bauer's work that is the most spectacular. His representations truly brought to life the flora and fauna of Australia, combining scientific accuracy with an artistic sensitivity of the highest order. His complex system of coding colours on unfinished drawings allowed him to complete them with accuracy after his return in 1805. He and Brown published only fifteen plates of his drawings in 1813 as a supplement to the *Prodromus*, but this *Illustrationes Florae Novae Hollandiae* sold pitifully few copies. Many of the original 2073 drawings were lost after Bauer's death in 1826, although some are now preserved in the Natural History Museum, London. Bauer's drawings, annotated with his detailed colour coding, are held by the Natural History Museum in Vienna.

Information from these voyages led by Baudin and Flinders at last delineated the entire coastline of Australia. It is sad that their successes were achieved at such a great human cost. Baudin lost many men to malaria, dysentery and scurvy and, like the five captains of the five ships of the previous three French expeditions that preceded him to Australia, he also died on the voyage. Flinders, one of the most able and likeable navigators of his time, died, having only just turned forty, after being weakened by his long incarceration in Mauritius. These unlucky voyages forged further links in the Flower Chain. As the nineteenth century progressed, this chain would become lost in a network of botanical connections created as the study of the Australian flora finally came into its own, and end in the 1870s with the first comprehensive flora in the form of Bentham's *Flora Australiensis*.

21
The Fate of the Flower Chain

After Robert Brown visited New South Wales, invisible chains of flowers and seeds stretched across the oceans from Botany Bay and linked the colony with the natural philosophers in Britain. Kew, under Banks' supervision, became the main repository of the living plant wealth of the British Empire. Barrels of plants covered in canvas were sent to Kew from New South Wales, and flora from the whole continent was displayed in the Botany Bay Glass House. In 1833 the invention of the Wardian case made transporting living plants much more successful. These were effectively mini greenhouses which both protected the plants from outside influences, and made it possible to maintain reasonably constant conditions inside.

Botanical expeditions from all over the world so enriched the scientific collections at Kew that the gardens and herbarium collections stood in relation to botanical science much as Greenwich does to astronomy. After Sir Joseph Banks' death in 1820 the gardens' status waned, but was

Before the advent of the Wardian case, effectively a mini greenhouse, plants had to suffer the rigours of a sea voyage and were tended diligently by the gardeners and plant collectors employed to care for them. Even so, many died from lack of water, sea spray or even being washed overboard. (Linnean Society collections.)

renewed in the middle of the century under the influence of William Jackson Hooker and his son Joseph Dalton Hooker.

Banks bequeathed his herbarium and library to Robert Brown — who had become his librarian in 1810 — for his use and enjoyment for life, and then to the British Museum. However, in 1827 Brown started the massive job of transferring the thousands of items earlier. Today this collection, including priceless drawings and paintings by Watling, Parkinson and Bauer, are in the Natural History Museum, London, which physically separated from the British Museum in the 1880s, eventually becoming an independent institution. Brown became Keeper of the museum's Department of Botany; his desk is still used by the Keeper today. Brown who survived Banks by nearly forty years, dying at the age of eighty-five in 1858, was buried in Kensal Green Cemetery, London.

In 1825, Bougainville's nephew Hyacinthe arrived in Sydney and began to erect a monument to the lost La Pérouse on the northern head of Botany Bay. At this point, La Pérouse's fate was still unknown but two years later an Irish sailor of fortune, Peter Dillon, voyaging in the Solomon Islands, acquired some European objects from the natives of Tikopia. Dillon guessed rightly that these were from La Pérouse's ships and secured the backing of the East India Company to investigate further. He found a array of relics, including a wooden panel decorated with the fleur-de-lys, astronomical instruments, crockery, guns and a large bell of French manufacture. At last the sea had yielded up its mystery, La Pérouse and his ships had met their end at Vanikoro. A French search party led by Dumont d'Urville in 1828 explored the site after hearing about Dillon's discoveries, and found evidence of La Pérouse's second ship. It appears they had been wrecked in a storm in 1788 and the survivors had probably been attacked and killed by the local islanders.

Labillardière, veteran of the first voyage in search of La Pérouse, died at 79 in 1834. His Australian collection was purchased by the British botanist, Phillip Webb, who bequeathed it to Leopold, the last Grand Duke of Florence. For years the pressed blooms of kangaroo paws and Tasmanian blue gum, the first collected and bought back to Europe, rested on the second floor of the Pitti Palace, Florence. They are now carefully preserved in the city's University Herbarium.

The discovery of the Australian flora continued with the visit of the British Admiralty ship HMS *Beagle* in 1836, captained by Charles Fitzroy (1805 – 65) with the young Charles Darwin on board as naturalist. Fitzroy was the great-great-great-grandson of Isabella Bennet, the first Duchess of Grafton, a relation of William Dampier's wife Judith. During the meanderings around the world of her husband, in which he had visited the west Australian coast in 1688, Judith Dampier had stayed with the Duchess at Arlington House (now the site of Buckingham Palace). After Darwin left Australia, knowledge of the Australian flora expanded into a web of connections between plant exchanges, books, papers and correspondents, as networks of skilled gardeners, botanists and collectors took over from the solitary pioneers. Australia at last had its own botanists such as the indefatigable German-born Ferdinand, later Baron, von Mueller, who arrived in 1847, and began to elucidate the flora. Mueller alone published 1330 books and papers, and despite deep philosophical differences and jealousies between them, also assisted Bentham in his compilation of *Flora Australiensis* by sending a vast number of his own herbarium specimens and descriptions.

In Europe, a change in the methods of heating greenhouses meant the death of thousands of hothouse Australian plants: the steam heating which came with the Industrial Revolution created too much humidity. Members of the Proteaceae such as hakeas, grevilleas and South African proteas, lost their popularity in favour of luxurious tropical plants from South America and South-East Asia. But Australian plants still found niches in Europe. The Marquis Cosimo Ridolfi grew several kinds of eucalypts in his park near Florence in 1818; by 1822 twenty-four acacia species and eighteen eucalypts were growing in the Botanic Gardens at Berlin; the Baron Cesati started growing Tasmanian blue gum at the former Naples Botanic Garden about 1829; the Botanic Gardens of Madrid distributed Australian eucalypts to Spanish provinces from about 1847.

THE FLOWER CHAIN

German-born Ferdinand von Mueller, was the first great resident botanist in Australia. His written output was prodigious and he collaborated with Bentham to produce the *Flora Australiensis*. (P. Olde & N. Marriott, *The Grevillea Book*, Sydney, Kangaroo Press, 1994.)

The capital of Ethiopia built in 1887 owes it name, Addis Ababa — 'new flower' — to the eucalypts planted there.

The work of the plant-hunters can now be seen throughout the world. Three hundred years after the first seeds and flowers left Australia with Dampier, Australian species comprise an important part of the cut-flower trade in the South of France, Israel, South America, California and elsewhere. The Norfolk pine towers over the horizon of Morocco and *Eucalyptus* species purport to be the fastest growing hardwood tree in the world. Eucalypts joined the olive trees and changed the appearance of the Mediterranean coastline forever, spreading so quickly that they have become a menace, displacing the native vegetation, creating silent forests which provide little for local birds, butterflies and other wildlife. Trees such as *Melaleuca quinquenervia* have spread and become rampant weeds abroad. *Melaleuca* has smothered surrounding vegetation, covering over 200 000 hectares in the Everglades, Florida, alone. Some acacia species have become wild in South America and the fern *Cyathea australis* has colonised Hawaii. In South Africa some species of hakea have become naturalised.

By the same token, although the major destruction of the Australian flora occurred during clearing for crops, grazing, cities and roads, tremendous damage has been done in Australia by introduced plants which escape, becoming prolific weeds in the bush. Seeds are spread by birds, with garden refuse, by winds, and by water during floods. It is estimated that over a third of all declared noxious plants in the Australian bush were once introduced garden plants. Australia has one of the most extravagant floras in the world, but the influx of foreign plants has been greater than the export of Australian natives. Alien plants and 'English flowers' have been naturalised since the first day of settlement, when Surgeon Bowes Smyth bought his flowering geranium ashore from his cabin on the *Lady Penhryn*.

Cook's 'fine meadows' on the northern shore of Botany Bay became a suburb of Sydney with backyards growing roses. Banks' marshes have been reclaimed into a long runway projecting into the sea — Australia's main airport. Thus most overseas visitors — just like Captain Cook, Joseph Banks and the First Fleet — still make their first landing at Botany Bay.

Acknowledgments

We are most grateful to the many people who helped us during the preparation of this book, particularly Professor Dalton of James Cook University and Professor Trevor Clifford, Emeritus Professor of Botany at the University of Queensland. Gina Douglas, the librarian at the Linnean Society of London, proved an endless source of information, books, images and most of all, encouragement. Dr E. Charles Nelson, generously lent us all his papers so that we could draw on his wide research into the early classification of Australian plants and the life of Surgeon General John White. Dr Ed Duyker in Sydney and Professor Chris Humphries of the Department of Botany, Natural History Museum, London, have provided prompt and invaluable help, especially during the latter stages of the book's preparation, for which many thanks are due. We are extremely grateful to Alex George for his timely comments and advice on the manuscript and to Professor David Mabberley of the Royal Botanic Gardens, Sydney.

Day-to-day help has been given to Jill Hamilton by neighbours on Magnetic Island, Liz Sellent and Maureen Sherriff. Greg Calvert, like many members of the Society for Growing Australian Plants (SOGAP) has been more than helpful.

Thanks are also due to Miriam Rothschild and Digby Neave.

To Mr David Robinson OBE endless thanks are due for introducing one of us (Julia Bruce), to the life and works of Joseph Banks.

This book owes a great debt of thanks to the librarians at so many libraries for their skilled advice, especially Allan Clarke at the library of the Royal Society, London; the library at James Cook University, Townsville; Kensington and Chelsea Libraries, London; the Department of Library and Information Services and the Banks Archive Project at the Natural History Museum, London; Miguel Garcia and the Library of the Royal Botanic Gardens, Sydney and finally the London Library, St James' Square London which also assisted us in our search for illustrations.

We would also like to thank the Literature Board of the Australia Council, who gave Jill Hamilton a fellowship over ten years ago to write a biography on William Dampier, from which this book originated.

Finally, we gratefully acknowledge the hundreds of authors who have previously researched the history of Australian discovery and the elucidation of its flora. Without their work, this book could not have been written.

Suggested Reading

Badger G., *Explorers of the Pacific,* Sydney: Kangaroo Press, 1996.

Beaglehole J.C. (ed.), *The Endeavour Journal of Joseph Banks 1768 – 1771,* Sydney: Angus & Robertson, 1962.

Beaglehole J.C.(ed.), *The Journals of Captain James Cook,* Cambridge: The Hakluyt Society, 1955 – 69.

Blunt W., *The Compleat Naturalist: A Life of Linnaeus.* London: Collins, 1971.

Bonnemains J., Forsyth E. & Smith B., *Baudin in Australian Waters: The Artwork of the French Voyage of Discovery to the Southern Lands, 1800 – 1804.* Melbourne: Oxford University Press in association with the Australian Academy of the Humanities, 1988.

Britten J., *Illustrations of the Botany of Captain Cook's Voyage Round the World in H.M.S. Endeavour in 1768 – 71.* London: British Museum (Natural History), 1900 – 1905.

Brosse J., *Great Voyages of Exploration.* David Bateman Ltd., 1983.

Bruce E., *Napoleon and Josephine: An Improbable Marriage.* London: Phoenix, 1996.

Carter H.B., *Sir Joseph Banks.* London: British Museum (Natural History), 1988.

Cathcart M., (abridger), *Manning Clark's History of Australia.* London: Chatto and Windus, 1993.

Christian G., *A Fragile Paradise: The Discovery of Fletcher Christian Bounty Mutineer.* London: Hamish Hamilton Ltd, 1982.

Drake-Brockman H., *Voyage to Disaster.* Perth: University of Western Australia Press, 1995.

Eisler W., Smith B., *Terra Australis: The Furthest Shore.* Sydney: International Cultural Corporation of Australia, 1988.

Flannery T.F., *The Future Eaters.* London: Secker and Warburg, 1994.

Gove Day A., et al. *The Spanish at Port Jackson: The Visit of the Corvettes Descubierta & Atrevida 1793.* Sydney: The Australian Documentary Facsimile Society, 1967.

Hughes R., *The Fatal Shore.* London: The Harvill Press, 1987.

Knapton E.J., *Empress Josephine.* Cambridge, Mass.: Harvard University Press, 1964.

Lyte C., *Sir Joseph Banks: 18th Century Explorer, Botanist and Entrepreneur.* London: David & Charles, 1980.

Mabberley D., *Jupiter Botanicus, Robert Brown of the British Museum.* Brunschweig Verlag von J. Cramer, 1985, British Museum (Natural History).

Miller D.P. & Reill P.H., *Visions of Empire.* Cambridge: Cambridge University Press, 1997.

Moorhead A., *The Fatal Impact.* London: The Reprint Society Ltd, 1966.

O'Brian P., *Joseph Banks: A Life.* London: Collins Harvell, 1987.

Olde P. & Marriott N., *The Grevillea Book*, Volume I. Sydney: Kangaroo Press, 1997.

Short S. (ed.), *History of Systematic Botany in Australiasia.* Melbourne: Australian Systematic Botany Society Inc., 1990.

Smith B., *European Vision and the South Pacific.* New Haven, Conn.: Yale University Press, 1985.

Tench, Captain W., *Sydney's First Four Years: Being a reprint of A Narrative of the Expedition to Botany Bay and A Complete Account of the Settlement at Port Jackson.* Sydney: Library of Australian History, 1979.

Walker R., Roberts D., *From Scarcity to Surfeit: a History of Food and Nutrition in New South Wales.* Sydney: University of NSW Press, 1988.

White J., *Journal of a Voyage to New South Wales.* London, 1790.

Withey L., *Voyages of Discovery: Captain Cook and the Exploration of the Pacific.* London: Hutchinson, 1987.

Index

Italic page numbers indicate illustrative material.

Aboriginal people, *40*, 74, *98*
   Banks' opinion, 97
   Cook's opinion, 86
   Dampier's description, 53
   firestick farming, 32, 33, 38
   knowledge of plants, 77
   land tenure, 40–1
   Péron's observations, 149
   use of plants, 38–9, 40–2, 53, 91
   –see also terra nullius
Acacia genus, 33, 84
   A. holosericea, 42
   A. rostellifera, 56
   A. saphorae, *34*
   A. truncata, 11, 43, *44*, 44–5
   Acmena smithii, 72
   Actinotis helianthi, *139*
Adams, John, 106–7
Adventure, 79, 81
Adventure Bay, Tasmania, 81–2, 103, 125
Ahu-Toru, 65
Aiton, William, 81, 93
   Hortus Kewensis, 93
Americas, European settlement of, 39
Anderson, William, 83, 84
Anigozanthus genus, 126
Apium prostratum, 48, 71, 125
Artocarpus altilis, *13*, 101
Astrolabe, 109–10
Athertonia sp., 41
Augusta, Princess of Wales, 28, 62
Augustine, Saint, 20
Austin, George, 114
Australia, early ideas of, 20–2
Australian east coast, 70–8
Australian plants
   adaptations and change, 31–3
   cultivation, 35–7
   early cultivation in Europe, 82–3, 93, 121–3, 140, 153–4

edible plants described by Banks, 76–7
European attitude to, 15–16, 41, 115
as exotic weeds, 154

Bacon, Roger, 20
bamboo, 75
Banks, Joseph, 12, 59–64, 68, 70–2, 73, 76–8, *88*, *96*, 116
   advice to Malaspina, 131
   assessment of Labillardière's collection, 128–9
   breadfruit scheme, 101–2, 107-8
   Florilegium, 12, 89–93
   Iceland journey, 89
   influence on Flinders' voyage, 144
   influence on settlement of Australia, 95–100, 114
   journal of *Endeavour* voyage, 87
   Kew, 16, 152
   member of Royal Society, 62, 95
   plant collection, 12, 88–9, 93–4, 153
   reception after *Endeavour* voyage, 87–9
   role in disseminating Australian plants, 122–3
   second voyage planned, 79, 81
Banksia genus, 34, 89, 90
   B. grandis, 136
   B. integrifolia, *36*
   B. praemorsa, 136
   B. serrata, *14*, *117*
   germinating, 36–7
Bass, George, 144–5
Batavia, 78
Baudin, Nicolas, 143, *144*, 146, 147, *148*, 149, 151
Bauer, Ferdinand, 144, 146, 150
   Illustrationes Florae Novae Hollandiae, *148*, 150–1
Beagle, HMS, 153

Bentham, George, *16*
   Flora Australiensis, 17, 58, 94, 151, 153
Bentham, Jeremy, 99
Billardiera genus, 126
Bligh, William, 15, 84, 102, 103, 107–8, 145
   second breadfruit voyage, 125
   voyage to Timor, 104–5
Boongaree, 149
botanic gardens, early, 28–30
Botany Bay, 70–2, 95, 97, 110–11, *111*
Boudeuse, 65
Bougainville, Louis Antoine de, 65–6, *66*
Bounty, 15, 102–4, *103*, 106, 109
   mutineers, 105–6
   mutiny, 104
Boussole, 109–10
breadfruit, *13*, 15, 17, 55, 101, *102*, 103–4, 108, 138
Briscoe, Peter, 63
British Museum, 88
Briton, 107
Britten, James, 61
Brooke, John, 53
Brougham, Henry, 59
Brown, Robert, 15, 17, 45, 89, 91, 114, 126, 135, 144–6, 151, 153
   Illustrationes Florae Novae Hollandiae, 151
   Prodromus Florae Novae Hollandiae et Insulae Van-Diemen, 17, 139, 149, 150–1
Brown, William, 15, 102, 103, 104, 106, 107
Buchan, Alexander, 63, 68
Burmann, Nicholas
   Flora Indica, 44
Burton, David, 114
bush tucker, 41–2
Byron, John, 66

Caley, George, 114, 122–3, 146
Cape of Good Hope botanic garden, 30
Cape Town, 84
Capel, Henry, 28
Carstensz, Jan, 46
Carteret, Philip, 66
Casuarina genus, 35
   C. equisetifolia, 56
   C. torulosa, 93
Casuarina (ship), 149
Cavanilles, Antonio José, 132
Chatham, 133
Chelsea Physic Garden, 28, *29*, 62
Christian, Fletcher, 104–6
coconuts, 75
Collignon, Jean-Nicolas, 109
Collins, David, 131–2
Collinson, Peter, 61, 62
Colocasia esculenta, 74
Commerson, Philibert, 66, 81
Cook, James, 63, 65, 67–8, 70–2, 73, 77–8, *80*, 84
   second Pacific voyage, 79–83
   third Pacific voyage, 83–6
Cook Islands, 106
Cumberland, 149
cut flower industry, 17–18, 154
Cybele, 138
cycads, 50, 75
Cygnet, 51, 52, 53, 54, 109

Dampier, William, 11–12, 27, 43, 51–8, *52*
   A New Voyage Round the World, 54–5, 101
   A Voyage to New Holland, 12, *12*, 57
Dampiera genus, 58
Dante Alighieri, 20–1
Darwin, Charles, 153
Davy, Humphry, 63
Delahaye, Felix, 124, 125, 137–8, 140
d'Entrecasteaux, Antoine-Raymond-Joseph de Bruni, 124, *124*, 125–6
desert rose, 34
Diderot, Denis, 98

Dieppe cartographers, 22
Dillon, Peter, 153
Dillwynia ericifolia, 122
Dioscorides, Pedanius
   De Materia Medica, 24
Discovery, 83–4, 133, 135
Dolphin, 65
domiculture, 40
Dufresne, Marion, 82
d'Urville, Dumont, 153
Dutch voyages, 22, 39, 43–50
Duyfken, 46

Elaeocarpus angustifolia, 41
Ellis, John, 61, 64
Endeavour, 12, 63–4, 65–78, *74*
Endeavour, New, 67
English garden plants, 23
Espérance, 124
Etoile, 65
eucalypt
   first collected, 81, 82
   first described, 51, 53, 84, 90
Eucalyptus genus, 33–4, 42
   E. cornuta, 136
   E. crebra, 93
   E. globulus, 34, 35, 125
   E. grandis, 34
   E. gummifera, 93
   E. marginata, 33
   E. obliqua, 82, 84, *85*
   E. perriniana, 35
   E. piperita, 34
   E. regnans, 33–4
exotic weeds, 154

fire adaptations in plants, 32–3
First Fleet, 99–100, 109, 110
Fitzroy, Charles, 153
flannel flower, *139*
Flannery, Tim
   The Future Eaters, 31
flax, 81, 83
Flinders, Matthew, 108, 114, 144–51, *145*
   A Biographical Tribute to the Memory of Trim, 150
   A Voyage to Terra Australis, 151
Flora Graeca, 145
Flora of Australia, 17, 45

Flora-for-Fauna campaign, 19
Folger, Mayhew, 106
Forster, Georg, 78, 81, 83
Forster, Johann Reinhold, 78, 81, *82*, 83
   Characteres Generum Plantarum, 83
   Florulae Insularum Australium, 83
French voyages, 109–10, 124–9, 143–4, 146, 147, 149
Freycinet, Louis, 149
Furneaux, Tobias, 81, 82–3

Gaertner, Joseph
   De Fructibus et Seminibus Plantarum, *92*, 93
Geelvinck, 43, 44
Géographe, 143, 146, 147
George, Alex, 17
Gerard
   Herball, 60, *61*
Gondwana, 31, 34
Good, Peter, 144, 146, 150
Gore, John, 65, 68, 75
Gorgon, 114
Green, Charles, 63, 78
Grevillea filifolium, 121
Grevillea pteridifolia, 87
Guardian, 114
gum tree *see* eucalypt
Guugu Yimidhirr people, 74, 77

Haenke, Thaddeus, 131, 132
Hamelin, Emmanuel, 149, 147
Hawkesworth, John, 57, 87, 99
herbals, European, 24
Herbert, Rev William
   Amaryllidaceae, 93
Hibiscus heterophyllus, 149
Hodges, William, 81
Home, Everard, 60
Hooghly, 128
Hooker, Joseph Dalton, 41, 153
Hooker, William Jackson, 135, 153
Howatson, Mr (gardener), 140
Humboldt, Alexander von, 30, 133, 140
Humea elegans, 122
Hunter, John, 125, 145

INDEX

Huon de Kermadec, Jean Michel, 124, 126

Investigator, 114, 144–50

Jansz, Willem, 39, 46
Jardin des Plantes, Paris, 28
Java-la-Grande, 22
Josephine, Empress, 16, 137, *138*, 140–2
  Jardin de la Malmaison, 141, 142, 149

kangaroo, 75, *75*
kangaroo paw, 126
Kennedy, Lewis, 30, 63
Kew Gardens, 16, 28–30, 62, 93, 152
King George Sound, 125-6, *134*, 145

La Pérouse, Jean-François de Galaup Comte de, *109*, 109–11, 124, 153
La Trianon, 138
Labillardière, Jacques-Julien Houtou de, 16, 124, 125, 126, 127, 138–40
  collections, 128–9, 135, 153
  Novae Hollandiae Plantarum Specimen, 17, 139
  Voyage in Search of La Pérouse, 139
Lamartinière, Joseph de, 109
Lécluse, Charles de
  physic garden, Leiden, Holland, 28
Lee, James, 30, 69, 83
  Introduction to Botany, 63
Leea rubra, 78
Leptospermum genus, 81
  L. lanigerum, 83
Leschenault de la Tour, 143
Lesueur, Charles Alexandre, 143, 149, 150
L'Héritier, Charles Louis, 84, 141
  Sertum Anglicum, 84, 141
lilly-pillies, 72
Linnaeus, Carl, *17*, 27, 62
  collections, 116–17, 119
  Historia Plantarum Generalis, 27
  Species Plantarum, 91
Linnaeus the younger, 89, 90

Linnean Society, 116, 119, 122–3
Lomatia ilicifolia, 146
Loudon, J.C.
  Encyclopaedia of Gardening, 23
Lyons, Israel, 61

Macadamia integrifolia, 41
Macadamia tetraphylla, 41
Macrozamia riedlei, 50
Mahogany Ship, 22
Malaspina, Alessandro, 130–3
Malmaison, 16, *137*, 137–42
Marie-Antoinette, Queen, 138
Masson, Francis, 81, 84
Matra, James Mario, 77, 96–100
  A Proposal for Establishing a Settlement in New South Wales, 95–6
Melaleuca sp., 122
  M. alternifolia, 42
  M. squarrosa, *127*
Menzies, Archibald, 89, *133*, 133–6, 145
Miller, John Frederick, 89
Mirbel, Charles-François Brisseau de, 140
Montague, Charles, Earl of Halifax, 54, 55
Morris, Valentine, 101
Mueller, Ferdinand, baron von, 17, 153, *154*
Murray, Alexander, 121
Mutis, José Celestine
  Flora of New Granada, 30
Myoporum acuminatum, 56

Nanbaree, 149
Naturaliste, 143, 149
Née, Luis, 131, 132
Nelson, David, 15, 83–4, 102, 103, 104–5
Nelsonia genus, 105, *105*
New South Wales, decision to colonise, 97–8
New Zealand, 70
New Zealand spinach, *71*, 72
Niger, HMS, 62
Nodder, Federick Polydore, 120
Nore, 108
Norfolk Island, 81, 83

oaks, 23
Ogilby, John
  America, 48
O'mai, 83
Ortelius, Abraham
  Theatrum Orbis Terrarum, 21, *21*
Oxylobum ellipticum, 84

Pamplemousses botanic garden, Isle-de-France, 30
Parkinson, Stanfield, 69, 70, 89
Parkinson, Sydney, 64, 68, *69*, 70, 75, 78, 89
Péron, François, 143, 149
Petit, Nicolas Martin, 143–4
Phillip, Arthur, 98, 113–14
Phipps, Constantine John, 62
pigs, first in Australia, 74–5
pigweed, 41
Pimelea linifolia, 121
Pineda, Antonio, 131
Pitcairn Island, 66, 106–7
plant classification, 23–4, 26–7, *27*, 91
plant collecting, early, 24–6
Pliny the Elder
  Historia Naturalis, 24
Plukenet, Leonardi
  Amaltheum Botanicum, *56*, 57, 59
Porpoise, 149
Port Jackson settlement, 110–11, 113–15, 146
  lack of botanist, 12, 15, 110-11, 113–14
Portuguese exploration, 21–2
Portulaca olearacea, 41
Possession Ceremony, 77
Pouteria sericea, 93
Presl, C.B.
  Reliquiae Haenkeana, 133
Providence, 107
Pryor, Lindsay, 18
Ptolemy, Claudius, 20
  Geography, 21
Pultenea stipularis, 121
Pythagorus, 20

quandongs, 41
Queensland, 73–8

Ray, John, 26–7
Historia Plantarum, 57, 59
Read, John, 51, 52, 53, 54, 109
Recherche, 124, 125
Redouté, Pierre-Joseph, 16, 84, 141–2
Les Roses, 141
Reliance, 145
Resolution, 79, 81, 83–4
Revesby Abbey, Lincolnshire, *60*
Roberts, James, 63
Roebuck, 54–7
Rotz, Jean
Boke of Idrography, 22
Royal Botanic Garden, Edinburgh, 28, 35
Royal Society, 26–7, 95
Banks elected to, 62

Sandwich, Lord, 61, 63, 79
Santalum acuminatum, 41
Sarcocornia quinqueflora, 48, *49*
Sceptre, 128
schleromorphy, 31–2
scurvy, 39–40, 65, 71, 147
sea celery, 71
sea parsley, 48, 125
seed collection, 93
Selkirk, Alexander, 68
Sesuvium portulacastrum, 76
Sherard, William, 58
Sibthorp, Humphrey, 59, 60–1
Sibthorp, John, 59, 145
Sloane, Hans, 28
Smilax glyciphylla, *112*, 120
Smith, Alexander, 106
Smith, Christopher, 125
Smith, James, 114
Smith, James Edward, 116–20, 120, 121–3, 135, 140
Exotic Botany, 15, 122, 123
A Specimen of the Botany of New Holland, 15, 120, 121–2, 123
Smyth, Arthur Bowes, 154

Solander, Daniel Carl, 12, 61–2, 63, 68, 70–1, 87–8, *88*, 89, 90
plant nomenclature, 91
Sowerby, James, 120, 122
Spanish voyages, 130–3
Sparrmann, Anders, 81, 83
Spöring, Hermann Diedrich, 64, 78
St Allouarn, François Alesne de, 53
St Vincent botanic garden, 30
Sturt's Desert Pea, 11, 51, *54*, 56
Styphelia tubiflora, 122
Swainsona formosa, 11, 51, *54*, 56
Swan, Captain, 51
Swift, Jonathan
Gulliver's Travels, 57
Synaphea spinulosa, 11, 43, *44*, 45

Tahiti, 15, 65, 68, 70, 83, 101, 103, 107
Targus, 107
taro, 74
Tasman, Abel, 22, 45, 47–8
journal, *47*, 48
Tasmania, 81–2, 84, 125, 126
Tasmanian waratah, 35
Tayeto, 68, 78
tea tree oil, 42
Telopea speciosissima, 121
Telopea truncata, 35
Tench, Watkin, 113, 114
Terra Australis Incognita, 20–2
terra nullius concept, 15, 77, 95, 97, 99
Tetragonia cornuta, 72
Tetragonia tetragonioides, *71*, 72
Theophrastus
De Historia Plantarum, 23–4
Tradescant, John, 25
travellers' gardens, 68, 103, 125, 126, 146
Tribulus cistoides, 91
Trollope, Anthony, 41
Tryal, 53
tulipomania, 45
Tupaia, 68, 74, 78

Turner, William
Names of Herbs, 26
van Diemen, Anthony, 47–8
Vancouver, George, 133, 134–5, 145
Vanikoro (Recherche Island), 126, 153
Ventenat, Etienne-Pierre, 122, 141, 142
Venus, Transit of, 63, 65, 70
Viminaria denudata, 122
'Vineyard, The,' 30, 63
Vlamingh, Willem Hesselsz de, 43, 48–50

Wallis, Samuel, 63, 65, 66
waratah, 121
Wardian case, 152, *152*
Watling, Thomas, 116, 120–1
Webb, Phillip, 153
West Indies, 101, 102
Westall, William, 145, 146, 151
Western Australia, 51–8, 134–5
White, John, 15, 114, 116, 119–20, 149
A Journal of a Voyage to New South Wales, 113, *118*, 119–20, 122
Wiles, James, 125
Williams, John
Narrative of a Missionary Enterprise in the South Sea Islands, 106
Wilson, Thomas, 116, 119, 120, 122
Witsen, Nicholaas, 43, 49, 50
Woodward, Dr, 11, 57–8
Wrigley, John, 45
Wytfliet, Cornelius
Descriptionis Ptolemaicae Augmentum, 22

Yencken, John, 17
Young, Edward, 106

Zoffany, John, 79, 81